NATIONS IN THE BALANCE

The India–Burma Campaigns, December 1943–August 1944

CHRISTOPHER L. KOLAKOWSKI

CASEMATE

Philadelphia & Oxford

Published in the United States of America and Great Britain in 2022 by
CASEMATE PUBLISHERS
1950 Lawrence Road, Havertown, PA 19083, USA
and
The Old Music Hall, 106–108 Cowley Road, Oxford OX4 1JE, UK

Hardcover Edition: ISBN 978-1-63624-096-1
Digital Edition: ISBN 978-1-63624-097-8

A CIP record for this book is available from the British Library

Printed and bound in the United Kingdom by TJ Books

Typeset in India by Lapiz Digital Services, Chennai.

For a complete list of Casemate titles, please contact:

CASEMATE PUBLISHERS (US)
Telephone (610) 853-9131
Fax (610) 853-9146
Email: casemate@casematepublishers.com
www.casematepublishers.com

CASEMATE PUBLISHERS (UK)
Telephone (01865) 241249
Email: casemate-uk@casematepublishers.co.uk
www.casematepublishers.co.uk

Contents

Acknowledgements

Of the 16 million Americans who served in the armed forces during World War II, only about 250,000 ever served in the China–Burma–India Theater. General William Slim referred to his army as the Forgotten Army, as its supplies and activities were usurped and overshadowed by larger operations in Europe, Africa, and the Pacific. It truly was, and is still, an overlooked battlefront.

I was aware of the fighting there, having read various accounts in years past. As a teenager, I recall reading John Masters's description of the Blackpool Block battle, which remains one of the finest battle accounts I've ever read. In 2016, I had finished my book on the defense of the Philippines and, in late spring, traveled to Britain to visit some family history sites and attend events surrounding the 75th anniversary of the loss of H.M.S. *Hood* and the centennial of the battle of Jutland. I had recently read about Imphal and Kohima in the British official history. During that trip, I re-discovered the events of the China–Burma–India front, and it fastened on to me with a strong grip. I published an article but found I had much more to say. This book is the result.

Writing a book like this is not a lone endeavor, and many people along the way have helped develop my understanding of these pivotal battles. First, thanks to Ted Savas, Ruth Sheppard, and the team at Casemate for their enthusiastic interest in this book and drive to make it the best it can be.

The response to this project from veterans, descendants, and people researching China–Burma–India (CBI) has been fantastic. John Easterbrook has been most supportive, and has freely given of his time to share perspectives on his grandfather, General Stilwell, and his campaigns. Nell Calloway shared information about her grandfather, General Chennault. Bob Passanisi of Merrill's Marauders and Jay Vinyard of the Hump Pilots Association both provided helpful memories and steered me toward useful sources. Lee Mandel, Paul Bevand, Chandar Sundaram, Keith Alexander, Nash Tysmans, Dave Powell, Steven Hantzis, Mal Murray, Bryan Hockensmith, Arambam Angaba Singh, Mary Cole, Dave Young, and Walter Borneman helped with encouragement, information, and perspectives.

Many people at various repositories helped with my research, in some cases providing the answers to questions I did not know I needed to ask. Thanks go to Jim Zobel of the MacArthur Memorial Archives, Carol Leadenham and staff at the Hoover Institution at Stanford University, Jim Atwater of the U.S. Army Transportation Museum, Jeffrey Kozak of the George C. Marshall Foundation, Clay Mountcastle and his staff at the Virginia War Memorial, and the staff of the Army Heritage and Education Center in Carlisle, Pennsylvania. Mark Frazier Lloyd and Tim Horning at the University of Pennsylvania Archives in Philadelphia were most helpful in mining the 20th General Hospital records. Andrew Newson copied many war diaries for me from the U.K. National Archives, and Cheyenne Campbell assisted with mining the CBI Theater records in the U.S. National Archives.

Research for this book took me to India, which was an incredible experience. My fraternity brother Lowrie Tucker left his family for two weeks to go along to Delhi and Northeast India, and we had the trip of a lifetime. Yaiphaba Kangjam (Yai) and Hemat Singh Katoch of Battle of Imphal Tours run a first-class tour operation of the Imphal–Kohima battlefields, and are expanding into Burma/Myanmar. Yai spent a week with me and Lowrie touring Imphal and Kohima, and it was wonderful to see the sites and share perspectives with such an expert.

Lastly, thanks to my parents for their unfailing support. Special thanks also go to my wife Alice for her support and encouragement. I was reading a biography of General Slim when we met, and she has known this project as long as she has known me.

Any and all errors are mine alone.

Introduction

World War II unleashed immense historical forces upon the globe, affecting every continent. While rising Axis powers Germany, Italy, and Japan sought to remake the world in their image, other nations led by the United States, the British Empire, and the Soviet Union combined as the Allies to crush the Axis menace. Within the Allied side, however, national goals were not always completely congruent. Some nations, such as Britain and France, sought to protect their global leadership positions; other nations like the United States, China, and the Soviet Union found new international influence. By the time the war ended, the world had undergone a shift more profound than any since Rome's fall in 476.

These historical forces—the Axis versus the Allies, coupled with the internal Allied national competition—intersected in every theater of the war, impacting the strategy of both sides to varying degrees. Yet only on the mainland of Asia, an area known as the China–Burma–India Theater (CBI), did the forces most fully come into conflict. The Japanese onslaught of 1941–42 destroyed colonial rule and gave many Asians their first glimpse of self-rule, while Japan sought to dominate India and China and establish hegemony as the preeminent Asian power. Britain tried to hold on to an empire that was slipping from its grip by defending India and working to avenge the defeats of 1942. The United States, less interested in British objectives, looked to reopen a land route to China and help that country stay in the war. Neither ally could achieve its objectives without the other's help, and that delicate and ongoing negotiation, with the United States holding very strong leverage, foreshadowed future postwar relationships.

These conflicts all came to a head in the titanic battles of 1944. Sino-American forces fought in north Burma to open the Ledo Road corridor to China, while the Japanese launched major offensives that culminated in an invasion of India, billed in Tokyo as the "March on Delhi." British forces also mounted Operation Thursday, a winged invasion of Burma that was the largest airborne operation in history to that point. Ultimately, these offensives grappled with each other and all reached conclusions around the same time in June and July 1944. The winners and losers of these battles both decided World War II in Asia and influenced the next 75 years of Asian history.

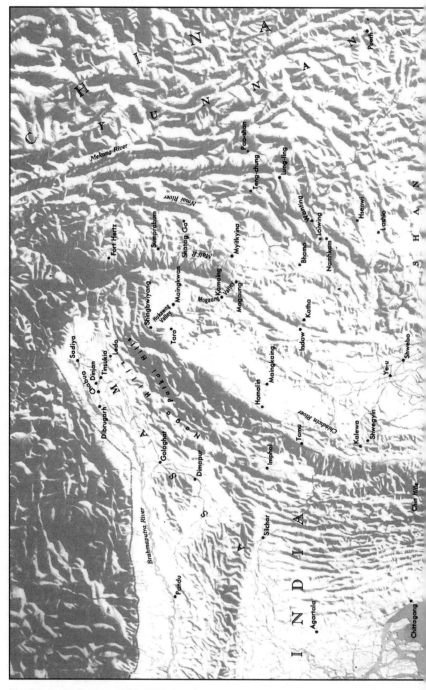

The Burma–India area, 1944. (U.S. Army)

For all of the geopolitical stakes, the fighting in Burma and India also involved some of the most dramatic battles and personalities of World War II. These intense human dramas are essential to understanding and appreciating the CBI in 1944, and make these stories even more compelling.

The CBI battles of 1944 touched a multitude of nations, involving troops from the United Kingdom, United States, Japan, China, Australia, India (including modern Pakistan and Bangladesh), Burma, Nigeria, Kenya, Nepal, and Sri Lanka, among others. Each nation remembers the battles as part of the heritage of their armed forces, and these institutional memories encase the stakes and decisions of the 1944 India–Burma Campaigns, when nations stood in the balance.

Names and Language

Among the people mentioned in the text, those with Chinese and Japanese names are rendered surname first. Language in quotes is authentic to the source and timeframe, and in some cases may be offensive to modern readers.

Place names in the text are rendered as they were in 1944. In the decades since World War II, the geography of the China–Burma–India Theater has changed. Some place names are different, while transliteration conventions have changed how other names are now rendered in English. Chinese names in particular are different, having abandoned the Wade–Giles system for Pinyin.

Below is a list, by country, of place names mentioned in the text and (if changed) how they are as of 2021.

Burma (since 1989 also called Myanmar)

Akyab	Sittwe
Arakan	Rakhine State
Fort Hertz	Putao
Irrawaddy River	Ayeyarwady River
Maymyo	Pyin U Lwin
Rangoon	Yangon
Shingbwiyang	Shing Bwi Yang
Tiddim	Tedim

China

Chengdu	Chengtu
Chungking	Chongqing
Kweilin	Guilin
Nanking	Nanjing
Peking	Beijing
Yenan Province	Ya'nan Province

India

Bengal (eastern section)	Bangladesh
Bombay	Mumbai
Calcutta	Kolkata
Ceylon	Sri Lanka

Other

Siam	Thailand
Malaya	Malaysia
Dutch East Indies	Indonesia

For my Ritson and Shelper relatives who did their bit for King and Country in both World Wars, and for their comrades, especially those who never came home.

When you go home
Tell them of us and say
For your tomorrow
We gave our today

John Maxwell Edmonds, inscribed on the
2nd Division monument at Kohima

Prologue: Longcloth

The Chindwin River flowed swiftly southward, as it had for millennia. The mile-wide river traced a winding course as it ran 750 miles generally southward to the mighty Irrawaddy. Silt colored and clouded the water; from the air, it looked like a brown line cutting through the green landscape, the westernmost of such lines in Burma. As the muddy water coursed on its way, a bright, tropical sun looked down upon it. Along the riverbanks was a thick mass of jungle green, interspersed with clearings and structures of human settlement. The flowing water made a gentle sound, one that joined the sounds of jungle—crying birds, roaring animals, and the rustle of foliage.

This day there entered a new sound and shape: a rustling of a man moving eastward toward the river. Clad in khaki and carrying a pack and rifle, he was something of a stranger to this land, but was determined to both exist and operate in it. It was mid-February 1943, and he represented the vanguard of a small invasion force that brought British troops back to Burma for the first time in nine months. This man was a *Chindit*, and he was soon followed by over 3,000 British, Burmese, and Gurkha comrades, plus over 1,000 horses and mules.

This invasion—known as Operation Longcloth—was the brainchild of the Chindit commander, Brigadier General Orde C. Wingate. A singular character, Wingate achieved both fame and infamy fighting Arabs in Palestine in the late 1930s, later leading Anglo-Ethiopian forces into Addis Ababa against the Italians in 1941. Wingate drove himself and his men hard with a single-minded determination to win that infused his Chindits with a very high *esprit de corps*. Wingate was also deeply eccentric in appearance, wearing an old pith helmet and an alarm clock. He would receive visitors completely naked, regularly ate onions because of their supposed curative properties, and ordered his officers to always move at a run. Major Bernard Fergusson, one of Wingate's acolytes, described him as "a broad-shouldered, uncouth, almost simian officer who used to drift gloomily into the office for two or three days at a time, audibly dream dreams, and drift out again ... he had the ear of the highest, [and] we paid more attention to his schemes. Soon we had fallen under the spell of his almost hypnotic talk." Longcloth was conceived in support of a general British advance into central Burma, but when the larger operation was cancelled, Wingate successfully argued to go ahead anyway.[1]

Wingate's force was the 77th Indian Brigade, containing a British battalion from the King's Liverpool Rifles, a Gurkha battalion, a battalion from the Burma Rifles, and attached units. The nickname "Chindit" came from a corruption of *chinthe*, the name of the Burmese lions that guarded that country's Buddhist temples. For speed and flexibility, the troops were organized into seven semi-independent columns, numbered 1 through 8 (omitting 6).[2]

Wingate's objective was to penetrate from Imphal through the hills separating Burma and India, cross the Chindwin River, and operate in the Japanese rear in northern Burma. The Chindits were to scout the area and the local population's loyalties, cause havoc through demolitions, and try to avoid a major engagement. Air drops by the Royal Air Force (RAF) would keep the men supplied, while limited air support was also available. Wingate could cross the mighty Irrawaddy River if he chose, but just east of the river he would reach the extreme limit of supply planes' range. Longcloth could only operate for about 90 days before exhaustion and monsoon rains would force its end. "This is a great adventure," stated Field Marshal Archibald Wavell, Commander in Chief India, to the Chindits. "It is not going to be an easy one. I wish you all the very best of luck."[3]

Wingate divided his brigade into two groups. No. 1 Group, with 1 and 2 Columns, would move southeast from Imphal and cross the Chindwin in daylight. This was a diversionary force under Lieutenant Colonel Henry Alexander; one of his officers would wear a brigadier's uniform and simulate brigade command. At the same time, Wingate would take No. 2 Group with 3, 4, 5, 7, and 8 Columns northeast by east and cross the Chindwin further upstream. Both groups would unite in Burma later if possible. The march began February 8.[4]

After crossing the Chindwin between February 13 and 15, the Chindits plunged eastward into Burma. Wingate issued an Order of the Day to his men as they left the river behind:

> Today we stand on the threshold of battle. The time of preparation is over, and we are moving on the enemy to prove ourselves and our methods. At this moment we stand beside the soldiers of the United Nations in the front line trenches throughout the world. It is always a minority that occupies the front line. It is still a smaller minority that accepts with a good heart tasks like this that we have chosen to carry out. We need not, therefore, as we go forward into the conflict, suspect ourselves of selfish or interested motives. We have all had opportunity of withdrawing and we are here because we have chosen to be here; that is, we have chosen to bear the burden and heat of the day. Men who make this choice are above the average in courage. we need therefore have no fear for the staunchness and guts of our comrades. The motive which had led each and all of us to devote ourselves to what lies ahead cannot conceivably have been a bad motive. Comfort and security are not sacrificed voluntarily for the sake of others by ill-disposed people. Our motive, therefore, may be taken to be the desire to serve our day and generation in the way that seems nearest to our hand. The battle is not always to the strong nor the race to the swift. Victory in war cannot be counted upon, but what can be counted upon is that we shall go forward determined to do what we can to bring this war to the end which we believe best for our friends and comrades in arms, without

boastfulness or forgetting our duty, resolved to do the right so far as we can see the right. Our aim is to make possible a government of the world in which all men can live at peace and with equal opportunity of service. Finally, knowing the vanity of man's effort and the confusion of his purpose, let us pray that God may accept our services and direct our endeavours, so that when we shall have done all we shall see the fruit of our labours and be satisfied.

These words moved at least one Chindit to tears.[5]

Within days, the Chindits encountered their first Japanese troops. Alexander's No. 1 Group had been spotted. On February 18, Japanese forces probed their camp, but were driven off. Further north, Wingate's No. 2 Group took a supply drop and massed near the key village of Tonmakeng. Hearing of a Japanese unit not far away at Sinlamaung, Wingate sent three columns to attack. The Chindit columns arrived on February 24–25 ready for battle, only to find a hastily abandoned camp. Wingate now set his sights eastward toward Pinlebu and the key Mandalay–Myitkyina Railroad.[6]

Wingate's incursion initially caught the Japanese by surprise, and they assumed it was simply a scouting mission of short duration. The Japanese Fifteenth Army had held Burma since conquering it a year before, and its commanders believed the Zibyu Hills between the Chindwin and the railway to be impassable to large bodies of troops. As a result, the Japanese had scattered outposts in the hills and disposed the main strength from their 18th and 33rd Divisions along the railway itself, in an arc running roughly from Myitkyina in the northeast to Mandalay in the south. At first British contact, the Japanese outposts had been pulled in to avoid battle.[7]

On March 1, Wingate gathered his column commanders together and issued his orders. While 7 and 8 Columns demonstrated south toward Pinlebu, 4 Column would push northeast as a diversion. Meanwhile, Major Michael Calvert's 3 Column and Fergusson's 5 Column would advance to the railway and blow several key bridges. The diversion against Pinlebu succeeded, but 4 Column was ambushed on March 4 and lost its radio and many mules; the commander, Major R. B. G. Bromhead,[8] ordered a retreat to India. Further south, No. 1 Group suffered a similar surprise on March 2, resulting in 2 Column retiring westward to India while 1 Column and the group headquarters continued eastward toward the Irrawaddy.

Despite these reverses, Calvert's and Fergusson's columns successfully reached the railroad on March 6. Lieutenant Jeffery Lockett of Calvert's 3 Column came to a bridge that "was just what we wished for—a three-span steel girder bridge with stone abutments stretching some 120 feet over a deep chaung [ravine] thirty feet below." He and his team quickly placed their charges and set a sixty-second fuse. "Exactly on the sixtieth second," Lockett recalled, "there was a roar accompanied by a flash and a column of black smoke spiraled into the air. Then chunks of steel, stone, and dirt began pelting down on us from the sky." Calvert destroyed two more bridges further south, while to the north Fergusson's men captured the station at Bonchaung before destroying a bridge and blocking a defile.[9]

It was now clear to the Japanese that this was no mere scouting party; Wingate's force presented a much more serious threat. The 18th and 33rd Divisions received orders to hunt down the Chindits. "Contact and destroy the invading enemy," Fifteenth Army commanded. Japanese battalions and regiments moved into the area north of Pinlebu.[10]

Nonetheless, Wingate pressed on. Both Chindit Groups crossed the Irrawaddy River between March 10 and 18, several columns meeting opposition in the process. Calvert set off to destroy the key Gokteik Viaduct, which ran 1,000 feet in the air over a ravine. This mission was personal, as Calvert had waited in vain for orders to destroy the viaduct the year before. As 3 Column undertook its mission, the bulk of the 77th Brigade reunited near Baw on March 23. Wingate and his men discovered the area east of the river was dry and difficult. "The soil was red laterite," remembered Fergusson, "and the jungle low dry teak; the only life that flourished there was red ants, with the most vicious sting imaginable." The men, already weakened by the exertions of a month behind enemy lines, became dehydrated. One officer estimated they were only 60% effective.[11]

The next day, March 24, 1943, Wingate received orders from his superiors to return to India. Wingate over radio directed Calvert's column and No. 1 Group to each make their way back independently, the latter via Bible verse: "Look not behind thee … escape to the mountain lest thou be consumed." Wingate attempted to cross the rest of the brigade over the Irrawaddy whence the same way he had come, but found the best crossing points covered by Japanese troops. Meanwhile, troops from the Japanese 56th Division began closing in from the east and northeast. It appeared the Chindits were trapped.

On March 28, Wingate had what he described as a "short and sad meeting" with his commanders. He ordered them to take one more supply airdrop, then destroy all communications equipment and disperse for India. On March 30, a large airdrop occurred and after a short rest period, 77th Brigade broke up into groups of between 50 and 100 men. Most of the Chindits headed west toward India, but a few bands turned east toward China or north toward the British-friendly Kachin territory and the Fort Hertz outpost beyond. These smaller units found it easier to cross the Irrawaddy and disappear into the jungles beyond. Rations grew short, forcing some Chindits to use Benzedrine tablets for the energy to keep going. Wounded and sick men who gave out on the march were left in villages with a note to the headman promising a reward if they were well treated.[12]

RAF planes buzzed the jungle looking for men, dropping supplies to those they found. They delivered supplies over a clearing in east-central Burma on April 11, based on a radio call from Lieutenant Colonel S. A. Cooke of No. 2 Group headquarters and Major W. P. Scott of 8 Column. Scott, concerned about some of his sick not being able to make it back to India, had placed parachute strips instructing the plane to land. The plane did not land, but the next day another plane arrived and dropped a message: "Mark out 1200 yards landing ground to hold 12-ton transport." The following day, April 13, an RAF C-47 arrived and landed on the marked field. Seventeen sick and wounded, including Scott, clambered aboard. The plane then took off for India, having spent just 12 minutes on the ground. A photographer for *Life* magazine documented the pickup—one of the first battlefield airborne medical evacuations in history.[13]

Calvert returned to Imphal with his column on April 21. They were the first group of Chindits to make it back to India since Wingate had ordered dispersal. Over the following weeks, other Chindits straggled in from Burma. Wingate himself recrossed the Chindwin on April 29, eluding Japanese pursuers in the process. Meanwhile, the Japanese put the railway back into operation after a few weeks. By June, Longcloth was over, and operations halted as monsoon rains took over Burma and India. Wingate's men had marched between 750 and 1,000 miles on average during the operation.

Wingate pronounced Operation Longcloth a complete success. Others were less sanguine, and many Chindits agreed with Fergusson's assessment: "What did we accomplish? Not much that was tangible … But we amassed experience on which a future has already begin to build." One-third of the 77th Brigade's 3,000 men did not return, having been killed, wounded, captured, or left behind. Six hundred of the 2,000 remaining Chindits were declared unfit for further active service. But these details mattered little to a British public starved for good news from the Far East; to them, the exploits of Wingate and his Chindits were just the positive tonic they needed. When Wingate returned to Britain that summer, he and his men were national heroes.[14]

One other person took note of Wingate's achievements: Lieutenant General Mutaguchi Renya,[15] the newly-appointed commander of Fifteenth Army, who had chased the Chindits while commanding the 18th Division. Mutaguchi was one of the officers who previously regarded the hills along the Chindwin as impenetrable to large numbers of troops, but after Longcloth his opinion changed. He began to think of how best to exploit this knowledge.

CHAPTER I

Nations in the Balance

The rain lashed the general's headquarters. It was early August 1943, and the monsoon was about halfway through its annual visit to the Burma–India borderland. Each day saw at least some rainfall, and in many places over 200 inches fell during the monsoon season. Road washouts and delayed planes were common occurrences, especially as most roads and airfields in this area were surfaced with dirt. Major operations on both sides had stopped in early May when the rain set upon both sides with equal fury. The pause would last until October—then battle would resume. The period almost felt like halftime at a football match, although the general resisted such comparisons.

His jaw set, the general looked over maps and documents that spelled out the situation in his corps sector. His creased face belied his 50 years, 30 of which he had spent in hard service with the Indian Army, in posts from the lowest frontier garrison to the highest headquarters. He had risen on merit and had a reputation as being "tough, cool, and well-balanced," according to a fellow corps commander. This was Lieutenant General Geoffrey A. P. Scoones, commanding the British IV Corps in Imphal.[1]

Scoones had been in command in Imphal for a year by this point. Imphal in 1943 was a city of 15,000 approximately 70 miles west of the India–Burma border. It sat in the northwest quadrant of an oval-shaped plain measuring 20 miles across by 40 miles deep, ringed by mountains of between 2,000 and 5,000 feet in elevation. Scoones used his limited forces to probe Japanese positions along the frontier and build the area into a major base for further incursions into Burma. He controlled two divisions: Major General Douglas A. Gracey's 20th Indian Division covered the east and southeast approach to the plain via the Palel Road, while Major General David T. "Punch" Cowan's veteran 17th Indian Division operated along the border along the road running south from Imphal to Tiddim in Burma. Scattered detachments, including irregular units recruited from the local Naga people, watched the hills north and east of Imphal.[2]

For Scoones and for the Allies as a whole, the past 21 months had been a dark time. After the outbreak of the Pacific War on December 8, 1941,[3] two Japanese armies moved into Southeast Asia; the Fifteenth Army marched into Siam while Twenty-Fifth Army targeted Malaya and the key bastion of Singapore. Singapore fell on February 15, 1942, after a 70-day campaign that netted 85,000 prisoners in the largest surrender in the British Army's history. Meanwhile, in January 1942, Fifteenth Army crossed into Burma's southeastern provinces.[4]

Burma, India's eastern neighbor, presented a significant obstacle. The country is the size of Texas, stretching 700 miles from Rangoon to Fort Hertz. The Bay of Bengal acts as Burma's southern border; the rest of the country is hemmed in by jungle-covered mountains along its other borders. Most road and rail connections ran north from Rangoon into the interior before stopping. Very few land routes, and most of those being poor quality, connected Burma with India and China across the mountains. The sole exception was the all-weather Burma Road from Lashio to Kunming, which the Japanese wanted to close to complete the land blockade of China. In early February, the Japanese Fifteenth Army slashed northward with the 33rd, 55th, and 56th Divisions, later reinforced with the 18th Division, to this end.

The Japanese pushed into an Allied command vacuum. Burma was part of the British India Command until it joined General Sir Archibald Wavell's ABDA (American-British-Dutch-Australian) Command in early 1942. Wavell's headquarters was in Java and was preoccupied with resisting Japanese advances into the Dutch East Indies; Burma was a distant afterthought. China, to the north, was in the separate China Theater, commanded by Generalissimo Chiang Kai-shek, ruler of China. The Chinese had been at war with Japan since 1937, and the Burma Road was their last remaining overland link with the outside world. Chiang offered Wavell Chinese troops to defend Burma, but Wavell caused great offense by refusing the offer outright.

Left to defend Burma were two understrength divisions: 17th Indian Division and 1st Burma Division, belatedly organized into Burma Corps (Burcorps) under Lieutenant General William Slim. The 17th Indian Division failed to hold back the Japanese advance, losing many men at the Sittang River in late February. Rangoon fell in early March and Slim drew his men northward, where they were joined by a Chinese expeditionary force under American Lieutenant General Joseph W. Stilwell, who came to China to act as Chiang's chief of staff. British Lieutenant General Harold R. L. G. Alexander commanded the overall force.

Stilwell and Slim planned a fast, aggressive campaign, but the Japanese moved faster. Flanking movements kept the Allied forces off-balance, and they were unable to recover their equilibrium as the lines moved northward. In late April, with the monsoon in the offing, Alexander ordered Burma's final evacuation. The Chinese troops escaped to India and China, while Slim marched Burcorps over the mountains to Imphal. Stilwell refused air transport to India, and led a multi-national party on foot across the mountains into India without loss.

The Japanese advance stopped at the Burma–India border, leaving the area around remote Fort Hertz in the north as the last Burmese territory in Allied hands. The 56th Division invaded China along the Burma Road and stopped at the rugged Salween River gorge. China was now cut off from outside help via land. "We got run out of Burma," said Stilwell at a press conference in Delhi, "and it is humiliating as hell. I think we ought to find out what caused it, and go back and retake it."

As the war's tide lapped at India's eastern frontiers, political tensions there boiled over. Since World War I, increasing friction existed between Indians demanding self-government and the desire of Britain to maintain maximum control of India, called "the crown jewel of the British Empire." Provincial self-government had come to India in 1935, but on the national level the British reigned supreme through its Viceroy and his administration. India entered World War II on September 3, 1939, when Viceroy Lord Linlithgow unilaterally declared war on Germany in solidarity with Britain's declaration on the same day. This action caused considerable unease among many Indians, but India had done its part to support the British so far in the war. The all-volunteer Indian Army grew to 2.5 million men during World War II, and in December 1941, Indian Army units were in action on a string of fronts from North Africa to Hong Kong.

As defeats mounted throughout 1942, and the prospect of invasion loomed, unrest among India's population and native political leaders reached a critical point. The Congress Party, inspired by Mohandas K. Gandhi and Jawaharlal Nehru, openly advocated peaceful nonresistance to any Japanese invasion. In March, Sir Stafford Cripps arrived from Britain with a proposal for India to become a British dominion after the war with national self-government and power-sharing between the Muslim and Hindu segments of the population. Both the majority Hindu Congress Party and Muhammad Ali Jinnah's Muslim League rejected Cripps's proposals, and he returned home empty-handed.

As the summer wore on, the Congress debated making a major push for independence. On August 7, the Congress party leaders debated and passed a resolution calling for the British to "Quit India." Gandhi called for non-violent non-cooperation with either side, but also asserted the mantra "do or die." "We shall either free India or die in the attempt," he told the assembly. "We shall not live to see the perpetuation of our slavery."[5]

The "Quit India" slogan and this revolutionary language, both reported in the newspapers, provoked a strong reaction from the British colonial authorities. They immediately arrested all of the Congress leadership. This action sparked weeks of local demonstrations and violent attacks around India, especially in the eastern regions of Bengal and Assam. The police, assisted by Indian Army soldiers, helped restore order and quell the disturbances; over 100,000 people were jailed in the process. By late September, the Quit India demonstrations had sputtered out. Nonetheless, a latent threat of recurrence remained. To prevent the Congress from again galvanizing such a movement, the party leadership stayed jailed for the war's duration. Jinnah and the Muslim League leadership, having supported the British authorities, remained free.[6]

As 1942 ended, the Allies turned their attention to the Japanese. Plans for a broad offensive from Imphal proved fruitless due to a lack of resources, but the British command decided to strike with what they had. The India Command's Eastern Army under Lieutenant General Noel Irwin launched a December offensive in the Arakan that sought to capture key airbases and the port of Akyab. Major General Wilfred L. Lloyd's 14th Indian Division attacked southward from the Buthidaung area, just inside Burma. Facing a weak Japanese regiment, the division made good progress until forced to pause and allow road building and supply crews to catch up. As the advance renewed, the Japanese made a stand at Donbaik in the tip of the Mayu Peninsula and at Rathedaung in the coastal area on the mainland opposite. A confident Irwin, exercising detailed control of the battle, pushed forward reinforcements until Lloyd's overwhelmed staff controlled nine brigades—three times the normal amount for a division.

Lloyd's infantry repeatedly attacked the Japanese positions without success. When the Major General requested tanks to help support his infantry, the squadron that arrived proved too small to make a difference. By March, the stalemate was clear. A frustrated Irwin ordered his troops to hold their ground until the monsoon. He relieved Lloyd, replacing him with Major General Cyril Lomax.

The Japanese had not been idle: the 55th Division arrived and launched a counteroffensive in early April. Japanese infantrymen flanked the British through the jungles, penetrating through areas that Irwin's men thought impassable. The appearance of Japanese in the 14th Indian Division's rear caused a disorganized retreat, which Lomax barely managed to prevent becoming a rout. Slim came forward to help Lomax regain control of the battle. The two men managed to stabilize the lines just north of Buthidaung by the monsoon's start in May. The British had advanced 30 miles with hope, but retreated the same distance in despair, having sustained 5,000 casualties against 1,700 Japanese for no gain. Irwin was replaced as Eastern Army commander by General Sir George Giffard, while Slim's XV Corps took over defense of Arakan.[7]

Against this backdrop of continual Allied failure on the battlefields of Southeast Asia, Wingate's Operation Longcloth stood out as a significant victory. The Chindit success also obscured another Allied disaster in 1943: the Bengal famine. Bengal, the state surrounding Calcutta and the Ganges-Brahmaputra River delta, did not produce enough food to provide for itself, and imported much of its rice from Burma. The Japanese conquest of Burma closed imports, and a typhoon in October 1942 destroyed much of Bengal's fall harvest. Wartime water and rail transportation disruptions limited the possibility of supply from elsewhere in India. These concurrent calamities reduced Bengal's food levels past the danger point. The result was a humanitarian catastrophe, a famine that killed three million people and caused considerable suffering.[8]

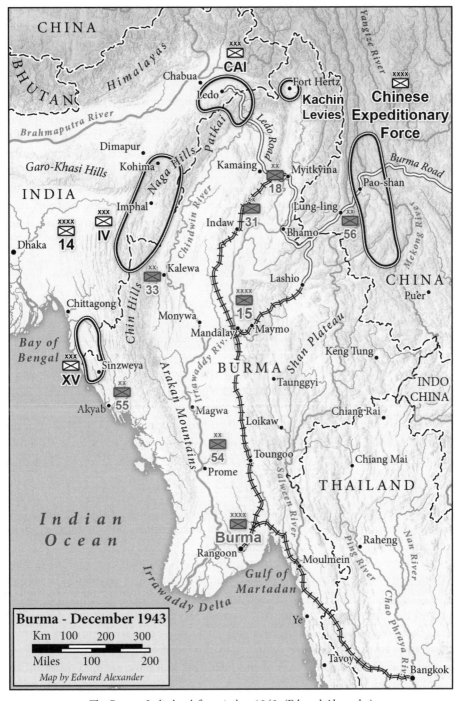

The Burma–India battlefront in late 1943. (Edward Alexander)

The monsoon in 1943 thus washed a very unsettled situation along the India–Burma border. It was clear that more fighting would come in the future.

Wingate's Chindits had departed from and returned to Imphal, and Scoones knew that other Allied offensives into Burma were under consideration. Weather permitting, engineers worked to add depots and airfields to the plain to sustain a major offensive buildup. They were already improving the IV Corps' lifeline, the Imphal–Kohima Road, which led 80 miles to Kohima and then 45 miles to Dimapur on the Bengal and Assam Railway. "Their great arc-lights lit up the dripping sides of the hill," recalled Bernard Fergusson, "while the bull-dozers and angle-dozers jerked screaming to and fro, shoving slithering tons of earth." Further plans called for upgrading the roads leading eastward to Burma for the corps' use and the construction of six airfields around Imphal. Scoones knew he had to be ready soon after the monsoon ended, as Imphal was likely again to be a major factor in any upcoming campaign.[9]

* * *

Three hundred miles to the east, the rain beat the roof and windows as General Mutaguchi reviewed maps and documents in his office. In contrast to Scoones's headquarters in the Imphal Plain, Mutaguchi's Fifteenth Army headquarters occupied the hilltop town of Maymyo, the former summer capital of British Burma. Elegant English-style houses,well-landscaped streets and views of the surrounding mountains and valleys made the war seem a distant prospect.

Maymyo was, from Mutaguchi's perspective, an excellent place to plan operations. An officer of long service, Mutaguchi joined the Japanese Army in 1910. He rose through the ranks quickly, developing a reputation for aggressiveness. As a colonel, Mutaguchi commanded the infantry regiment involved in the Marco Polo Bridge Incident on July 7, 1937, which set off the Second Sino-Japanese War (known as the China Incident by the Japanese). From 1941 to spring 1943, Mutaguchi commanded the Japanese 18th "Chrysanthemum" Division in the Malaya Campaign and later in Burma, helping force the British surrender at Singapore and the longest retreat in British history (from Rangoon to India).[10]

His record of victories caused Mutaguchi to view himself as a man of destiny, fated to be tied to some of Japan's greatest military moments. Invading India seemed to be a logical next step. "I started off the Marco Polo Incident which broadened out into the China Incident and then expanded until it turned into the Great East Asian War," Mutaguchi wrote in his diary. "If I march into India now, by my own efforts and can exert a decisive influence in the Great East Asian War, I, who was the remote cause of the outbreak of this great war, will have justified myself in the eyes of our nation."[11]

Fifteenth Army fell under Lieutenant General Kawabe Masakazu's Burma Area Army, which held the country with forces scattered along the major invasion routes. Opposite XV Corps stood the 55th Division. In central Burma, the 33rd Division faced IV Corps. The 18th Division, now under Major General Tanaka Shinichi, stood near Ledo at the northern end of the Hukawng Valley. Major General Matsuyama Yuzo's 56th Division held the Burma Road against the Chinese.[12]

After they captured Burma, the Japanese planned an invasion of India under the name 'Plan 21'. Plan 21 was prepared in September 1942 as the Quit India movement subsided, and envisioned the 33rd Division and part of the 55th Division attacking through Imphal to Kohima and Dimapur. Meanwhile, the 18th Division would capture Ledo and march southward toward Dimapur. When all three divisions were in the Brahmaputra River Valley, it was expected that a decisive battle would occur, hopefully in conjunction with an Indian popular uprising.

As 18th Division commander in 1942, Mutaguchi had argued that Plan 21 was impossible. But Wingate's expedition had converted him: even before Longcloth's conclusion, Mutaguchi started advocating for an offensive into India. He explained his ideas to Kawabe, and pushed them forward during a wargame in June involving officers from Fifteenth Army and Burma Area Army. The Southern Army staff, which oversaw all Japanese forces in Southeast Asia and the Southwest Pacific, also sent representatives to participate in the game. Mutaguchi's proposals met with opposition from many of his colleagues on the grounds that it would overextend Japan's limited forces in the region. The matter was referred to Imperial General Headquarters in Tokyo and Premier Tojo Hideki's government. In early August, Tojo ruled that planning and preparations could continue pending a final decision.[13]

* * *

On the other side of the world, Allied leaders assembled in a sunny and breezy Quebec City to discuss strategy. British and American delegations met in the city's imposing Citadel and the Chateau Frontenac, overlooking the mighty St Lawrence River. British Prime Minister Winston Churchill and his senior military leaders attended, as did U.S. President Franklin D. Roosevelt and the top American military leaders. Over eight days, August 17–24, they examined all aspects of the war and discussed future operations.

The Quebec Conference took place during a bright time for the Allies. Since their last meeting at Casablanca in January 1943, Allied forces had met with considerable success against the Axis. German and Italian forces had been evicted from North Africa in May, while Russian forces had battered the Germans in eastern Ukraine and Kursk. The 38-day battle of Sicily ended on the conference's first day, leaving the Allies in control of the central Mediterranean. Italy was on the brink of surrender as Allied forces prepared to invade the peninsula in September. In the Pacific, Japan had lost the initiative at Guadalcanal and Papua, and been driven out of the Aleutians. Now General Douglas MacArthur's U.S. and Australian forces were moving to neutralize the key base of Rabaul. In Hawaii, Admiral Chester Nimitz prepared his Central Pacific Area forces to drive westward into the Japanese defenses.[14]

The China–Burma–India front also was on the agenda, driven partly by the presence of General Wingate. He had arrived in London wearing the same uniform he used in Burma, and called on Churchill at 10 Downing Street. Churchill was having dinner, and invited Wingate to join him. "We had not talked for half an hour before I felt myself in the presence of a man of the highest quality," recalled Churchill. "I decided at once to take him with me" to Quebec. Wingate agreed to make the trip, but expressed sadness at not seeing his wife Lorna. Churchill arranged for her to go along, too.[15]

In Quebec, Wingate made a presentation to the Combined Chiefs of Staff, made up of the U.S. Joint Chiefs and the British Chiefs of Staff Committee. He recounted his experiences during Longcloth, and explained how it validated his overall concept of what he termed "Long Range Penetration" into enemy territory. Wingate advocated for a force to do more, for longer, in the Japanese rear areas. He also wore his unwashed battle uniform, which contrasted with the senior leaders in their polished dress uniforms. Wingate's forceful words and appearance made a deep impression. "You took one look at that face," recalled General Henry H. "Hap" Arnold, Chief of the U.S. Army Air Forces, "like the face of a pale Indian chieftain, topping the uniform still smelling of jungle and sweat and war, and you thought: 'Hell, this man is serious.'"[16]

As the Combined Chiefs discussed Wingate's proposals, the complexities of the China–Burma–India front came into sharp relief. Administratively, the area fell under two separate theater-level commands: China Theater, which directed Allied forces in China and Indochina; and India Command, which oversaw the defense of India and Burma. China Theater was under U.S. strategic direction, while India Command was a British headquarters. On top of these, U.S. forces in the area fell under a third headquarters—U.S. Army Forces China–Burma–India, or USAF CBI. Unlike China Theater or India Command, which oversaw operations, USAF CBI was a purely administrative headquarters.[17]

Aside from the administrative factors, the personalities of the senior leaders in the area added a further complicating factor. China Theater had been created in late 1941 with an Allied staff grafted onto the Chinese national command structure. Because most of the theater's forces would always be Chinese, theater command went to Generalissimo Chiang Kai-shek, who was head of state of China and commander of all Chinese armed forces. Chiang, a graduate of Whampoa Military Academy, had led China since 1927. His country had been at war with Japan since 1937, and had lost most of its eastern third to Japanese forces before December 1941. Chiang centralized as much power as he could in himself, and his Kuomintang party ruled the areas it controlled in a proto-fascist style. By 1943, he had weathered several internal challenges to his supremacy.[18]

Chiang, governing from Chungking, also faced a Communist insurgency in the north led by Mao Zedong, based in Yenan. Although an uneasy truce existed between them, over half-a-million of Chiang's troops watched the Communist stronghold around Yenan. Both Chiang and Mao knew a final showdown awaited them after the war. "The bitterness between the Communists and most of the Kuomintang leaders I talked to, including the Generalissimo, cannot hardly be exaggerated," wrote Ernest Hemingway in 1941 after a trip to China. "As one Kuomintang official put it to me, they still regard Communism as the HEART DISEASE from which China suffers while the Japanese invasion is only a SKIN DISEASE."[19]

Chiang's appointment to theater command, made for what seemed to be pressing reasons in 1941, produced unintended consequences. His status as a head of state meant that virtually any matter involving Chiang, his strategy, command structure, or operations involving China Theater, rose to a matter of state to be solved only between Chiang, Churchill, and Roosevelt. This political complication limited the Combined Chiefs' influence over what was ostensibly a subordinate theater.

The senior Allied officer assigned to China was American Lieutenant General Joseph W. Stilwell. A 1904 graduate of West Point, Stilwell was one of the most complex American commanders of World War II. He and his contemporary, Douglas MacArthur, were the Army's top Asian experts in 1941. Stilwell had served several tours in China in the 1920s and 1930s, and had been present as an observer at the Marco Polo Bridge in 1937. The general had a deep personality—introspective, but very in tune with the people and cultures around him. He had an excellent command of language, and spoke fluent Chinese. Stilwell held himself to a code of values that stressed modesty, loyalty, and duty above all; anyone who violated Stilwell's code met with public and private venom, the latter usually expressed in his diary. His vitriol had earned him the nickname "Vinegar Joe."[20]

Roosevelt had sent him to Chungking in the spring of 1942 to "help China," bestowed with broad powers to equip, train, and command Chinese units under Chiang's overall direction. This meant that, by 1943, Stilwell occupied several roles at once. He was Lend-Lease administrator of aid to China, Chiang's Chief of Staff and commander of any Chinese units Chiang chose to assign to him, and Commanding General of USAF CBI. This necessitated that Stilwell maintain two headquarters, one in Chungking and one in Delhi, and split the running of CBI between them. Major General Thomas B. Hearn oversaw operations in Chungking as USAF CBI Chief of Staff, while Major General Daniel I. Sultan, Deputy Commanding General of USAF CBI, ran the Delhi headquarters. Hearn's Chungking operation occupied an estate overlooking the city, while officers in Delhi lived and worked in the palatial Imperial Hotel.[21]

The command setup and geographic dispersion complicated Stilwell's operations. "The mission of CBI had to be executed in China," recalled the theater's adjutant, "but it had to be implemented in large measure in India." Depending on what role he was inhabiting at the given time, Stilwell answered to Chiang, the British, or the U.S. Joint Chiefs of Staff. "I could never have drawn an organization chart for Stilwell's role—and, therefore, mine—in CBI," recalled Major Dean Rusk, an operations officer in the Delhi headquarters. "Because command arrangements were so complicated, we had to work on the basis of cooperation and negotiation rather than direct command." Stilwell's many hats also gave him considerable influence and power beyond his positions in the chain of command. "To watch Stilwell," remembered Slim, "when hard pressed, shift ... from one of the several strong points he held by virtue of his numerous Allied, American, and Chinese offices, to another, was a lesson in the mobile offensive-defensive." Nonetheless, trying to get anything done while working with such disconnected partners and unusual command setup could be frustrating, especially for Vinegar Joe. "If St Francis of Assisi had been given Stilwell's jobs," observed Colonel Robert M. Cannon of Stilwell's staff, "he would have been known as 'Vinegar Frank.'"[22]

Stilwell continually advocated for a campaign to reopen the Burma Road, urging that U.S. combat troops be committed to that effort. He also butted heads with Chiang over his recommendations to improve organization and training in the Chinese Army. Most of the Chinese senior military leaders were known more for their loyalty to Chiang than for their military ability; many had also used their positions, which they owed to the Generalissimo, for personal enrichment. If they were removed from their roles—as Stilwell wanted—Chiang would lose control of his army and possibly of his government. John S. Service of the U.S. State Department summed up the situation in 1944: "In the last analysis the power of [Chiang's] Central Government rests on its military might. This all boils down to the facts of the incomplete unification of China, the continuing struggle for power, and the universally accepted inevitability of civil war."[23]

Another source of friction in CBI was Stilwell's Anglophobia. Following an encounter with pompous officers in 1918, Stilwell developed an antipathy toward those Brits he found "smugly complacent about their own superiority." Interactions with other British people between the wars seemed to reinforce this general impression, while the many status-conscious Brits in India Command headquarters seemed to be the same type. "The Britisher cannot be himself," Stilwell wrote. "He must be, or rather appear to be, one of the Clives or Rhodes who helped build that grandest work of man, the British Empire. Granted that they have integrity, are more or less incorruptible and coldly business-like for Jolly Old England, they spoil it all for anyone else by making such a blare about it. They have a monopoly on all the virtues and they carry this critical attitude into the smallest details of life." This ill-concealed attitude did not endear him to many of his British allies.[24]

Another American officer played an outsized role in the theater: Major General Claire Lee Chennault, commander of U.S. Fourteenth Air Force. A Louisianan, Chennault had developed a prewar reputation as an expert on fighter aviation and tactics. In 1937, he retired from the U.S. Army and took a contract job with Chiang and the Chinese Air Force. After Japan invaded, he helped train Chinese pilots and worked with U.S. firms to obtain new planes and equipment. In 1941, Chennault assembled the American Volunteer Group (AVG), the famous "Flying Tigers," which amassed an impressive record against Japanese fliers before being absorbed into the U.S. Army Air Forces on July 4, 1942. By March of 1943, Chennault was a U.S. Major General and in command of Fourteenth Air Force, a collection of 110 P-40 fighters under 23rd Fighter Group and 48 B-24 bombers of the 308th Bombardment Group based in China. He still wore Chinese Air Force pilot wings on his U.S. uniform.[25]

Stilwell's refusal of air transport out of Burma in 1942 had offended Chennault. He was convinced that General Stilwell was "indifferent to the achievements and problems" of his fliers. In reality, Stilwell had a good grasp of airpower's capabilities and limits. An Air Force "can do a great deal of damage," Stilwell stated to Chiang in 1942, "but it is still only an auxiliary of the ground forces, indispensable if a decision is to be reached, but incapable of reaching that decision by itself. The great limitation is that … it cannot hold ground. Only troops on the ground can do that, and only by doing so can a decision be reached."[26]

In 1942 and early 1943, Chennault pushed for a major air effort in China. "Japan can be defeated in China," he wrote to President Roosevelt. "It can be defeated by an air force so small that in other theaters it would be called ridiculous." He requested a force of "105 fighter aircraft of modern design, 30 medium bombers, and … 12 heavy bombers" plus replacements. "I am confident this force can destroy the Japanese Air Force probably within six months, within one year at the outside," after which "the complete military subjugation of Japan is certain and easy." Roosevelt summoned Stilwell and Chennault to Washington in May, and approved Chennault's proposals. He placed priority for U.S. forces in China to support the air campaign.[27]

Roosevelt's decision reordered priorities in CBI, and touched a nerve regarding supplies to China. A check on Allied operations—and a periodic source of friction between Stilwell and Chiang—was the airlift over the Himalayas, known to the pilots as the Hump. The cutting of the Burma Road left China surrounded. Japanese troops lay to the south and east, while the mighty Himalaya Mountains barred the way from India. To the west and north stretched the vast Asian expanse into the Soviet Union, which was neutral in the war with Japan. China was, in effect, surrounded, and cut off from the Allies. While the country could supply food, Allied forces in China needed munitions and fuel from the outside to fight.

The solution was to ferry supplies by air from Northeast India to Kunming. Starting with a few aircraft in the spring of 1942, U.S. Army Air Forces C-47s and C-46s flew from airfields around Jorhat in the far northeast of India into Kunming, as the India–China Wing (ICW) of the Air Transport Command (ATC). Contract pilots from the civilian China National Aviation Corporation (CNAC) also participated. These fliers made daily trips across the mountains in all weathers, often multiple trips in one day. The airlift was one of the primary American efforts in CBI, and impacted operations in both India and China. The roar of Hump planes provided constant background noise for everything else in CBI.[28]

The Hump route took between five and seven hours to fly round trip, including turnaround time in China. After take-off, most planes would fly the "high Hump," a northern route designed to avoid the Japanese fighters based at Myitkyina. The high route took pilots through mountains at over 15,000 feet, where planes suffered from powerful air drafts and flew through large cloud banks. "Weather was always a factor in our flights," recalled Lieutenant Jay Vinyard of the ATC. "Weather reporting was not too good. Navigational facilities were also a problem. They were low frequency nondirectional homing beacons, not very strong, operating from around 200KC to 550KC. When we flew in the clouds static electricity would build up on our aircraft and block out the beacons … winter monsoons had a lot a very bad thunderstorms, icing, and extreme winds aloft, often over 100 miles per hour. But some days the Hump were clear and from the cockpit quite beautiful." A southern route ran closer to Myitkyina and went through lower mountains, but the risk of encountering enemy fighters, which took a toll on the slow and unarmed transports, was far greater. Wrecked planes soon accumulated into what pilots dubbed the "Aluminum Trail." Despite the risks, some pilots found the terrain quite striking. "The scenery here is probably the finest anywhere, and undoubtedly the wildest and most isolated of any on the world," recalled CNAC pilot Donald McBride. "Very few people have ever seen it. There are places in the Himalayas where we fly over dense tropical jungles and a few seconds later are over regions of eternal ice and snow and beautiful sea-green rivers winding through canyons with vertical asides two and three miles high."[29]

By the summer of 1943, over 5,000 tons were coming over the Hump each month, well short of the target of 10,000 tons. This volume did not meet Chennault's requirements and almost halted Stilwell's efforts to train and equip Chinese ground troops. Unless the supply route situation could be improved, it would limit the scope of any operations in China. More planes were on the way to increase the tonnage, but the buildup would take time.[30]

All of these factors weighed on the Combined Chiefs as they considered plans for Burma and India. The consensus was for an offensive into Burma after the monsoon: while the Americans favored an overland advance to open the Ledo Road, the British pushed for an amphibious operation against Akyab. Everyone also saw the need to find a way to solve what Stilwell called the "Chinese puzzle" of overlapping command relationships. The solution was a new headquarters:

Southeast Asia Command (SEAC). It would combine air, ground, and naval units under one commander, and be responsible for the war in Burma, Siam, Ceylon, Sumatra, and Malaya. As the area was under British strategic direction, the Supreme Allied Commander (SACSEA) would be nominated by the British Chiefs of Staff for approval by Roosevelt and Churchill. Stilwell would be the deputy commander and a key liaison between SACSEA and Chiang.[31]

The British initially nominated Air Marshal Sir Sholto Douglas of the RAF for the post; the Americans, led by Army Chief of Staff General George C. Marshall, vetoed him because of his well-known anti-American feelings. Marshall suggested either Admiral Andrew B. Cunningham of the Royal Navy or the RAF's Air Marshal Arthur Tedder, both serving in the Mediterranean, but neither could be spared from their current positions. Both sides finally agreed on Vice Admiral Lord Louis Mountbatten, the 43-year-old Chief of Combined Operations. Mountbatten was in attendance at Quebec and eagerly accepted the position. He was made an acting Admiral, the youngest of that rank in the Royal Navy since Horatio Nelson in the Napoleonic Wars.[32]

Lord Louis, the youngest Supreme Commander of the war, brought a singular background to the table. Born in 1900 to German-English parents, Prince Louis Francis Albert Victor Nicholas of Battenberg was a cousin to the British Royal Family and grew up with future monarchs as his playmates. Queen Victoria held him at his christening and nicknamed him "Dickie." His German father, also named Louis, had a remarkable career in the Royal Navy and was First Sea Lord at World War I's outbreak in 1914. Anti-German feeling swept Britain that fall; the elder Louis was hounded out of office, and the family was forced to change its name to Mountbatten. These developments devastated the teenage Louis, then a naval cadet. "I shall take his place," he told a friend. He determined to protect the family honor and position, and becoming First Sea Lord was the as-yet-unrealized goal of his existence.[33]

Mountbatten had spent the first three years of World War II in command of the destroyer H.M.S. *Kelly*, during which it spent more time in drydock, repairing damage, than it did on active service. He survived *Kelly's* sinking off the coast of Crete in May 1941. After a short period in command of an aircraft carrier, he took charge of Combined Operations in London, a role that included preparing the raids on St. Nazaire and Dieppe and developing specialized equipment (later famous as "Hobart's Funnies") for the invasion of Normandy. It was in this capacity that Mountbatten attended the Quebec meetings.[34]

The new SACSEA possessed a boyish charm and enthusiasm that attracted attention but gave an impression of shallowness. Mountbatten was vain and fond of luxury. Married since 1922 with two daughters, neither he nor his wife kept to their marriage vows. "Some senior officers, both British and American, were apt to regard me as an upstart, which indeed I was," recalled Mountbatten. An exception was General Marshall, who "invariably treated me as an absolute equal in age, experience and seniority. He never talked down on me. He made me feel that he regarded me as an equal."[35]

The Combined Chiefs laid out their vision to Mountbatten: "We have decided that our main effort should be put into offensive operations with the object of establishing land communications with China and improving and securing the air route [the Hump]. Priorities cannot be rigid ... regard this decision as a guide." They then asked Mountbatten to examine possible offensives against Sumatra, north Burma, across the Bay of Bengal, and southern Burma. All of these operations except north Burma had an amphibious element, which Mountbatten welcomed. "Winston had sent me out primarily to conduct amphibious operations to beat the Japs quickly," Mountbatten later said. "[But] we seemed fated to slog our way through the Burmese jungle and the worst terrain in the world."[36]

August turned unto September, and both the Allied and Japanese high commands were thus separately considering major efforts on the Burma–India front for 1944. While the exact nature of each effort remained undecided, it was clear that both sides wanted to tip the balance in their favor. As the monsoon ran its course, the strategies and their required forces coalesced for action.

CHAPTER 2

The Gathering Forces

Mountbatten set about nurturing the key relationships for his new command. During the Quebec Conference's final sessions, Mountbatten approached the heads of the British Army and the RAF—Field Marshal Sir Alan Brooke and Air Chief Marshal Sir Charles Portal respectively—asking each for a uniform button for him to wear; since he was going to be a supreme commander over all land, sea, and air units in Southeast Asia, Mountbatten wanted all services represented on his person. Stunned, both men handed over a button. Mountbatten then traveled to New York, where he met with General William Donovan of the Office of Strategic Services (OSS) about his office's operations in Mountbatten's theater. The new SACSEA decided to test Donovan's skills, and asked for tickets to the sold-out Broadway show *Oklahoma*. When Donovan came through, Mountbatten gave OSS full backing in SEAC. Mountbatten then went on to Washington for more discussions. Before leaving, he also obtained buttons from Marshall, Arnold, and Admiral Ernest J. King, the U.S. Navy's Chief of Naval Operations.[1]

Hap Arnold left Quebec impressed with Wingate and determined to help him. Wingate's presentation had dwelt on the fraught necessity of leaving wounded behind due to lack of transport. In Quebec, Arnold had offered up to 300 light planes for the Chindits to use in their next expedition, but upon returning to Washington his thoughts grew beyond medical evacuation. He looked for a way to use airpower to help the Chindits move and fight. Arnold offered Mountbatten a larger unit to support Wingate, one that included bombers, fighters, gliders, and transport planes in addition to light aircraft. A somewhat surprised Mountbatten eagerly accepted.[2]

Thus encouraged, Arnold gave his personal attention to what he called Project 9. Arnold sent for two of his best young officers, Lieutenant Colonels Philip Cochran and John Alison. The two were good friends, and greeted each other warmly upon arrival in Washington. Both had seen considerable fighting: Cochran in North Africa and Alison in Asia. Cochran even found fame as the model for maverick Flip Corkin in the comic strip *Terry and the Pirates*. Both men were smart and energetic, good leaders and proven fighters. Unable to choose between them, Arnold decided to make them co-commanders of this new force, officially designated as 5318th Provisional Air Unit but informally referred to as 1st Air Commando. The two decided between themselves that the outgoing Cochran would be in charge, with the reserved Alison as second-in-command.[3]

Cochran traveled to England to meet with Wingate. His reception was initially cool, but after a few days Cochran began to understand Wingate's methods. He realized the radio direction of columns was analogous to vectoring aircraft. "I saw it as an adaptation of air to jungle, and application of radio-controlled air-war tactics to a walking war in the trees and weeds," remembered Cochran. "I realized there was something very deep about him."

Arnold told Cochran and Alison to "draw up a list of what you want," and the men used the opportunity to create a miniature air force. The 1st Air Commando left for India with 30 P-51 Mustangs, 20 B-25 Mitchell bombers, 32 C-47 transports, 225 gliders, 100 L-1 and L-5 liaison aircraft, and six prototype Sikorsky helicopters. Aviation engineers of the 900th Field Unit also joined the burgeoning Chindit support force.[4]

Marshall contributed a U.S. ground force to the Burma effort. A request for 3,000 volunteers for a "dangerous and hazardous mission" went out from Washington in early September; by the 18th of that month, two infantry battalions had been formed with men in training in the United States, and a third in New Caledonia with veterans of the South and Southwest Pacific Theaters. After organizing into battalion-size groupings designated Casual Detachments 1688A, 1688B, and 1688C under the overall command of Colonel Charles N. Hunter, the volunteers set sail for India. They were expected to arrive in late October 1943.[5]

Meanwhile, Mountbatten returned to London and organized his headquarters, which was scheduled to become operational on November 16, 1943. In September British General Henry Pownall became SEAC Chief of Staff, with American Major General Albert C. Wedemeyer the Deputy Chief of Staff. Pownall viewed his assignment, and his new boss, with some trepidation. "Mountbatten, aged 43, will certainly have all the necessary drive and initiative to conduct this war," he confided to his diary. "The difficulty will be to restrain him, or rather to direct his energies into really useful directions ... Most of his staff have already confided this to me and they obviously rely on me to keep him on the rails; which won't be too easy."[6]

Most of the area within SEAC's boundaries was under Japanese control, and SEAC depended on India as its base. Mountbatten had decided to locate his headquarters in Delhi for the time being. He negotiated with Wavell, who had just replaced Linlithgow as Viceroy of India, and General Claude Auchinleck, the new Commander in Chief for India, for support and agreement on operational responsibilities within India itself.[7]

SEAC's structure followed the model of the Allied headquarters under General Dwight D. Eisenhower in the Mediterranean and General Douglas MacArthur's

Southwest Pacific Area in Australia. As Supreme Commander, Mountbatten would have three senior leaders below him, one each in charge of air, ground, and sea operations. The highly capable Vice Admiral Sir James Somerville, renowned for his role in the sinking of the German battleship *Bismarck* and actions in the Mediterranean, commanded the Royal Navy's Eastern Fleet. General George Giffard, a modest and experienced soldier of long African service, moved up from Eastern Army to command SEAC's land forces, now designated 11th Army Group. Air Chief Marshal Sir Richard Peirse—a dignified, professional, and experienced bomber commander—directed SEAC's British air units. U.S. air units initially stayed under Stilwell, but Major General George E. Stratemeyer's U.S. Tenth Air Force came under Peirse's command starting in December 1943. The combined force was known as Eastern Air Command from that point.[8]

Mountbatten flew to India in October and began to organize his headquarters. It soon became clear that his three chief subordinates each had a very different approach to working with him. Peirse was open and cooperative, and both he and Stratemeyer were anxious to move forward with the new arrangement. Giffard proved willing to help, but his modesty and deliberative personality soon generated friction with the energetic and decisive Mountbatten—a development that foreshadowed problems in the future. Somerville, who in 1940–41 had been an admiral in command of a fleet when Mountbatten was a destroyer commander, was openly hostile, and insistent on his prerogatives of direct subordination to and communication with the Admiralty in London. "James Somerville has been tiresome again," mused Pownall in his diary at the end of 1943, "and is deliberately not playing the game."[9]

Giffard's promotion meant a new commander had to be found for Eastern Army. On October 15, 1943, General Slim was appointed to take Giffard's place. Lieutenant General Philip Christison assumed command of XV Corps. "I left with many regrets," recalled Slim of his departure from XV Corps. "As we drove out to Barrackpore, I watched an army commander's black-and-red flag fluttering over the bonnet of my car, and wondered where I was really going."[10]

Slim had much to do. He was now in charge of half-a-million men stretched over 300 miles, from the Arakan to the north of Imphal. He commanded two corps—Christison's XV Corps in Bengal and Scoones's IV Corps at Imphal—plus rear-area units stretching back to Calcutta. His men came from all over India, but also included British, African, Burmese, and Nepalese troops. Among the air forces and support units were Americans, Australians, Canadians, Poles, and Chinese. It was arguably one of the most diverse forces ever assembled for battle. Slim decreed there would be "no distinction between races or castes in treatment" of his soldiers.[11]

The new commander knew he would soon be fighting, and needed to get his army ready. A critical issue for Slim to address was maintaining troop health in the hills and jungles of eastern India. "Assam and Burma constitute one of the most dangerously malarious zones in the world," reported Major General A. Campbell

Munro, India Command's Director of Medical Services. "The whole of Assam below a height above sea level of 4,000 feet is affected." Based on performance in 1942 and 1943, sick rates were at least 10% and sometimes 25% in many units. Men were issued mepacrine as a malaria prophylactic, but the drug turned the skin yellow and was rumored to cause impotence; many refused to take the pills. At this rate, the army's physical and moral strength would quickly slip away even before battle was joined.[12]

Slim set about counteracting the spread of the disease, which he tracked on a chart in his headquarters. He educated his troops about the need for hygiene and prevention of cuts and infections. His medical staff set up malaria treatment centers behind the lines for quick treatment. Taking the pills became a command responsibility; if less than 95% of a battalion was up to date on the dosage, the commander was relieved. "I only had to sack three," declared Slim, "by then the rest had got my meaning." As 1944 started, the line showing the disease rate was going down; by 1945, the army-wide average stood at 1 per 1000.[13]

Morale was another major factor that needed improvement. At Slim's insistence, mail delivery was increased. He also traveled around to his troops, giving speeches. Slim was good at languages, and often talked in a unit's native tongue. Mountbatten later joined this effort, giving seemingly impromptu speeches about future plans, the overall war situation, and local conditions. He also played on the army's nickname for itself: The Forgotten Army. "You're not the Forgotten Army on the Forgotten Front," Mountbatten would say. "No, make no mistake about it. Nobody's ever *heard* of you!" This line usually generated a hearty laugh.[14]

One of the most important changes that occurred was the army's designation. "Let's change this ghastly name 'Eastern Army,'" Slim told Mountbatten. "Let's just get a number." All other major Allied field armies were numbered and several, such as U.S. Seventh Army and British Eighth Army, had won considerable renown by the fall of 1943. Eastern Army, by contrast, was an internal India Command formation with an implicit mission to protect India and keep internal order in the eastern states. Having a numerical designation would effectively give Slim's army a broad offensive mission as part of a larger global effort. Mountbatten agreed with Slim's suggestion, and pressed the point with his superiors in London. Slim's force was soon named Fourteenth Army, a designation destined to earn great fame in the last two years of the war. Its patch of a sword, red shield, and XIV across it was worn with pride by everyone under Slim's command. Fourteenth Army's creation also enabled Slim to jettison responsibility for rear-area security and administration, except for the area immediately behind the fighting front within SEAC's boundaries.[15]

The last concern Slim needed to address that fall was his troops' tactical prowess. Almost two years of consecutive defeats had convinced many of his soldiers that the Japanese were jungle supermen, able to move and fight at will in even the most difficult terrain. "We had first to get the feel through the army that it was we who were hunting the Jap, not he us," stated Slim. Aggressive training, followed by patrolling and ambushing the enemy, helped demonstrate to his men that the Japanese could be beaten in the jungle. Larger actions involving battalions and brigades built on those lessons. "The myth of Japanese 'invisibility' was exploded," recalled a brigadier in 7th Indian Division, a new formation committed to the Arakan in the fall of 1943. "While our own troops found that they were able to see without themselves being discovered, and that the reputed iron-nerved yellow man was just as prone to jitters as anyone else when faced with the unexpected."[16]

Major General Harold R. Briggs, commander of the 5th Indian Division, who had recently transferred from North Africa, summed up the new attitude in commandments to his men: "Be prepared to kill every Jap you meet and then some. Be determined not to let the Jap frighten you with ruse and induce you to disclose your position and waste ammunition. Ambush him and do unto him as he would unto you. Be determined to hold fast when ordered, whatever happens. The Jap will then have to give you the target you want, whilst our reserves are on the way to help you. Be determined to carry out to the letter every task given to you … Be observant and suspicious. Be determined—even fanatical."[17]

Slim's army would be ready for the next campaign, but it remained to be decided when and how it would fight.

* * *

Under the terms of Mountbatten's appointment, General Stilwell was to retain command of all U.S. and Chinese forces in SEAC as Deputy Supreme Commander. On October 16, Mountbatten flew to China to obtain Chiang's concurrence for this arrangement. He arrived to find that Chiang was fed up with Stilwell, and on the point of formally asking Roosevelt to recall him. Chiang's stated reason was that Stilwell had "lost the confidence of the troops." "The real reason is hard to guess," mused Stilwell in a private note to himself. "It may be with me out, nobody else will push the campaign … or it may just be the suspicious Oriental mind" not willing to let a foreigner "upset the equilibrium of mediocrity through which he [Chiang] maintains control." Undoubtedly there was a personal factor involved, as Stilwell's proposals and observations challenged Chiang's competence and threatened the Generalissimo with a loss of face and prestige. Stilwell's habit of referring to Chiang by his assigned codename of Peanut, which came across as derogatory, didn't help either.[18]

Mountbatten was taken aback by Chiang's attitude. The SACSEA talked with Stilwell, who wanted to stay, and made it known to the Chinese that he wanted to retain Stilwell. Chiang's wife and sister-in-law also lobbied the Generalissimo to change his mind. In the end, Chiang and Stilwell met for a bit of face-saving theater on the evening of the 17th. Stilwell admitted "I have only one aim, the good of

China, and if I had made mistakes it was from misunderstanding and not intent, and that I was ready to cooperate fully." Chiang reiterated the relationship between a commander and chief of staff, and asked Stilwell to "avoid any superiority complex." Stilwell agreed to do so, and Chiang decided not to request Stilwell's relief.[19]

Mountbatten met with Chiang the next day to coordinate plans. The nervous attitude of his Chinese companions toward Chiang struck Mountbatten as odd. "I have never come across such awesome reverence as they show for the Generalissimo," he recorded. "I very much doubt whether the devout Christians could show any more reverence for 'Our Lord' if he were to appear on earth again." Mountbatten met with Chiang and his wife, Madame Chiang Soong May-ling, who Mountbatten believed to be "most striking looking." With Madame translating, the three spoke for over two hours. Mountbatten flattered Chiang by calling him "the best and most renowned soldier of our generation." This set the tone for another day of meetings, which garnered Chiang's support for and understanding of the new SEAC setup and plans. When Mountbatten flew back to India on October 20, he and the Chiangs had developed a "real feeling of affection and regard" for each other.[20]

One of the plans the two commanders discussed was an attack into northern Burma from Ledo by the Sino-American force, then based in India. This small army numbered 38,845 men, almost all of them contained in the Chinese 22nd, 30th, and 38th Divisions. Most of these units had retreated into Burma in 1942, and all had since been retrained and equipped with U.S. and British weapons. In support was the battalion-sized Sino-American 1st Provisional Tank Group under Colonel Rothwell Brown, and 2,000 U.S. advisors. The overall command had an array of names: the Chinese called it New 1st Army, the Americans knew it as the Chinese Army in India (CAI, translated *Chih Hui Pu*), and SEAC used the name X Force.[21]

This offensive would be the big test for Stilwell's concept of training Chinese soldiers. Stilwell believed in the overall fighting quality of the Chinese, provided they received good training, equipment, and leadership. In June 1942, Stilwell obtained from the Government of India use of the camp at Ramgarh in Bihar State, northwest of Calcutta. The camp had previously held Italian prisoners of war. Brigadier General Frederick McCabe took command of what became known as the Ramgarh Training Center, and Chinese troops arrived over 10 weeks beginning July 17, 1942. Replacements flown over the Hump brought the three divisions up to regulation strength and provided personnel to create support and service units. Uniforms and small arms for the Chinese came from British and American stocks in India, while American Lend-Lease provided heavier weapons like mortars, bazookas, artillery, trucks, jeeps, and tanks.[22]

McCabe and his trainers put together a series of courses over several months to get the Chinese proficient in modern war. Infantry units started with weapon and individual training, moving up to platoon and company maneuvers that emphasized basic battlefield movement, communication, and coordination. Intensive jungle training then drilled moving, fighting, and survival in the terrain in Burma. Other specialist courses covered signals, transportation, medical, veterinary, and engineer activities—many new to the Chinese. Field and general officers also trained in how to efficiently administer and fight regiments and divisions.[23]

Some of the cultural differences caused complications, but were not unamusing. Chinese soldiers, in the habit of foraging liberally, stole anything not nailed down or otherwise secured. The fluid Chinese concept of time contrasted with the structured class schedule. Many soldiers were surprised when they were paid to the penny what they were due; they were used to paymasters in China skimming off the payroll with various excuses. The language barrier was a problem, as working through translators slowed down instruction and sometimes obscured meaning. It was less a problem in weapons instruction, as the Chinese quickly learned to imitate their teachers in how to operate individual weapons. Some senior Chinese officers, veterans of six years of war, resisted instruction from U.S. officers. Nonetheless, by the fall of 1943, the 38th and 22nd Divisions were ready for battle, with the 30th and the tankers not far behind.[24]

In the field, the CAI would enjoy a strong U.S. support network. U.S. engineer units, many all-black segregated units, had been around Ledo and Jorhat since 1942 building airfields for the Hump transports and for combat planes. They had also made the first efforts toward improving the road into northern Burma. A few medical units had arrived, but were overwhelmed by the needs of the area.

In early April 1943, the 20th General Hospital arrived from the United States and set up at Ledo. For the next two years, it would be the major medical center for Allied forces in northeast India and northern Burma.[25]

The 20th General Hospital was a reserve unit recruited from the staffs of the University of Pennsylvania's medical school and university hospital. After activation in May 1942 and a period of training in Texas, the unit docked in Bombay in early March. It took weeks of train travel across India before the Pennsylvanians arrived in Ledo. "The first view of the hospital was something never to be forgotten," recalled an officer. "We splashed out of the trucks into nearly six inches of soft slippery mud." The facilities consisted of clusters of bamboo huts with dirt floors, called *bashas*, surrounding a polo field. "We spent the next nine days getting used to mud, rain, wet feet, mosquitos, jackals, fog and cold." They were a long way from Philadelphia.[26]

By late 1943, the hospital staff had scrounged and built a facility that could handle 2,000 patients at any one time, up from the 300-patient capacity in April 1943. "In bamboo bashas, using American hospital equipment," recalled the hospital commander, Colonel I. S. Ravdin, "we for the first time brought modern methods of medical and surgical care, on a large scale," to the troops in the area.[27]

Also in the area, and destined to trail behind the CAI, was a small legion of engineers and road builders to cut the Ledo Road. General Stilwell described his planned advance as needing to "go in through a rat hole and dig the hole as we go," and these were the men to do the digging. They numbered a total of 9,000 U.S. troops under Colonel Lewis A. Pick, a personable and direct Virginian who had taken command in October 1943. Sixty percent of his engineer force was African-American in segregated units. Over 60,000 Indian, Burmese, and Chinese contract laborers assisted in the project. As the front advanced, part of Pick's command staked out the route and cut rough trails. Work crews would widen the trails into roads, while others would improve drainage and run pipelines along the corridor. In this way, the Ledo Road (nicknamed "Pick's Pike" by the men) would move ahead toward Lashio. But Pick's progress was dependent upon the success of the CAI. Its ability to fight—and win—remained to be seen.[28]

* * *

In Maymyo, General Mutaguchi put the finishing touches on his proposed India invasion. As he and his commanders deliberated, they had for reference the latest report on lessons from earlier battles against the British and Indians in the Arakan. After commending British use of machine guns and mortars, it offered observations about the troops themselves. "The quality, compared to that during the [spring 1942] Burma offensive, was excellent and the will to fight was on the whole good," it said. "The tactical abilities of the senior commanders and subordinates were poor and the fighting ability of each soldier was inferior. Apparently Indian soldiers blindly followed the leadership of the English. The quality of the white soldiers without any doubt was bad." As for how the British fought, "the enemy places extreme emphasis on material power ... Enemy infantry depends on firepower, and as long as they are under its cover, their power of resistance is great. However, if the firepower support is insufficient, they give up easily." Attacks came at predictable times—dawn, dusk, early afternoon—and flanking movements often resulted in a hasty retreat. "Seek out the white forces at the start of the battle and administer a crushing blow upon them," the report counseled. "In attacking it is important to direct the attacks incessantly day and night at the enemy's flanks and rear, and in this way penetrate the enemy line at numerous points. After this has been achieved, if necessary, these elements will attack the enemy from the opposite direction."[29]

Mutaguchi took this advice into consideration as he planned the invasion of India, His plan, codenamed U-Go, envisioned a two-stage advance. The first stage would involve a diversionary attack in the Arakan by one division, designed to draw British reserves to that area. Two to three weeks after the Arakan operation's start, the main attack of Fifteenth Army would jump off for the Imphal–Kohima area with three divisions and support units totaling 84,000 men. Within a month, they would push into India and capture the base at Imphal, as well as a blocking position further north at Kohima. His troops would only carry supplies for three weeks, after which they expected to use captured British stores. Although his orders only mentioned the Imphal area as an objective, Mutaguchi dreamed of pushing deeper into India, to Bengal and possibly all the way to Delhi.[30]

A unique element of the U-Go plan was the presence of Subhas Chandra Bose and the Indian National Army (INA), rendered in Hindi as *Azad Hind Fauj.* The INA was created in 1942 from men recruited from the 45,000 Indian soldiers surrendered at Singapore. The Japanese enticed Indians to join with statements of solidarity and appeals to anti-British sentiment. Many Indians remained wary, but others volunteered for the cause with enthusiasm. The INA's first commander, General Mohan Singh, fell out with the Japanese over strategy and policy and, by early 1943, the INA was in considerable disorganization.[31]

The INA received new purpose and direction when Bose arrived in Singapore in early July 1943. By any measure, he was having a remarkable war experience. A prominent Congress Party leader, he advocated more direct action to obtain India's independence and had fallen out with Gandhi over the latter's non-violent stance. In 1941, he escaped from house arrest in Calcutta and made his way to Nazi Germany via the Soviet Union. There, he recruited an Indian Legion among captured Indian soldiers and took the title of *Netaji,* or "Respected Leader." He hoped to lead the legion to India, but by early 1943 it was clear that the fortunes of war made that prospect unlikely. Bose then traveled by German and Japanese submarines to Asia and flew to Singapore to take charge.

Bose's arrival galvanized the INA and the Indian expatriate community in Malaya. His presence also lent new energy and legitimacy to the cause of Indian independence. On October 21, 1943, Bose declared himself head of the Provisional Government of Free India, raised a flag, appointed a cabinet, and took the INA under his wing. He expanded INA recruiting to expatriate Indians living in Malaya. He soon amassed a force of some 50,000 men and women, including the all-female Rani of Jhansi Regiment. Bose's government also took administrative control of the Andaman Islands, the only Indian territory then under Japanese occupation. On November 5/6, 1943, Tojo convened the leaders of his collaborationist governments for the Greater East Asia Conference in Tokyo; Bose attended with the status of an observer.[32]

The Japanese greeted these activities with mixed feelings. Some politicians in Tokyo felt Bose was too independent, and not completely aligned with Japan's war aims. For Japanese military men, who believed that surrender was dishonorable in the extreme, the INA was tainted because of its origin among prisoners. Nonetheless, the Japanese planned to make use of Bose and his followers.[33]

The INA unit assigned to U-Go was the small 1st Division, 7,000 men in the Gandhi, Nehru, and Azad Brigades, under the overall command of Major General Shah Nawaz Khan. The INA brigades would be attached to Japanese divisions, and hopefully entice desertions among the British Indian Army troops they encountered. They also would work toward a larger goal: "Upon the occupation of Imphal," directed General Kawabe to Mutaguchi, "the Provisional Government of Free India will be established there in order to accelerate the political campaign in India."[34]

Over the last weeks of 1943, Mutaguchi worked feverishly to develop and refine the U-Go plan. Nonetheless, it was still far from clear whether it would be approved.[35]

* * *

SEAC came into being on November 16, 1943. Two days later, the major Allied commanders in SEAC met in New Delhi to discuss plans. Mountbatten chaired the meeting. Among the operations discussed was Operation Champion, a converging attack on Burma by X Force, the Fourteenth Army, and associated units to open land communications to China. It was expected that the large Chinese Y Force under General "Hundred Victories" Wei Li-Huang would advance from the east and meet X Force near the key town of Myitkyina. In addition to Champion, Mountbatten envisioned an amphibious attack called Buccaneer on the Andaman Islands. These two plans illustrated the divergent strategic interests of the United States and the United Kingdom: the former looked to support China in playing a major role in the defeat of Japan, while the latter looked to liberate its colonies and avenge the humiliations of 1942.[36]

The multi-pronged nature of Operation Champion created questions regarding the overall coordination of operations. Most of the forces were from SEAC, but Y Force was in China and therefore under Chiang's direct command. Moreover, Stilwell refused to serve under General Giffard for national and personal reasons. After considerable wrangling, Stilwell proposed to serve under Slim until his forces advanced to Kamaing. The two men, who regarded each other with great respect, left the room and worked out a handshake deal. Stilwell outlined his plans to Slim. "Tactically we were in agreement," recalled Slim, "and, wisely, we avoided strategic discussion ... I assured him that, as long as he went on those lines, he would not be bothered by a spate of directives from me." The two men returned and reported their solution. As the conference ended, Stilwell saluted Slim and asked "Sir, as Fourteenth Army commander, do you have any orders for me?" With a smile, Slim replied, "No, sir. As Deputy Supreme Commander, do you have any orders for me?" "Not on your life," replied the American with a grin. Their personal relationship solved the command issue.[37]

Four days later, Mountbatten joined Stilwell, the Chiangs, and other leaders in Cairo for a major strategy session. As at Quebec, the major British and American military leaders attended along with Roosevelt and Churchill. For four days, November 22–26, 1943, the group debated Allied strategy for 1944 and beyond. Chiang's presence was a watershed in Chinese international relations, marking the first seating of China as one of the four Great Powers (along with the United States, Britain, and Soviet Union) among the Allies.

Very quickly, the frustrations and complications of the China–Burma–India Theater became clear to the participants. Stilwell made most of the early presentations to the Combined Chiefs for the Chinese, while Mountbatten briefed both Champion and Buccaneer. Madame Chiang made quite an impression in the opening plenary session with a revealing dress and coquettish manner. For his part, Chiang viewed only the head-of-state-level discussions with Roosevelt and Churchill as decisive; he largely ignored the Combined Chiefs—his nominal superiors as China Theater commander—except for issuing demands for more resources. The language barrier further complicated all discussions.[38]

The upshot of all this was confusion. In separate meetings with Roosevelt, Mountbatten, and Churchill, Chiang agreed to support Champion with a Y Force attack on the condition the British could dominate the Bay of Bengal and launch an amphibious operation, for which Buccaneer would suffice. He rejected Churchill's suggestion of a Sumatra invasion and advocated for a push to Mandalay instead. When he was informed by Mountbatten that a Mandalay attack was not feasible logistically, Chiang had his staff demand more planes to fly the Hump and asked for a loan of $1 billion. They claimed China's right to be supported as an ally. "Now let me get this straight," an exasperated Marshall reminded them. "You are talking about your 'rights' in this matter. I thought those were *American* planes, and *American* personnel, and *American* material."[39]

In the end, Champion and Buccaneer were both sanctioned. A joint British-American-Chinese declaration stated "that all the territories Japan has stolen from the Chinese, such as Manchuria, Formosa, and The Pescadores, shall be restored to the Republic of China. Japan will also be expelled from all other territories which she has taken by violence and greed. The aforesaid three great powers, mindful of the enslavement of the people of Korea, are determined that in due course Korea shall become free and independent." But the feeling of resentment engendered by the Chinese behavior lingered as the Combined Chiefs, Roosevelt, and Churchill left for Tehran to meet with Soviet leader Joseph Stalin. For his part, Chiang left feeling triumphant, and planned to stop in Ramgarh on his way back to Chungking.[40]

At Tehran, discussions centered on the war with Germany and the postwar world. Stalin agreed to join a postwar United Nations, and offered to come into the war with Japan 90 days after Germany's defeat. After much debate, Operation Overlord—the long-awaited invasion of France—was set for May 1944; a subsidiary landing in Southern France, Operation Anvil, received Stalin's endorsement. He promised to match these attacks with a major Red Army offensive against the Germans in June 1944. The meeting ended on December 1 and the Combined Chiefs, Roosevelt, and Churchill all returned to Cairo to reassess the previous decisions in light of the discussions with Stalin.[41]

The Tehran decisions made Operation Buccaneer impossible to execute, as its landing craft were needed for the operations against France. This development left the agreements with Chiang, and therefore the entire strategy for China–Burma–India, in the air. "What precisely were the final military decisions of the conference?" asked Stilwell's political advisor, John Paton Davies. "Nobody seemed definitely to know … Even George Marshall wasn't sure what the score was."[42]

Stilwell and Marshall conferred one-on-one. Marshall sounded out Stilwell's feelings on coming home and taking command of Fourth Army, mentioning that he had almost offered this post to Stilwell in September. Stilwell indicated that he wished to stay and finish what he had started. Marshall then scolded him on his "outrageous talking." Stilwell denied any such loose conversation, or publicly calling Chiang "Peanut." "My God," Marshall said, "You have never lied. Don't start now."[43]

Just before the conference broke up, Stilwell and Davies met with Roosevelt to discuss policy. The president announced Buccaneer's cancellation. "I am interested to know how this affects our policy in China," inquired Stilwell. Roosevelt deflected the question, instead reminiscing about his family's business in China years ago. The conversation drifted from there. "We heard a good deal about his ancestors," recalled Davies. "He never directly came to grips with the real subject at hand—what did he want the General to say to Chiang about the change in plans, what instructions as to policy in China did he have?" At one point, Roosevelt asked about Chiang's chance of being overthrown, and commented on the need to identify and cultivate a successor or successors to "carry on" in case of the Generalissimo's fall. "They would probably be looking for us," replied Stilwell. The meeting ended abruptly when Churchill arrived, and Roosevelt dismissed Stilwell and Davies with a hearty "Remember, you're both Ambassadors; both Ambassadors."[44]

During the car ride back to the hotel, Stilwell sat with his head in his hands. "A brief experience with international politics confirms me in my preference for driving a garbage truck," he mused in a note to himself. "This is admittedly not the proper approach to the matter of international politics. It is a very serious business." And with that he returned to India to salvage what he could of his offensive.[45]

* * *

On the way back from Cairo to Chungking, Generalissimo and Madame Chiang visited CAI's headquarters at Shingbwiyang, on the Burma–India border. They met with the commanders of the two divisions at the front, Lieutenant Generals Sun Li-jen of the 38th Division and Liao Yu-sheng of the 22nd Division, on November 30. Both were capable officers who had fought well in the 1942 Burma campaign. Both were also Western-educated, Sun a graduate of the Virginia Military Institute and Liao of the French military academy at St. Cyr. U.S. Brigadier General Haydon L. Boatner, a bluff Louisianan commanding CAI in Stilwell's name, also attended the meeting.[46]

The three generals reviewed the situation with Chiang. Sun's division was in contact with the Japanese along the Tarung Hka (River) and Tanai Hka, while elements of Liao's division were on line, with more coming up to join. A general stalemate had persisted for several weeks.[47]

Chiang chatted in Chinese with Sun and Liao, which Boatner (who had a limited command of the language) could not follow in detail. Madame Chiang asked Boatner if he needed reinforcements to envelop the Japanese and move forward, and Boatner answered in the affirmative. Chiang then gave his views to the three men. Boatner reported Chiang's points to General Stilwell: "Our forces were at a big disadvantage, that supply was most difficult, that no road was available for rapid troop movements and the Japanese had every advantage to include large forces in our immediate front ... we should not provoke a large-scale battle with the Japanese and we should not cross the Tarung-Tanai River until February, because at that time the British would move to the South and the Chinese would move from Yunnan." Chiang also "stated that the Chinese force used to hold the present river line should not exceed one regiment. He explained that this force was desirable because we had only six regiments and if two were cut off by the enemy we would have only four regiments left."[48]

The Chiangs and the generals then went to dinner. An alarmed Boatner understood that Chiang's statements, left unchallenged, would be taken by Sun and Liao as inviolable guidance. His concern increased during the meal when Chiang repeated the comment about using only one regiment. Boatner pressed Chiang about what to do if the lone regiment was not enough force. "Well, of course you will have to think up a method," replied Chiang. Boatner "immediately told Madame Chiang," he recalled to Stilwell, "that I considered the Generalissimo's statement in reference to using only one regiment of the utmost importance; that if he told his division commanders that only one regiment would be used and if thereupon he, the Generalissimo, left the area, the situation might change abruptly and a catastrophe result before he could make necessary changes in orders. I quickly added, again to Madame Chiang, that this was of utmost importance and the Generalissimo must realize that many of his officers took his views and wishes as explicit orders, and that such would severely handicap future operations in this sector." After his wife translated these thoughts to him, Chiang agreed that his statements were only opinion, not orders; he formally confirmed this after dinner with Sun and Liao, and directed them to follow Stilwell's directives. The Chiangs then flew up to Jorhat, then over the Hump to Chungking.[49]

Stilwell arrived back in Chungking on December 13. He confirmed the news of the revised decisions that had been telegraphed to Chiang. In conversations with Stilwell and a note to Roosevelt, Chiang threatened the collapse of China within six months unless they were loaned one billion dollars by the United States. Chiang also floated the idea that the United States pay in full for airfield construction near

Chengtu for the new B-29 bombers set to arrive in early March. These requests produced consternation in Washington, and an immediate reply from Roosevelt pushing for a northern Burma campaign to open the Ledo Road corridor. Faced with this response, Chiang vacillated.[50]

Stilwell understood that any postponement likely meant no campaign would be possible before the monsoon, and insisted on an immediate decision. Madame Chiang and a number of other advisors also pushed the stubborn Generalissimo to authorize Stilwell to move with the CAI. After much wrangling, Chiang gave in on December 18. He formally tasked Stilwell with command of X Force, and gave him the official insignia, or *chop*, to command Chinese troops in Chiang's name with full powers. "*Surprise*," Stilwell wrote in his diary. "*I really command the X-Force. Without interference! And with the power to hire and fire* ... It took a long time, but apparently confidence has been established. A month or so ago I was to be fired and now he gives me a blank check."

This appointment was a landmark in Chinese military history. "For the first time in history," an exultant Stilwell told his wife, "a foreigner was given command of Chinese troops with full control over all officers and no strings attached. Can you believe it?"

Stilwell departed Chungking for Ledo two days later.[51]

CHAPTER 3

Stilwell's Advance

General Stilwell arrived at X Force headquarters on December 21, 1943. He wore standard U.S. field uniform and carried a musette bag, carbine, bedroll, and a change of clothes, and took up residence in a standard GI tent. "The décor of the Stilwell field headquarters was somewhat unorthodox in comparison with the normal establishments of lieutenant generals in or out of the field," recalled Lieutenant Colonel Fred Eldridge, Stilwell's press officer. "The general had an ordinary camp cot to sleep on. His desk was a packing box, but he had the luxury of a couple of wicker chairs. He shaved and bathed out of a helmet the same as everyone else." Stilwell took his meals at a simple bamboo table with other officers, eating normal rations off standard-issue mess kits. This included Christmas dinner 1943, which Stilwell was photographed enjoying.[1]

For essentially the entire next seven months, Stilwell stayed in the field and left other tasks to Hearn in Chungking and Sultan in Delhi. For Stilwell, the top priority was to help China by opening land communications, which meant a campaign in northern Burma under his personal command to ensure success. This decision, which appeared to some observers as an abdication of responsibility, generated considerable comment in both SEAC and China Theater. "Personally, I think he was right," said General Slim. "The most important thing of all was to ensure that the American-trained Chinese not only fought, but fought successfully. No one could do that was well as Stilwell himself. Indeed, he was the only American who had authority to actually command the Chinese."[2]

Stilwell found X Force's divisions in disarray. The situation had not improved since the Chiangs' visit at the end of November. Sun's 38th Division was inside Burma, facing the 18th Division along the Tarung Hka at the northern end of the Hukawng Valley. Three battalions of the division were surrounded by Japanese forces and receiving air supply; Sun planned a limited relief attack in a few days' time. Behind Sun, Liao's 22nd Division was moving up from Ledo. The pace and aggression of operations were not to Stilwell's liking. "No action for past ten days.

Sun's 'attack' would have been a bust," he confided to his diary. "How long would they have sat on their asses here?"[3]

Stilwell underestimated his opponents. The Japanese 18th Division was an elite formation from Kyushu. Formed in 1907, by 1943 the division carried battle honors from World War I, the China campaigns of 1937 to 1941, the capture of Singapore, and the conquest of Burma. The men wore the division's nickname "Chrysanthemum" with pride. The division's commander, Lieutenant General Tanaka Shinichi, was a veteran officer who had come to Burma from Imperial General Headquarters after a difference of opinion with Tojo over strategy for the Solomon Islands. Tanaka opposed Stilwell with two of the division's three regiments, the 55th and 56th; the 114th Regiment garrisoned the area around Myitkyina and points south. Tanaka had been ordered to make an offensive, but in mid-December those plans were cancelled.[4]

Stilwell's plan, called Albacore, envisioned a southward advance in stages from Shingbwiyang to Mogaung and Myitkyina, a distance of 155 miles. This would take his forces though the Hukawng Valley, an area of 15,000 square miles between mountains of 4,000 and 5,000 feet. The valley itself was quite flat, with elephant grass plains interspersed with jungle clumps and swampy areas. Halfway down, the Jambu Bum ridge divided the valley into northern and southern halves. The southern half was also known as the Mogaung Valley, as it ended at that city. A rough dirt road traced the approximate path of the advance; it would be improved by Pick's crews as the soldiers advanced. Small villages of between four and nine huts lined the route—about one every 14 miles—and contained most of the valley's 9,000 inhabitants. Maingkwan, Kamaing, and Shaduzup were the three largest settlements on the route of advance. Malaria was prevalent, by one estimate affecting 90% of residents. This would be the scene of battle for the next eight months.[5]

On Christmas Eve, X Force started the drive to Myitkyina. Stilwell understood that the Chinese Army generally had a poor offensive combat record against the Japanese, which translated into a lack of confidence among the men and highlighted the need for an initial success. In consultation with Sun, Stilwell ordered the Chinese 114th Regiment to attack in succession each of the Japanese companies that blocked connection with the surrounded battalions. The attack started with a preparatory artillery bombardment, followed by an infantry assault signaled by a bugle call. Sun's men wiped out all Japanese in 36 hours of fighting and restored the position. Chinese morale soared, while Tanaka realized that these Chinese "were far superior in both the quality of their fighting and their equipment" to Chinese units he had previously encountered.[6]

General Stilwell led from the front, going out each day to personally supervise operations. This involved "walking the muddy jungle trails to small troop concentrations scattered over a wide perimeter," recalled Eldridge. "Stilwell ignored warnings and traveled the trails accompanied by no more than two or three Americans and, upon occasion, a Chinese bodyguard." Stilwell's standard uniform of field jacket,

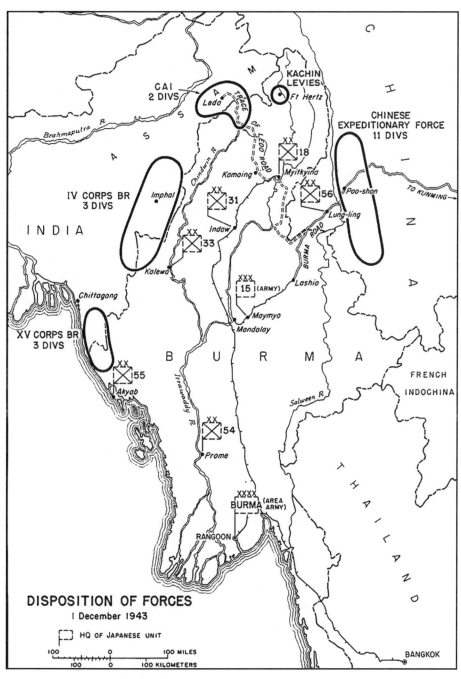

DISPOSITION OF FORCES
1 December 1943

⌐ ⌐ HQ OF JAPANESE UNIT
└ ┘

100   0   100 MILES
100   0   100 KILOMETERS

Stilwell's advance through January 1944. (U.S. Army)

tunic, trousers, boots, and leggings was topped alternately with his signature World War I-style campaign hat or, more commonly, a Chinese Army field cap. He initially wore no rank insignia, but relented following a few weeks of persuasion by his staff.[7]

These actions made a deep impression on the Chinese troops. Sun and Stilwell had a "heart-to-heart talk" on December 26. "[Sun] swears they are trying to do a good job for the *liao hsien sheng* [Old Man]," recorded Stilwell. "The troops are all bucked up to have me with them, but commanders are uneasy for fear I get hit and they be held responsible. Insistent that I stay back and let them do it. Says everybody appreciative of my backing and interest in them."[8]

The Chinese advance continued on December 28. Stilwell had received intelligence of a possible Japanese attack, and decided to secure positions to meet it and sustain the advance. Sun attacked the Japanese at Yupbang Ga, securing the position in heavy fighting. "Good work by Chinese," noted Stilwell in his diary. "Aggressive attack, good fire control, quick action. They are full of beans and tickled to death at beating the Japs." By January 1, 1944, the Chinese had relieved all the surrounded units and stood along the Tarung Hka, although mopping up of isolated Japanese units would continue until the middle of January. Stilwell had directed a flanking force against the remaining Japanese, but the troops moved too slowly and Tanaka escaped the trap by retreating southward.[9]

As the battle raged, Stilwell learned that his rear headquarters were clamoring for decisions. On New Year's Eve, Stilwell made a quick trip to Delhi, landing amid a firework display at 1am on January 1, 1944. He met with staff at the Imperial Hotel, and then attended a general conference with Mountbatten and the SEAC leadership at 2pm. Among the topics on the agenda was the American infantry, now coalesced into the Galahad Force and formally designated the 5307th Composite Regiment (Provisional). The unit had been training in India and Wingate wanted it for his use. "I would like it placed on the record," Stilwell said, "that I am responsible for the training of all American forces in this theater and I am the person to decide when they are adequately trained and can move forward."

This statement raised Mountbatten's hackles. "I accept that in principle," he replied, "but would remind you that the troops are being trained under British officers. I am responsible for operations and will decide when units move to the fighting lines. In other words, General, I should like to place on the record that I am the Supreme Commander out here and that what I say goes." Stilwell laughed and said, "We none of us dispute that." The meeting broke up soon after, and that night Stilwell flew back to the battle.[10]

Wingate visited Stilwell on January 3, 1944. The Chindit force had been very active since Quebec: Wingate had assembled a staff in London, and left for India in mid-September. Brigadier Derek Tulloch, an old friend, went out as Wingate's chief of staff. The Chindit force also received a new name: Special Force. For official and deception purposes, the Chindits would be called the 3rd Indian Division.[11]

Special Force contained six brigades numbering 30,000 men. One was Wingate's former command, 77th Brigade under Brigadier Mike Calvert. Brigadier W. D. A. "Joe" Lentaigne's 111th Brigade, already training in Long Range Penetration at General Auchinleck's behest, also joined Calvert. The veteran 70th British Division was broken up and reorganized into 14th, 16th, and 23rd Brigades under Brigadiers Thomas Brodie, Bernard Fergusson, and Lance Perowne, respectively. The sixth brigade was Nigerian troops of Brigadier A. H. Gillmore's 3rd West African Brigade, which joined in December. Galahad also trained with Special Force.[12]

Wingate set out an eight-week training program for his troops. Based on the experiences of Operation Longcloth, it emphasized "marching, watermanship, mules, air supply, jungle shooting; air support with live bombs; digging, column marching, column bivouac, patrols, R.E. [field engineering] and Signal exercises, medical and veterinary tests," recalled Calvert. Wingate wanted to weed out older men and unfit personnel and replace them with volunteers from other units. In addition, each brigade rehearsed their part of their operation, including cooperation with the Air Commandos for glider landings, air supply, casualty evacuation, and air support. The units' trust in each other became apparent after a training accident in which two gliders crashed, killing 10 Chindits. "Please be assured," said Lieutenant Colonel D.C. Herring, the victims' commander, to the Air Commando leadership, "that that we will go with your boys any place, any time, anywhere." The latter part of this statement became the 1st Air Commando motto.[13]

A key part of Wingate's plan was a system of fixed bases for his men to use behind enemy lines. Known as Strongholds, these fortified centers would hold airstrips, supplies, and artillery. Floater units would operate nearby to ambush the Japanese and if possible draw them into the Stronghold itself. "The Stronghold," instructed Wingate, "is an orbit around which columns of the brigade circulate … The motto of the Stronghold is 'No Surrender.'"[14]

Much of Special Force's successful preparation was the result of Derek Tulloch's hard work as chief of staff, for Wingate had come down with typhoid during the multi-stage flight from London. Wingate and his party had stopped in Tripoli at dawn, and airport services were not yet open. A vexed and thirsty Wingate, recalled Tulloch, "impatiently threw some flowers out of a vase in the canteen and drank the water." Symptoms of typhoid began appearing soon after Wingate got to India, but Wingate, who believed most diseases were signs of mental weakness, pressed on. By early October, he was seriously ill and reluctantly went to the hospital. "Wingate was a difficult patient," recalled Tulloch. "He had little faith either in the desire or the ability of the hospital authorities to cure him." Tulloch arranged for the woman who had nursed the Chindits in Imphal after Longcloth to come. "As soon as Matron McGeary arrived, Wingate settled down and ceased to worry about his condition. He had complete faith in her and obeyed her instructions implicitly." Wingate was in the hospital from October 8 to November 10, and did not take full command of Special Force until December 1.[15]

By the time of the meeting with Stilwell, Wingate had made a full recovery. Stilwell met Wingate and Tulloch in his headquarters tent, where Wingate explained his general plans for Special Force's operation, codenamed Thursday. He would use three brigades—77th, 111th, and 16th—to get into the area around Indaw, where he could cut supplies for Tanaka's division and hopefully part of Fifteenth Army. The first two brigades would fly in, while Fergusson's 16th would march south from Shingbwiyang. Wingate hoped that Fergusson's men might be able to help Stilwell's advance as they passed by. After 90 days, the other three Special Force brigades, 14th, 23rd, and 3rd West African, would fly in and relieve the first three, extending operations into and throughout the monsoon. Wingate also formally released Galahad to Stilwell. "The meeting ended in a most friendly atmosphere," recalled Tulloch, "and Stilwell's previous suspicions appeared to have been replaced by respect."[16]

Two days after this meeting, Stilwell appointed Brigadier General Frank D. Merrill of his staff to command Galahad, officially redesignated the 5307th Composite Unit (Provisional). The press seized on the alliterative possibilities combined with Galahad's rough reputation and quickly dubbed the unit "Merrill's Marauders." It was a task force in the truest sense, not designed to permanently exist on the Army's rolls and slated to go away after a few months. Indeed, its formal designation, 5307th Composite Unit (Provisional), sounded to one Marauder like an address in Los Angeles.[17]

Stilwell ordered Merrill to join him by early February; Merrill reported he could have his men on the scene by February 15. "My God what speed," noted Stilwell sarcastically. "Snorted at him and he allowed they might better the time."[18]

Meanwhile, the campaign went on. It was apparent the Japanese attack was not coming. Stilwell turned to the next steps in his advance.

* * *

As Stilwell's troops prepared to again press south, Tokyo issued its verdict on U-Go. The Southern Army Chief of Staff, General Ayabe Kitsuji, arrived in the capital in early January with the latest version of the plan, worked out over Christmas 1943 in war games with Mutaguchi and Kawabe's staff. Ayabe presented the scheme for an advance to Imphal and Kohima to an attentive General Staff. Premier Tojo also reviewed the plans in his capacity as Minister of War.[19]

General Ayabe arrived at a dark time for the Japanese. The year just ended, which Tojo called "the year of decisive battles," had seen a virtually unbroken series of Japanese strategic reverses. First was the twin defeats at Guadalcanal and Buna-Gona in early February 1943, followed by repeated failures to stop Allied offensives in the Solomons and New Guinea throughout the year. In November, strong American forces from Hawaii captured the Gilbert Islands, a key part of Japan's outer defense perimeter in the Pacific. The Americans were now poised to push west into the Marshall Islands and Mariana Islands, the latter of which Tojo had declared part of what he called the "Absolute National Defense Zone," the penetration of which would lead to direct attacks on the home islands and vital resource areas. Burma had provided the lone major strategic victory for Japan that year with the Akyab success in the spring. "The real war is only just beginning," summarized Tojo to the Japanese legislature at the end of 1943.[20]

Tojo and the staff of Imperial General Headquarters, faced with this litany of defeats and dark prospects in the Pacific, thus regarded the U-Go proposition with optimism. However, there were concerns about opening a new commitment in view of the challenges in the Pacific. After Ayabe briefed the plan to the highest Japanese commanders, they grilled him for three days on its details. Questions arose about the sufficiency of force levels, air support, and supply availability. Ayabe was asked what would happen if an amphibious attack came from the Bay of Bengal during the operation, and faced concerns about U-Go impairing the continued defense of Burma. Ayabe's answers on these points appeared to satisfy his interviewers.[21]

All that remained was to get Tojo's assent, in his capacity as War Minister and Premier. A staff officer was sent to Tojo's residence to present the outcome of the discussions. Tojo was taking a bath, but spoke to the officer, Colonel Nishiura Susumu, through a glass partition. The premier barked questions about supplies, forces, and air support to Nishiura, who telephoned Imperial General Headquarters and confirmed the issues had been resolved to the staff's satisfaction. By then the bath was over, and Tojo emerged to put his seal of approval on the plan for the India invasion. "Impress on Ayabe," Tojo told Nishiura, "he's not to attempt the impossible!"[22]

On January 7, Tokyo formally authorized Southern Army to "occupy and secure the vital areas of northeastern India, in the vicinity of Imphal, by defeating the enemy in that area at an opportune time." Imperial General Headquarters left the attack's timing up to local commanders, but urged that, once launched, the offensive be concluded quickly. Twelve days later, Kawabe told Mutaguchi to "destroy the enemy at Imphal and establish strong defense positions covering Kohima and Imphal before the coming of the rainy season."[23]

Final preparations for the offensive started in earnest. Japanese and Indian reinforcements entered Burma via the recently-completed Burma–Siam Railway. The Japanese also modified their command structure for the operation: Burma Area Army would control two Japanese field armies and two independent divisions. Opposite XV Corps stood Lieutenant General Sakurai Shozo's new Twenty-Eighth Army with the 54th, 55th, and 2nd Divisions, the latter having just recovered from a mauling at the battle of Guadalcanal. In central Burma, Mutaguchi's Fifteenth Army faced IV Corps with the 15th, 31st, and 33rd Divisions, supported by a contingent of

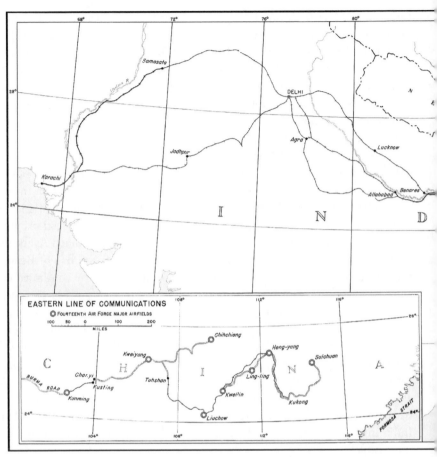

Lines of communication in the China–Burma–India Theater, 1943–44. (U.S. Army)

the Indian National Army. Tanaka's 18th Division opposite Stilwell's troops stayed independent, as did Major General Matsuyama Yuzo's 56th Division, which was holding the Burma Road against Y Force. Sakurai's forces would make a diversion into the Arakan in early February, to lure British reserves to that front. Two to three weeks later Mutaguchi would launch the main attack.[24]

Mutaguchi now sped up plans and preparations for Fifteenth Army. Each of his three infantry divisions received interlocking missions as they attacked into India on three separate axes of advance. The northernmost thrust, by Lieutenant General Sato Kotoku's 31st Division, aimed for Kohima and the road to Dimapur with the mission of capturing the area and shielding "the flank and rear of the main force of the Army until the capture of Imphal has been completed." In the center, Lieutenant General Yamauchi Masabumi's 15th Division would "move through the enemy

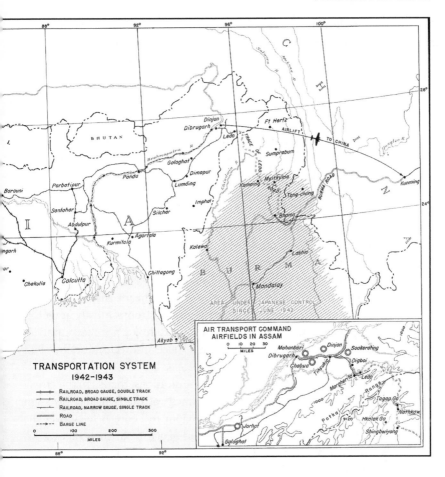

troops into the mountain district northwest of the Imphal Plain and rush to the sector west of Imphal" from the north. The southernmost attack would come from Lieutenant General Yanagida Genzo's 33rd Division, with his men slashing toward Imphal from the south and southeast in an "offensive drive" on the town itself.[25]

The plan had its limitations, as all three division commanders pointed out to Mutaguchi. The need for speed and the element of surprise while moving masses of men, animals, and equipment across mountain ranges up to 8,000 feet in elevation was a major concern. The plan's chief weakness was the necessity of capturing Imphal and its supplies within three weeks of commencing the invasion. Failure to do so would create serious and ever-mounting supply issues. "The success of the Imphal Operation was dependent upon a surprise assault," stated a postwar staff report. "It was evident that the bold tactics of the Army, aimed at the capture of

Kohima and Imphal within three weeks by making a long march across the steep Manipur Mountains [sic], could be upset by well prepared enemy resistance and reinforcements from the eastern Assam area." Mutaguchi dismissed these concerns and predicted a quick victory.[26]

* * *

Mutaguchi's preparations did not go unnoticed by Slim and Fourteenth Army. Both of Slim's corps commanders, Scoones and Christison, reported increased aggression among the Japanese. Patrols in front of IV Corps captured documents outlining Japanese dispositions and future operations. XV Corps, advancing slowly beyond the Burma–India frontier, had discovered the presence of Japanese reinforcements opposite. Codebreaking intelligence confirmed the expanded Japanese order of battle in Burma, but offered little understanding of their intentions.[27]

Slim concluded that both of his corps would soon face major Japanese attacks, and considered how best to meet them. He realized that he had air superiority on his side, an advantage denied to his predecessors. This meant that Eastern Air Command's fighters and bombers could support his ground troops mostly at will. It also meant that cargo planes could be used with impunity to keep forces supplied; indeed, RAF and USAAF crews had developed some successful techniques in 1943 that were being used to sustain Stilwell's Chinese troops.[28]

Slim also knew he could expect improved rail communications, thanks to the arrival of U.S. railway units. One of Fourteenth Army's lifelines was the Bengal and Assam Railway, which ran 738 miles from Calcutta via Dimapur to Ledo. A ferry over the Brahmaputra at Pandu marked the transition from broad-gauge to narrow-gauge tracks. Designed to service the tea plantations of Assam, the railway had, to date, proven inadequate to supplying the needs of Fourteenth Army, not to mention the increasing needs of Stilwell's forces and the Hump airlift. In early January, U.S. railway troops recruited from the New York Central and other major American railroads arrived to help run the railway. On March 1, they took full control of the rail line, bringing new maintenance standards and more efficient operating processes. The British had expected 4,400 tons to go over the line per day by October 1944; the Americans beat that average in April, and kept improving. In April, the Americans also accommodated 64 unscheduled troop trains, all running at least as far as Dimapur.[29]

These important advantages influenced Slim's strategy and the orders he gave to both Christison and Scoones when he visited their respective headquarters. Based on experiences in Burma in 1942 and Arakan in 1943, Slim expected the Japanese to try to force his divisions to retreat by enveloping their flanks and rear. "Christison and I agreed that if any 15 Corps troops were cut off they would stand fast," wrote Slim. "I promised that, when necessary, they would be supplied by air and that they would be relieved by our counter-attacking forces, with whom they were to co-operate."[30]

Scoones had a more complex problem on his hands with his wider front and more dispersed forces and threats. "To gain a decisive success [against Mutaguchi]," Slim said, "I needed to concentrate against him a force superior in both numbers and armament." Both Scoones and Slim considered and rejected spoiling attacks and defending in place, choosing instead to withdraw to Imphal and lure the Japanese into battle around and near the plain. They would have the advantage of shorter communication lines, while Mutaguchi would be at the end of long supply lines over the mountains back into Burma. Air support and air supply could sustain and reinforce IV Corps as needed. Scoones was preparing Imphal to withstand a major siege.[31]

* * *

As January 1944 continued, Stilwell's Chinese forces resumed their advance. More of Liao's infantry arrived, and for the first time CAI was operating as a multi-division force. Stilwell also got armor support from Colonel Rothwell H. Brown's 1st Provisional Tank Group, made up of between 100 and 125 U.S. M3 and M4 tanks, crewed mostly by Chinese soldiers with some American personnel. The all-American 527th Ordnance Company provided maintenance.[32]

As the size of his force grew, Stilwell expanded a system of liaison teams embedded within each Chinese division, regiment, and battalion headquarters. These men had no command authority except over supplies, and could only advise. Each team also had a four-man radio unit to communicate and coordinate supplies and operations. Stilwell exploited this network to get reliable information from the front, which he would then check against reports from his Chinese officers. Liao spoke good English, and Sun was fluent, but for most Chinese officers a language barrier existed. Liaison work was hard and lonely duty. "In many instances, a single American officer with a four-man radio team found himself living out in the jungle six or seven days' march from headquarters with a small Chinese outpost unit," recalled an officer. "Some of the officers assigned to this duty remained in these positions for periods of six months or more ... The willingness to share the hardships of the jungle and the risk of battle shown by American personnel accompanying the Chinese was, in large part, responsible for increasing the confidence of the Chinese in the Americans."[33]

The Americans soon detected a competition of sorts between the 22nd and 38th Divisions, something they turned to their advantage. "This rivalry between the two divisions proved to be a very effective weapon in headquarters," recalled Boatner, "for it enabled us to send them down the valley side by side, giving each a task to do and calling attention of the other division as to their manner of accomplishment."[34]

On January 6, Stilwell sent the 65th Regiment of Liao's division to secure X Force's west flank by methodically clearing the Taro Plain, an off-shoot of the Hukawng Valley that extended southwest into a dead end surrounded by mountains. The regiment's commander, Colonel Fu, assured Stilwell he will "go after 'em." After two weeks, however, the 65th had not moved very far, which prompted Stilwell to order Fu's relief and state to a shaken Liao that "Fu really should be shot" as an example to other commanders. The next day, the Chinese attacked and met with success. Unknown to Stilwell, the Chinese regiment faced nearly one full Japanese regiment guarding the Taro Plain's entrance; only when Tanaka withdrew most of his forces on the 23rd to face Sun's division did the 65th get moving. On January 26, Stilwell restored Fu to command, and four days later the Taro Plain was cleared. Fu got the point, and for the rest of the campaign proved an excellent commander.[35]

While the Taro operations progressed, Sun's infantry probed the Japanese position at Taipha Ga. His division advanced on January 17, with Brown's tankers in support. The Japanese gave ground, in at least one case leaving a sign in a bunker saying, "Beat us this time; we'll get you next time." Taipha Ga fell in heavy fighting, but flanking forces again failed to move fast enough to trap Tanaka's men. In a meeting with Sun, Stilwell threatened to resign and report everything to his superiors in Washington. "If I am double crossed by the people I'm trying to help," he told Sun, "I am through for good and will recommend very radical measures." Sun proved stubborn in his methods, and failed to speed up the advance. By late January 1944, the five weeks of multiple Chinese offensives had only pushed the front line 10–15 miles from where it had been on Christmas Eve 1943.[36]

The sluggish pace of the Chinese divisions was attributable to several factors. The first was the weather. January 1944 was proving to be more rainy than usual, with near-daily rain for the last two weeks of the month. On January 30, Stilwell found mud three feet deep in places; the main base at Shingbwiyang he called "a sea of mud." For an army dependent on dirt roads and trails to move and fight, these conditions hampered every type of movement. They also slowed Pick's crews as they built the Ledo Road.[37]

Perhaps the biggest factor affecting CAI's performance was leadership. "The Chinese soldier is doing his stuff, as I knew he would if he had half a chance," Stilwell wrote his wife. "It's only the higher-ups who are weak." Sun and Liao were capable leaders and had proven themselves in battles between 1937 and 1943, but they and their senior commanders understood that they belonged first to Chiang Kai-shek. Chiang's comments in November carried weight with the Chinese officers. Chiang also secretly communicated with his commanders during the campaign, although Sun denied it when confronted by Stilwell. On top of all this, there was the question of face: as Sun told Lieutenant Colonel Trevor N. Dupuy, a liaison with his headquarters, he had never lost a battle and was not about to start now.[38]

Still, nothing could disguise the fact that Chinese forces were besting elite Japanese troops, a fact that caused morale to soar among the troops. Another factor that helped morale was something new to the Chinese Army: medical care and evacuation. U.S. field hospitals accompanied Chinese regiments to provide on-the-spot care, while more serious cases went to Major Gordon Seagrave's hospital or back to the 20th General Hospital. Light planes evacuated casualties by air to Ledo. Over the course of the campaign, more than 20,000 Chinese were treated for wounds.[39]

The wounded gave Stilwell an opportunity to demonstrate his priorities. He tried to visit hospitals at least once a week, and did what he could to support the doctors. At one point during the campaign, Ravdin requested fans and air conditioners for his facility to help treat urgent cases. "Dig up 150 ceiling fans, 160 standing fans, and 11 air conditioning units," Stilwell radioed from the field to Sultan in New Delhi. "You and I both know where a lot of it can be dug up." A furious Sultan went to the Imperial Hotel and ordered staff officers to surrender their fans and air conditioners. "We had air conditioners all over our offices," recalled Dean Rusk. "We tore those units out and sent them to Assam, but that kind of incident does not endear staffers to troops in the field."[40]

Stilwell also enjoyed support of a different kind: local Kachin peoples from the hill area east of the Hukawng Valley. They had been organized into the Kachin Rangers, a scattered guerrilla force of local tribesmen trained and equipped by the U.S. OSS Detachment 101 under Lieutenant Colonel William R. Peers. He had taken over when the detachment's original commander, Colonel Carl Eifler, was invalided home in December 1943. Eifler and Peers had set up a network of OSS agents controlled from a base at Nazira on the Indian border. These agents organized the local anti-Japanese Kachin tribes to provide intelligence, rescue downed Allied airmen, and harass the Japanese forces in northern Burma. This force, which by war's end numbered 10,000 Kachins and 500 American officers, was ordered by Stilwell to support his advance and help liberate the area south of Fort Hertz. Peers traveled with CAI's headquarters throughout the campaign, and Stilwell conferred with him often.[41]

On January 24, Wingate and Fergusson returned to Stilwell's headquarters to talk further about 16th Brigade's march, set to begin in two weeks. Stilwell agreed to provide supplies and facilities along the Ledo Road, in return for Fergusson making a strike on Lonkin, west of the key Japanese base at Kamaing. This was designed to worry Tanaka and force him to divert strength away from the main front. The wiry Fergusson shifted his monocle and agreed to uphold his end of the bargain. "I like the sound of that," replied Stilwell, and the meeting broke up. "Help this guy," Stilwell told Boatner. "He looks like a dude, but I think he's a soldier."[42]

As the month progressed, Stilwell received repeated indications that SEAC was considering a different strategy, one that did not necessarily involve his campaign or the Ledo Road. Indeed, it appeared that Mountbatten wanted to attack Sumatra, and shut down the north Burma offensive. "The limies are welshing," Stilwell bitterly noted in his diary. Worse, SEAC's strategic vacillation was weakening Chiang's support for Stilwell's campaign, which meant no Y Force attack and more stalling by Sun and Liao unless something was done. Stilwell would now have to fight his superiors behind as well as the Japanese in front.[43]

CHAPTER 4

Battles Front and Rear

Throughout January, Dan Sultan in New Delhi had monitored the planning discussions in Mountbatten's headquarters. By January 8, SEAC's basic program was clear: stop the Ledo Road offensive, enhance the China airlift, contain the Japanese along the India–Burma border, and pause until fall 1944, when Germany would hopefully be defeated. In October or November 1944, SEAC forces would launch Operation Culverin, a landing in northern Sumatra preparatory to a move into Malaya or Thailand. The forces for Culverin would come from Slim's army, transported by landing craft presumably no longer needed in Europe.[1]

Sultan advised Stilwell of this plan and the progress of discussions. Stilwell saw that Culverin would completely undo the strategy set at Cairo, threatening any hope of opening a road to China. He was determined to thwart it any way he could.

Mountbatten called a conference in New Delhi for the morning of January 31, and Stilwell left the field to attend. All of SEAC's senior commanders and staff, some of whom also harbored doubts about the plan, attended what Mountbatten billed as "a full dress meeting." The SACSEA had also laid on a dinner party that night with Wavell and Auchinleck to boost the spirits of the assembled generals.[2]

At the conference, U.S. Major General Albert C. Wedemeyer of SEAC's staff predicted that Stilwell's Ledo Road campaign was impossible of completion before at least 1946. Wedemeyer also outlined the plan to halt all operations before the monsoon and conserve strength for the Culverin attack to come that fall. It all seemed to Stilwell nothing more than "fancy charts, false figures, and dirty intentions." "To hell with logistics," he responded, and proceeded to argue forcefully for continuation of the overland advance into northern Burma. He also reminded the attendees (almost all British) that Robert Clive had conquered India with 123 soldiers. "Dead silence," recorded Stilwell. The meeting broke up soon after.[3]

Mountbatten knew that without the British and American Chiefs of Staff committed to it, Culverin would be impossible to execute. During the meeting, he announced the imminent dispatch of an Anglo-American delegation to advocate for Culverin; they would travel first to Mountbatten's superiors in London and later move on to Washington for final approval from the U.S. Joint Chiefs. Wedemeyer would head the mission of 17 officers, codenamed Axiom. At the end of the meeting, Mountbatten promised that Stilwell's views would be carried forward by the Axiom Mission, even though none of Stilwell's staff would go along in the party.

Stilwell had anticipated this development, and on January 20, he met with his staff in Shingbwiyang. Davies and Brigadier General Benjamin G. Ferris, CBI's Deputy Chief of Staff, also flew in for the conference. As a U.S. theater commander, Stilwell had the right of direct contact with the U.S. Joint Chiefs and decided to use that right to send a deputation of his own to Washington. Ferris and Davies would go, and stay as long as they needed to defeat Mountbatten's plans.[4]

Afterward, Davies pulled Stilwell outside the tent. "I told him," recalled Davies, "that the forthcoming conference was for him the most important yet and that he was sending the weakest delegation he had ever dispatched." Davies stated that Ferris's "Anglophobia would not go down" with General Marshall, and Stilwell agreed. Davies also noted that Ferris "would be overawed by the people he had to deal with in Washington and would not make a very good presentation of the case." What was needed was "a positive personality such as General Joe himself," Merrill, or Boatner. After a short discussion, Stilwell agreed that Boatner should join Ferris and Davies on the team.

On January 31, not long after the conference with Mountbatten, Stilwell gave his final instructions to Boatner, Davies, and Ferris. The three men then took off from New Delhi for Washington accompanied by two staff officers, Colonel Francis G. Brink and Lieutenant Colonel Francis Hill. Stilwell chose not to inform Mountbatten of their dispatch, and returned to Burma late that night, after Mountbatten's dinner.[5]

Five days later, on February 5, the Axiom Mission took off from New Delhi for London at 7:45am. Mountbatten and over 100 SEAC staff came to attend the departure of Wedemeyer and his team. "Nothing could have shown more clearly the splendid Anglo-American family feeling that exists than that so many hard-worked officers should voluntarily have gone to the airport at this early hour to see the party off," mused Mountbatten. "It was rather like saying goodbye to a football team with metaphorical cries of 'Don't come back without the cup!'"[6]

The jubilant mood dissipated somewhat when Mountbatten and his staff returned to headquarters and reviewed the latest reports from the battlefront. "A great battle," noted Mountbatten, "has started in the Arakan."[7]

* * *

As SEAC's commanders debated over whether to fight in Burma, the first phase of the Japanese offensive, codenamed Ha-Go, got underway against Christison's XV Corps in the Arakan.

In early February, Christison's corps stood in a rough east–west line not far over the Burma frontier near Buthidaung. For much of January, his three divisions—Major General Harold "Briggo" Briggs's 5th Indian Division on the left, Major General Frank W. Messervy's 7th Indian Division directly to its east, and Major General C. G. Woolner's 81st West African Division spread out in the mountains further east—had slogged their way south against determined Japanese resistance. The rolling and virtually roadless terrain, cut up into compartmented valleys by steep mountain ranges, were as much of an obstacle to the advance as the enemy. By the first week of February, Christison's corps stood just north of Buthidaung, a key town and road junction in the region. His troops were in the process of regrouping in preparation for a major attack on Buthidaung scheduled for February 8.[8]

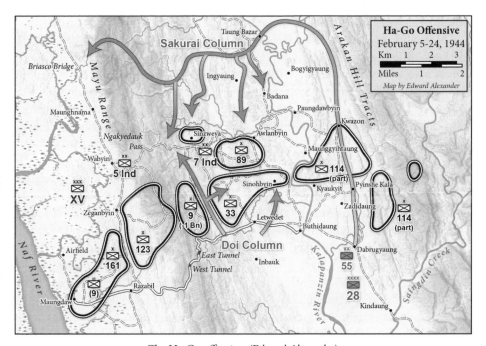

The Ha-Go offensive. (Edward Alexander)

Christison's troops were strung out along a front of 40 miles, stretching from the Naf River in the west to the Kaladan River and valley to the east. The 5th and 7th Indian Divisions occupied the westernmost 20 miles to the Kalapanzin River, opposite Buthidaung and the main Japanese defenses. The rest of the area, mostly remote jungle and hills, was covered by Woolner's two West African brigades. They had been assigned that sector for a reason, recalled Slim: "Their discipline and smartness were impressive, and they were more obviously at home in the jungle than any troops I had yet seen."[9]

Dispositions on the main front faced more rolling terrain, cut up by the Mayu Range mountains between 1,500 and 2,000 feet in elevation. Two roads crossed them behind British lines at Goppe Pass and Ngakyedauk (nicknamed "Okeydoke") Pass. About one mile in front of British lines was the third crossing, consisting of two prewar rail tunnels; the Buthidaung attack was expected to force the Japanese to give them up. Briggs's division stood at Maungdaw with 9th, 123rd, and 161st Brigades in order from east to west. The 9th Brigade had crossed the Mayu to take over a portion of the 7th Indian Division's line, so the latter could prepare for the planned offensive. Messervy's division linked to it with 33rd and 114th Brigades on line from west to east, and 89th Brigade in reserve. In preparation for the drive, Christison had established a Corps Administrative Area for supplies, transport, and hospitals at Sinzweya, five miles behind 33rd Brigade.[10]

"Briggo" Briggs and his men were veterans of hard service in Africa dating back to 1940. "Briggs was every inch a soldier, and a fighting one," recalled Antony Brett-James, who served on his staff. "He was not the showman, he did not advertise, but none was more successful, more trusted, more 'true blue.'" Messervy's division had only been in battle since the previous November, but had already developed what Slim called "a freshness and a keenness in all it did." This was Messervy's influence; he was a tall man who one brigadier described as "a cavalry officer of great dash and verve who was always itching to get there the fighting was fiercest … He was a great leg-puller, as well as being a thrusting commander." Messervy was commanding his fourth division in battle after leading 4th Indian Division, 1st Armoured Division, and 7th Armoured Division in North Africa during 1941 and 1942. He had escaped a short captivity when German troops overran his headquarters in May 1942, and based on that experience trained all his subsequent headquarters and rear-echelon troops to fight as infantry if required. In 1943, Messervy successfully persuaded the high command in New Delhi that heavy tanks could be used in the jungle. Later that year, he assumed command of 7th Indian Division and took it into action.[11]

The Japanese entrusted Ha-Go to the 55th Division, reinforced with elements of the 54th Division. The divisional commander, Lieutenant General Hanaya Tadashi, planned the same type of flanking operation that had so discomfited the British in 1943. His infantry commander, Major General Sakurai "Tokuta" Tokutaro, would flank 7th Indian Division with 6,000 men and attack it from the rear. Once behind Messervy's flank, a battalion known as Kubo Force would split off to capture the mountain passes and block the road along the Naf River connecting Briggs's division with the corps' main supply base at Chittagong. At the same time the balance of Sakurai's troops would slash into Messervy's rear. This was Tanahashi Force, named after its commander, who had played an important role in the 1943 victories. Tanahashi had his 112th Infantry Regiment, reinforced by a regiment of engineers and part of the 143rd Infantry Regiment, and a mission to destroy all enemy units in his path. While these forces caused havoc in the British rear, a reinforced battalion known as Doi Force would attack Messervy's front. The balance of Hanaya's division, known as Yoshida Force, would stand firm against Briggs's division.

The 55th Division was the same unit that stopped the British incursion into the Arakan a year before. That experience produced great confidence among its men. "As they have previously suffered defeat," announced Sakurai in reference to his British opponents, "should a portion of them waver the whole of them will get confused and victory is certain." The Japanese expected to rout the British again, and hoped that this attack would destroy at least one of the two divisions that it struck. Some commanders even hoped to press into India and capture the key British base at Chittagong.[12]

Ha-Go got underway on the night of February 3, when Sakurai's men moved out into the dark jungle. Rain and mist helped conceal their movements as the men made their way past Messervy's flank. At 7am on February 4, a patrol of 114th Brigade detected what they reported as a "large party of Japs, coolies, and mules moving North." Artillery fire dispersed the Japanese. Reports continued to come in of Japanese units to the east of his division that morning, so Messervy ordered 89th Brigade to move east and "destroy" them. He also successfully appealed for two squadrons of the 25th Dragoons, and late in the day on the 4th the Lee-Grant tanks clanked over Ngakyedauk Pass. The next day, the 89th Brigade reported significant fighting along the division's east flank, while patrols found Japanese still moving north. Messervy considered moving the division headquarters a mile south to Sinzweya, but decided to stay put.[13]

Messervy's reaction had delayed the rear battalion of Sakurai's column and scattered the column's supplies. Tanahashi's lead elements had successfully reached the 7th Indian Division's rear and stood to the northeast at Taung, where they crossed the Kalapanzin River. The middle battalion of the column was strung out in between. The Japanese attackers now divided, with Kubo Force striking west toward the Mayu Range. On the night of the February 5, Tanahashi sent the middle battalion advancing directly westward toward Sinzweya, and personally led the lead battalion in a wide swing to approach Sinzweya from the north. This latter battalion was unknowingly marching directly toward Messervy's headquarters.[14]

At 5am on February 6, the 7th Indian Division's headquarters staff heard shouting and commotion in the distance, but in the mist and wet the sounds were indistinct. Upon discovering Messervy's headquarters, Tanahashi attacked with his headquarters guard and immediately called up his infantry. At 6:30, the Japanese attacked out of the mist, hitting the signals tents. The signalmen fought back as other staff sections mobilized to help defend. Messervy awoke to gunfire, dressed hastily, and joined his senior staff to see what was happening. Japanese fire quickly pinned them down, and they were soon forced to abandon the HQ when the Japanese placed a machine gun on a commanding hill. The battle grew fiercer as more of Tanahashi's infantry arrived on the scene. A troop of British tanks approached and opened fire, but soon withdrew lest they be bogged down in the mud and rain. By 10:30am, the division's Chief of Artillery realized the situation was hopeless and ordered the headquarters staff to scatter and make for Sinzweya. Japanese soldiers swarmed in to the headquarters behind them, capturing papers, codes, equipment, and food. The 7th Indian Division had been decapitated.[15]

The first news of this disaster came via a message to 89th Brigade on the artillery radio net. Brigadier M. R. Roberts of 114th Brigade tuned in to the division radio frequency and heard "Put a pick through that set," followed by silence. Messervy's three brigade commanders— Roberts, Brigadier Frederick J. Loftus-Tottenham of 33rd Brigade, and Brigadier W. A. Crowther of 89th Brigade—talked among each other via field telephone. As Loftus-Tottenham was in touch with Briggs's division and XV Corps headquarters, the three men agreed that he would assume temporary command of the division until either Messervy reappeared or Christison directed otherwise. In the meantime, 89th Brigade would pull back toward Sinzweya and all the brigades would assume positions for an all-around defense.[16]

Messervy's headquarters going off the air galvanized the rest of XV Corps. Over in the 5th Indian Division sector, General Briggs received an order from Christison to secure Ngakyedauk Pass and the Administrative Area. Briggs called Brigadier Geoffrey C. Evans, a hard-charging officer who had taken over 9th Brigade from Brigadier Joseph "Sally" Salomons just the day before. "The situation is obscure, to say the least of it, but obviously a large enemy force has got round behind 7th Division," Briggs said. "The Corps Commander wants to you take command of the Corps Administrative Area … Put it in a state of defense and hold it at all costs." "To say that I was staggered," recalled Evans, "was to put it mildly."[17]

Evans turned command of 9th Brigade back to Salomons, and ordered the 400 men of 2rd West Yorkshires to march for the Administrative Area at once. He also called the 25th Dragoons and ordered a troop of tanks to join the infantry. Salomons received directions to get the brigade front organized and then move his headquarters to Sinzweya. Having given these orders, Evans had just one more task: "to discover," as he wrote, "just where the Administrative Area was!" Salomons showed him on a map and pointed the way.[18]

After a muddy trip, Evans arrived at his destination about 11:30am. The Administrative Area was in a roughly circular clearing 1,200 yards in diameter. "Surrounding it were high hills covered with dense jungle, so that an attacker could get right up close without being seen," recalled Evans. "In the middle of the clearing was a small scrub-covered hill [soon dubbed Ammunition Hill], about two hundred yards in length and perhaps a hundred fifty feet high, around which was stacked all the ammunition. In other parts of the area were big dumps of petrol and supplies, the supply echelons of the various brigades, a mule company and such installations as an officer's shop and a main dressing station. I did not know there was a hospital until the following night."[19]

The senior officer present, Lieutenant Colonel R. B. Cole of the 24th Anti-Aircraft/Anti-Tank Regiment, had already organized the units of clerks, quartermasters, mechanics, muleteers, and artillerymen into something of a defense perimeter—a "Box," in British Army parlance. The Administrative Area now became the Admin Box. Evans strengthened the perimeter with men as they came in, but had to leave the eastern face open due to a shortage of personnel. Two companies of the 4/8 Gurkhas of 89th Brigade moved in to cover that area during the night. Evans held the 25th Dragoons' tanks and two companies of the West Yorkshires as a reserve and counterattack force. Salomons arrived with 9th Brigade headquarters in the early afternoon, and Evans converted it into the Admin Box's nerve center. The calm atmosphere within the Box struck Evans forcefully. "It was heartening to see the determination with which they set about their defense tasks," he said of the men. "Yet I could not help wondering how these administrative unit commanders and their men would fare."[20]

As Evans's defenders settled in, the first men from 7th Indian Division headquarters appeared. More arrived during the afternoon, and by evening most of the headquarters personnel had assembled in the Admin Box. They had inflicted over 50 Japanese losses in the headquarters battle, but sustained 100 casualties, mostly among the signals section. Enough of the organization had survived that it could function as a headquarters. At 2pm, General Messervy emerged from the jungle. He gratefully accepted a mug of tea fortified with whiskey, and set about resuming command of his division. A radio borrowed from the 25th Dragoons got him back on the air, to the pleasure and relief of all concerned. Messervy told Evans to command the Box, while he would resume leadership of the 7th Indian Division.[21]

An hour after Messervy's arrival, Japanese fighters strafed the Box, killing two mules near Evans's headquarters. The carcasses remained there for the rest of the battle. At 5pm, Evans summoned his commanders and told them, "Your job is to stay put and keep the Japanese out. Hold your fire and conserve ammunition. Wait till you see the yellow of their eyes before you shoot. Make sure one round means one dead Jap." Two hours later, these instructions were put into practice as the first Japanese probe hit the northwest side of the Box. "There was a great deal of shouting by the Japs," wrote Evans, "But the attack was not pressed home and after an hour it died down."[22]

The next morning, February 7, Tanahashi's Japanese attacked the Gurkhas, who had recently taken up their positions on the Box's east face. The defenders fell back after heavy fighting, but a quick counterattack by the West Yorkshires restored the situation. Meanwhile, Tanahashi sent another infantry battalion around the Admin Box's western side, both to complete the encirclement and probe for a weak point. A British patrol that had been sent to Ngakyedauk Pass reported that it was in Japanese hands. The Admin Box was surrounded.

The Admin Box position. (India Ministry of Defence)

Shortly after dark, the Japanese, preceded by INA troops calling for Indian troops to surrender, assaulted the Box's southwest perimeter near Messervy's and Evans's headquarters. The defenders withdrew under pressure after a short and sharp battle. As the firing died down, screams carried through the darkness. "Good God," exclaimed an officer. "They've got into the hospital!"[23]

Japanese troops had indeed overrun the Admin Box's main dressing station, manned by personnel of 66th Indian Field Ambulance, 12th Mobile Surgical Unit, 48th Indian Dental Unit, and 28th Indian Blood Transfusion Unit. Many walking wounded had been transferred to a location near Messervy's headquarters, but at least 30 stretcher cases were present along with the medical staff when the Japanese troops arrived. The result was a very great tragedy.[24]

Around 8pm, the first Japanese soldiers entered the hospital. They fired upon any personnel they saw, drawing no distinction between the medical staff and the wounded on cots or operating tables. Some staff escaped in the confusion, but many, including at least one wounded officer, were killed in the melee. In a very short time, the Japanese captured the entire facility, taking over 30 staff prisoner. They bound everyone and interrogated the officers, many quite brutally. Anyone who asked for water, including those seriously wounded men lying in cots, received death by bayonet, sword, or gunfire. Japanese troops ransacked the place for supplies and medicine. The next day, some prisoners were used as human shields, while the remaining men were exposed to incoming shelling from the Box. The fire caused casualties among the prisoners. No medical care was made available, and food and water arrived only in the smallest amounts. Those asking for a cigarette were instead burned by lit cigarettes. A group of Indian prisoners were forced to carry Japanese wounded to Buthidaung; seven were executed near the tunnels on February 11.

On February 9, the Japanese herded the remaining 20 prisoners, all with their hands bound behind their backs, to a gully not far west of the dressing station. At least two doctors still wore stethoscopes around their necks. The men were given no food or water, and their pleas for medical treatment generated no response. The men who complained the most were killed. As evening set in, the Japanese gathered around the prisoners in what one of the doctors, Lieutenant Basu of the Royal Indian Army Medical Corps, described as "a very suspicious manner." Basu soon discovered their intent: "when they shot the B.O.R.s [British Other Ranks, or enlisted soldiers] we all knew we were going to be shot down, one and all." The doctors desperately protested that they were noncombatants, and motioned toward their Red Cross armbands. These efforts were futile. "They shot every one of us," recalled Basu, "most being killed then and there." Basu was only stunned by the bullet that struck him, and he played dead until the Japanese left the area. Two enlisted orderlies did the same. A British patrol later arrived on the scene and rescued them. Of over 30 prisoners taken at the hospital, these three men, plus two who escaped from the group taken to Buthidaung, were the only survivors.

A counterattack by the West Yorkshires had started at daylight on February 8. After a 36-hour battle, the British recovered the hospital on the morning of February 9. The extent of the carnage was apparent and soon known to all. "If there had been in the mind of anyone in the Box any previous doubts about the nature of the enemy," said Evans, "these would have been dispelled by the attack on the hospital."[25]

* * *

A world away, Stilwell's delegation arrived in Washington. "Boatner and I promptly went to see Brigadier General Frank Roberts, a China specialist whom I had known in Peking and the first Burma campaign and who was now impressively installed as head of army planning," recalled Davies. "Boatner stated the Stilwell case. Roberts agreed with it." The men then had a series of meetings with the highest echelons of American leadership, including General Marshall and Secretary of War Henry Stimson, about the situation in CBI.[26]

One of the meetings was a private session between Boatner and President Roosevelt in the White House's Oval Office. "Tell me about Burma, young man," said Roosevelt to open the meeting. Boatner spread a large map of the front on the floor next to Roosevelt's chair. The two were soon in an earnest discussion about recent operations, the nature of the terrain, and possible courses of action. The meeting ran over the allotted time, but Roosevelt did not seem to mind. Boatner sensed an opportunity, and asked Roosevelt to "put pressure on the British in India to help and not hinder General Stilwell." Roosevelt agreed, and on the spot the two men drafted a telegram to that effect. After approval by the Joint Chiefs, it arrived in London on February 14.[27]

It quickly became clear to Stilwell's delegation that the senior American leaders would not welcome the Axiom proposals. In addition to its questionable assumption about the timing of Germany's defeat, Mountbatten's plans did not serve U.S. objectives at all. Capturing Myitkyina, even without the Ledo Road yet opening, would improve the supply line to China by freeing up the Hump's easier southern route. This would, in turn, mean more supplies could be transported over the Hump for the projected air operations from Chinese bases, which the Ledo Road would augment when it finally opened to traffic. The air support from B-29s and Fourteenth Air Force was considered critical for the Pacific offensives, now heating up after the capture of the Marshall Islands and the nearly-complete isolation of Rabaul. Viewed in this light, Mountbatten's proposals seemed a needless diversion of resources. The United States was also firmly committed to a policy of not being seen as helping Britain re-establish colonial rule in Asia, which further militated against supporting any campaign into Sumatra and Malaya. As far as the leadership in Washington was concerned, Stilwell would have his campaign into northern Burma, and that was that. Boatner, Ferris, Davies, Brink, and Hall returned to India after two weeks to report success.[28]

A week after Boatner's arrival in Washington, the Axiom Mission landed in London. On February 14, the team met with Churchill and the British Chiefs of Staff. Wedemeyer briskly laid out the plans for Culverin and shutting down the Burma operations. It soon became apparent that the senior British leaders were divided on the proposal. "My presentation was received courteously but coolly by the Chiefs of Staff and enthusiastically by the Prime Minister," recalled Wedemeyer. "He kept urging me to say more, even to the point of repetition. Upon breaking up the meeting the Prime Minister gave instructions to the British planners to prepare a report on Culverin as soon as practicable." Wedemeyer dined at 10 Downing Street with Churchill, King George VI, and senior British commanders, and Churchill used the opportunity to press again for Culverin.[29]

Roosevelt's telegram, prepared with Boatner, arrived during these discussions. The British deferred a reply, pending further study. When asked for his comments, Mountbatten pointed to the logistical issues of an overland advance into Burma, and restated his belief that the Ledo Road would never be opened. He also took a swipe at his deputy commander: "While I regret that General Stilwell should have made representations in Washington without reference to me, and before General Wedemeyer had had an opportunity of presenting my proposals," he said, "I have complete confidence in General Wedemeyer and do not wish to change or add to his instructions in any way."[30]

The British Chiefs came back to Churchill on February 23 with a recommendation to table Culverin for the moment. The required resources, including landing craft, could not be spared from the Pacific offensive and the upcoming invasion of France. The Japanese main battle fleet had recently moved to Singapore, and posed a serious threat to any amphibious operation in Southeast Asia. The Royal Navy could not guarantee sufficient ships to defend an invasion force. Instead, the Chiefs endorsed improving the airlift to China and defending India.[31]

Three days later, the Axiom Mission flew to Washington. Over the first weeks of March, Wedemeyer tried in vain to change the American Joint Chiefs' minds; his arguments only strengthened their resolve to continue with the current strategy, as decided at Cairo. "There appears much more to be gained," summarized General Marshall, "by employing all the resources we now have available in an all-out drive into upper Burma so we can build our air strength in China and ensure the essential support for our westward advance to the Formosa–China–Luzon area." Since the Americans controlled the needed amphibious resources, this opinion, which was shared by Marshall's colleagues on the Joint Chiefs, effectively vetoed Culverin.[32]

In late March, the Axiom Mission flew back to London with this verdict. After two more weeks of discussions, the Mission returned to India in mid-April.[33]

* * *

Back at the front, the fighting went on. By February 9, the Japanese offensive had reached its apogee. Kubo Force had struck Goppe Pass, but a determined stand by an Indian mule transport unit held them at bay. Turning south, the battalion-sized unit hacked its own trail over the Mayu, including manhandling its heavy guns up and down a 1,000-foot elevation, and cut the road behind 5th Indian Division. Briggs's division was receiving supplies via barges on the Naf River, and 123rd Brigade was moving into position to reopen the road and force Ngakyedauk Pass from the west. Messervy's 7th Indian Division was surrounded in a series of circular positions, one for each brigade plus the Admin Box. Tanahashi's regimental-size force surrounded the Admin Box, while Doi Force had infiltrated between 33rd and 114th Brigades to form a tenuous link with Tanahashi's infantry.[34]

General Slim had anticipated the general course of this battle. He assigned Major General Lomax's 26th Indian Division and Major General Francis W. Festing's 36th Division to Christison's corps as a relief force. Lomax, a veteran of the 1943 Arakan battles, would lead the relief attack, with Festing's men in support.[35]

Slim also summoned Brigadier Arthur "Alf" Snelling, Fourteenth Army's supply officer, and ordered him to start supplying Messervy's division by air. Snelling's staff had already assembled supplies and planned an airlift down to individual planeloads, and improvised parachutes out of jute fabric to solve a shortage of actual parachutes. "The switchover [to air supply], as far as I was concerned," said Slim, "was simple, thanks to the preparation that Fourteenth Army, Third Tactical Air Force, and Troop Carrier Command together had made—it required only the word, 'Go!'"[36]

To make the airlift work, Fourteenth Army would also more cargo aircraft. On February 15, Mountbatten asked Stilwell for 38 American planes to be temporarily diverted from the Hump flights to China. Stilwell refused, as he did not want to create difficulties with Chiang. He also misunderstood and underestimated the size of the Japanese force involved in the Arakan attack. Five days later, Mountbatten appealed to the U.S. Joint Chiefs. They released 30 C-47s to SEAC on a temporary emergency authorization. This boost gave Fourteenth Army what it needed, at the cost of reduced Hump tonnage for February by 3,500 tons.[37]

Back in the Admin Box, the defenders grimly held on. Dawn and dusk usually brought Japanese attacks on various parts of the perimeter, which were beaten off by rifle fire and sometimes by bayonet. The Japanese used the night to harass the defenders and deny them rest. "Those long hours of darkness brought shivers," wrote Scott Gilmore, an American-born lieutenant in 4/8 Gurkhas. Japanese artillery detonated some of the ammunition, producing great fireworks, while the firing from both sides denuded the hills of most foliage by February 12. On the that day, the Japanese wrested Artillery Hill from the defenders along the Admin Box's southern perimeter, which brought them into a position overlooking Messervy's and Evans's headquarters. An immediate counterattack by the West Yorkshires, supported by tanks firing high explosives and machine guns, recovered the hill.[38]

Regimental Sergeant Major Jim Maloney of the West Yorkshires held a position close to the former dressing station, in command of a group of orderlies and clerks. It overlooked a steep-sided creek bed. On the fourth night of the siege, Maloney's men killed two Japanese in the creek bed. The next night, 40 Japanese moved down the same, evidently preparing to make an attack. "Do nothing until I give the signal," ordered Maloney, "then let them have everything you've got." When the enemy was just below the bank, Maloney and his men threw grenades and poured fire into them. One officer got into the British trenches but was killed; over 30 bodies were counted the next day in the creek. The dead officer was carrying a map of Japanese assembly points and attack routes, which promptly provided targets for Messervy's artillery. The creek bed below Maloney's position turned out to be one of these assembly points, and remained so throughout the battle. "This meeting point continued to prove a magnet to small Japanese parties," said Evans. "While the battle lasted, no fewer than one hundred and ten of the enemy were actually accounted for and there were probably many more."[39]

Air battles raged over the Box as the RAF and Japanese Army Air Force planes wheeled and whirled in a battle for supremacy. The Japanese mounted a major air effort, with large fighter sweeps over the battlefield. Third Tactical Air Force countered with its Hurricanes and Spitfires, the latter new to the theater. By mid-February, over 150 Japanese planes had been shot down, and the British owned the skies over the Arakan.[40]

During the day on the 11th, the drone of a different kind of aircraft came from the west, and the first groups of C-47s appeared over the Admin Box. This was the second lift attempt, the first having been turned back by Japanese fighters. This time, Troop Carrier Command's leader, U.S. Brigadier General William D. Old, personally piloted the lead plane. He bored in on the drop zone through Japanese ground fire at an altitude of 250 feet, with the rest of the transports following. Parachutes erupted from the rear of each transport as the supplies were pushed out the door. The planes circled and made repeated runs to make sure all supplies were dropped. Separate lifts brought supplies to the other brigade positions. "It is difficult to describe the light-heartedness these low and slow-flying Dakotas produced among the troops," recalled Roberts. "Ammunition, food, medical comforts, rum, and cigarettes poured out of the sky." General Evans also marveled at the supply operation. "The thoroughness of the air supply was remarkable," he said. "Everything that was ordered was flown in, even such items as razors and toothbrushes" for those who had escaped the division headquarters. Mule fodder came in, as did mail, issues of *SEAC* (the theater newspaper), fuel and oil for the tanks, and replacement clothing. Morale soared among the defenders.[41]

The battle settled down into a routine: the Japanese harassed and attacked at night, lasting from 7pm until about 6am the following day. Days were filled with supply drops and maintenance of the defensive positions. Everyone snatched what rest they could, but the strain of operations was becoming apparent. As the siege entered its second week, it was clear the men were holding—but relief was needed soon.

General Messervy directed his division by wireless, all phone lines having been cut. Every evening between 5 and 6pm, Messervy had his three brigade commanders—Crowther, Loftus-Tottenham, and Roberts—gather at their radio sets for what quickly became known as "Frank's Bedtime Stories." The four men would discuss the day's events and make plans. The conversations took place in plain language, as all codes had been compromised when the divisional headquarters was overrun. "Accounts of actions with the enemy or of his moves could of course be spoken of openly," remembered Roberts. "Anything concerning our own moves and plans had to be cloaked in parables or by reference to events which could not be known to the enemy. When all else failed there was always school-boy French and that would have defeated even a Frenchman!" After the battle the division staff recorded that "on NO occasion was there any indication of the Jap having taken tactical advantage of information intercepted over the air."[42]

Captured maps and messages revealed enemy confusion. Tanahashi's men had started with battle with 10 days' rations, which were exhausted on February 14. A courier carrying orders and call signs for all of Sakurai's units had been killed. "The loss of this message," reported a Fourteenth Army intelligence officer, "caused widespread disruption in [Japanese] communications." On February 11, the first wireless contact between 7th Indian Division and 26th Indian Division occurred. It was clear that the Japanese were running out of time.[43]

Messervy called in the 89th Brigade to take over defense of the Admin Box's eastern perimeter. Meanwhile, the 123rd Brigade slowly cleared Ngakyedauk Pass, while 26th Indian Division advanced southward. After a tenacious defense, Kubo Force was annihilated almost to a man. Feeling boxed in, Tanahashi launched one last charge against the Admin Box on the February 21, which was repelled in heavy fighting. The worn-out Japanese could do little more, and on his own initiative Tanahashi ordered a retreat. Christison's relief forces opened the pass at midday on February 24, and reached the Admin Box that afternoon. Messervy immediately ordered his division to regroup in preparation for resuming the offensive in early March.[44]

That same day, Hanaya approved a general retreat. The Japanese stole away and tried to infiltrate back to their lines. Of the 6,000 men who started the march into Messervy's rear, 5,000 never returned. British forces hunted down stragglers throughout the 7th Indian Division's rear, and in the process recovered all of General Messervy's possessions, which Japanese soldiers had taken as souvenirs, including his unique large-size general officer's hat.[45]

The British had just won their first major land victory against the Japanese in World War II. It was also the first victory for Fourteenth Army and SEAC. "You have given the Japanese a crack they will remember," said Mountbatten in a message to the troops. Slim could not help letting his pride show: "The battle of Arakan was the first occasion in this war in which a British Force has withstood the full weight of a major Japanese offensive—held it, broken it, smashed it into little pieces and pursued it," he announced to the Fourteenth Army. "Anybody who was in the 7th and 5th Indian Divisions and was there has something of which he can be very proud indeed."[46]

Captain R. A. Scaramanga, the keeper of Messervy's divisional War Diary for the battle, could not resist commemorating the moment using a cricket analogy: "England first Innings score."[47]

* * *

In Maymyo, an undeterred General Mutaguchi put the finishing touches on his orders for the Imphal attack. His confidence remained as high as ever. "The Army has now reached the stage of invincibility and the day when the Rising Sun will proclaim our definite victory in India is not far off," he announced.[48]

On February 11, at the height of the Admin Box battle, Mutaguchi formally issued his instructions for the Fifteenth Army's attack. Mutaguchi's three subordinate divisions—31st in the north, 15th in the center, and 33rd in the south—each accompanied by INA forces, found their missions unchanged. Food would be carried or driven on the hoof for later slaughter and consumption.[49]

"The capture of Imphal will be completed, by mid-April," Mutaguchi commanded; he later admitted that he wanted to present Imphal to the Emperor as a gift on his birthday of April 29. "Thereafter," Mutaguchi went on, "the mountain ranges east of Dimapur and Silchar and the Chin Hills will be secured and the necessary defensive preparations made before the advent of the rainy season."[50]

Significantly, Mutaguchi and his staff made no attempt to analyze or alter their plans based on lessons learned from the Arakan fighting. Only one element of the plan was changed: the start date. The 15th Division was slow in assembling, and so Mutaguchi fixed U-Go's start as March 15, three weeks later than originally planned. The one exception to this timing was 33rd Division, which was furthest from its objectives and would therefore start its attack on March 8, a week before the other elements of Fifteenth Army. Mutaguchi again pushed his men to move quickly: "Speedy and successful advance is the keynote," he said. "We must sweep aside the paltry opposition we encounter and add luster to the army's tradition by achieving a victory of annihilation."[51]

As the invasion date drew closer, Bose sent a message to his troops, who he addressed as "Officers and Men of India's Army of Liberation." "Let there be one solemn resolve in your hearts—'Either Liberty or Death!'" he exhorted. "And let there be but one slogan on your lips— 'Onward to Delhi.'"[52]

Japanese leaders echoed this enthusiasm. Colonel Miyamoto Kaoru, the commander of the 31st Division's 124th Regiment issued the following statement to his troops:

> This operation can become a decisive factor in the Great East Asia War, which has reached a deadlock recently. It will deliver a telling blow against Britain and America, who are staging a counter-offensive for the so-called recapture of Burma, and will free 400 million Indians from the British yoke after a hundred years of bondage.
>
> Yours is the glory of participating as a soldier in this decisive war of survival, and this should be a source of deep gratification to you. With the shades of our Imperial ancestors above us, and led by our demi-god Generalissimo, we officers and men of the divine army will have faith in our invincibility and will devote ourselves whole-heartedly to our country. Helped as we are by the Gods, does it still seem difficult to climb the steep mountains of the Arakan or to cross those accursed Chindwin torrents which still block our path?

Having thus spiritually charged his men, he offered them some advice. "Army discipline will be strictly observed throughout the operation, and for those who ignore this there will be no victory ... We shall invariably seek out and destroy British and Americans, but Indian units will only be annihilated if they persist in offering resistance to our attacks" and any Indian prisoners will be handed over to the INA. "Brave and loyal officers and men of my regiment, I ask you to devote yourselves proudly to the task."

Miyamoto also offered this passage: "Those who issue orders are simply passing on the orders of their superiors, so all orders should be strictly obeyed."[53]

* * *

In contrast to the determined fighting in Arakan and the confident planning of Mutaguchi, February had mostly produced frustration for General Stilwell and his advance into northern Burma.

As of February 1, the forces had a new designation: Northern Combat Area Command (NCAC). The command, in effect a field army-level headquarters, included all troops in northern Burma north and east of a line from Bhamo to Lonkin. Boatner took command of NCAC, and received administrative control over all U.S. units in the area. General Stilwell retained command of CAI, and Boatner retained his title as CAI Chief of Staff. To avoid confusion, Stilwell drew a sharp line on who commanded combat operations. "The command of all combat troops in the Northern Combat Area Command remains as heretofore under the Commanding General, Chinese Army in India," he ordered. "All matters pertaining to the operations and administration of combat troops within the Northern Combat Area Command will be addressed to the Commanding General, Chinese Army in

India." This organization would henceforth be the primary force to capture Myitkyina and open the road to China.[54]

Stilwell acutely felt the need for speed, as the monsoon's arrival in the first half of May loomed. But rains of January did not let up in the new month, with multiple rain and thunderstorms over the first three weeks of February. "Just a matter now of weather," mused Stilwell on February 2. "God give us a few dry days, and we can go." But NCAC remained literally stuck in the mud, as the rains arrived with such frequency that the ground rarely dried enough to permit major operations. By February 21, Stilwell was frustrated: "It *rained* last night from 11 to 1 and I lay there cursing till long after it finally stopped," he reported to his diary. "About one more day of that and I'll be a raving maniac."[55]

Stilwell publicly kept up a brave face to his staff and commanders. "We were a team," recalled Colonel Robert M. Cannon, who was filling in as CAI Chief of Staff while Boatner was in Washington. "He [Stilwell] was our director and he was properly nicknamed, 'The Quarterback' ... Many a night when I was feeling low mentally because of the rain, the jungle, and the problems of the day, I have invented reasons for going to his tent to visit. No matter how low I felt or how impossible everything appeared to be, I never left his presence with any feeling except that everything was on the up, or that it rained today but the sun will be out tomorrow. He affected everyone the same way."[56]

General Pick and his Ledo Road crews proved undaunted. Once the road reached the Shingbwiyang area, it was past the major mountains and into the valley. The operation turned into one of cutting and grading roadbeds, bridging rivers, and laying the crushed gravel road surface. Fuel pipelines also ran along the route. Survey teams kept ahead, staking the road's trace almost to the front line. The road averaged one bridge or culvert every 2.8 miles, and measured between 12 and 24 feet wide. "Rare it was that his trace was far behind the front line troops," recalled Colonel Ravdin, "and the lead bulldozers were armor plated." Pick's men also built airstrips for light planes to use for casualty evacuation and other missions. "Such was the devotion of men to Pick," continued Ravdin, "that the negro who ran the bulldozer worked for 44 hours without rest to complete [one airfield]. The General was devoted to the men who could run those 'dozers' ... He exemplifies the finest traditions of the Army."[57]

Pick's crews lived in work camps along the roadway, and soon a sort of community was established. By late February, the Ledo Road appeared to one observer, Lieutenant Charlton Ogburn, as "a great, broad, raw gash through the forest dipping, rising, winding, cutting back, going on days without end." He was struck by how "some of the world's most diverse strands [came] into juxtaposition," as Indians, Chinese, Burmese, and American troops all intermingled at stations along the way.[58]

Despite the weather, the Chinese forces did manage some gains in the first three weeks of the month. The fighting of the past few months had depleted and exhausted Sun's division, so Stilwell assigned them a supporting role of pushing south and east from Taipha Ga. Liao's 65th and 66th Regiments would swing in from the west and northwest in an effort to flank the Japanese. Rain delayed all of these moves, and the Chinese did not advance in strength until February 14. Liao's men reported success two days later, but it soon turned out they were lost and confused an unnamed village with their objective. On February 18, Stilwell "blew up at breakfast and bawled Liao out. Dumb performance has bitched up our chance to catch Japs. Told him he and 22d had lost face." The delay gave Tanaka time to detect the threat to his western flank, and he pulled his Japanese back five miles to just north of Maingkwan. Stilwell's front had moved five miles further forward, but without a decisive battle. Nonetheless, Japanese prisoners admitted their division had lost more men in this campaign than it had taking Singapore in 1942.[59]

Stilwell was again active on the front line, visiting the 38th Division's positions near Taipha Ga and later ranging into Liao's sector. Several times he came under enemy shelling and small-arms fire; the most serious occasion was with a group of newsmen escaped a shelling by Japanese artillery on February 13. Stilwell's staff created a bodyguard for him of three enlisted Americans and Dara Singh, an ex-boxer from Singapore who held a colonel's rank in the Chinese Army and according to Cannon "spoke every language used in that part of the world." He doubled as Stilwell's interpreter and went everywhere with the general. Singh took his duties very seriously, and carried a Thompson submachine gun, a carbine, an American .45 pistol, a Mauser pistol, and extra ammunition for all weapons. "He was a one-man arsenal," recalled Eldridge.[60]

As the Chinese lurched forward, in their rear the 3,000 Chindits of Fergusson's 16th Brigade started their march south. Wingate had ordered the men to be near Indaw, 350 miles away, in six weeks' time. After Giffard and Wingate saw him off on February 5, Fergusson dispatched his eight columns in succession southward over the rugged Patkai Hills. The narrow trails combined with rough terrain to slow movement and make Wingate's schedule ambitious at best. The Chindits were soon strung out along the path. "Until we eventually reached [the first good stopping point at the village of] Hkalak," recalled Fergusson, "I do not recollect one single stretch of level track so much as one hundred yards in length ... It was no unusual thing for a column to sleep in two halves, with one of those major hills dividing the two; and supper was often a dry meal, with no water within reach, save that which we caught in our mugs or groundsheets from the rain." Nonetheless, the advance continued.[61]

On February 21, Stilwell at last received the promised American infantry. The 2,997 men of General Merrill's Galahad Force arrived that day after a long trip across India via riverboat and rail. As a final effort of conditioning, Merrill ordered the men to march in from Ledo. The 1st and 2nd Battalions passed Stilwell's headquarters, but the man himself did not appear; some men were disappointed that he did not take a salute that they were prepared to give. Stilwell paid Merrill and his men a visit in their camp at Ningbyen. Lieutenant Ogburn recalled that Stilwell "made a good impression" on the Americans. Stilwell stated that Galahad was "what he and everyone had been waiting for." Stilwell passed Galahad's 3rd Battalion on his way back to headquarters. "Tough looking lot of babies," noted the general that night.[62]

Heartened by these reinforcements, and with the prospect of drier weather to come, Stilwell felt prepared to resume the attack. "With M. [Merrill] ready and Brown ready," he told his diary on February 21, "we can go now." Three days later, the next stage in Stilwell's drive began.[63]

CHAPTER 5

The Triple Invasions

For the next stage of his campaign, General Stilwell planned another enveloping attack against his Japanese opponents. He expected Tanaka to fight for Maingkwan, as it was the most sizeable village in the Hukawng Valley. Accordingly, Stilwell decided to use his Chinese divisions and Brown's tanks to attack toward Maingkwan. At the same time, a Sino-American force of two regiments would swing to the east, march down the valley's east side, and then move into the rear of the Japanese to cut the Kamaing Road. Initially, the envelopment was aimed for Shaduzup, but the rougher terrain in that area would have slowed the march too much; instead, the flanking force would aim for Walawbum, where the road turned east for about six miles before resuming its southward course. It was also the last village before crossing the Jambu Bum ridge from the Hukawng Valley into the Mogaung Valley, which ran to the Irrawaddy River and the Myitkyina area. Victory at Walawbum would have strategic consequences.[1]

The spearhead for this attack into Tanaka's rear would be Merrill's Marauders, with the 113th Infantry Regiment of Sun's division in support. Merrill received great discretion in how to execute his mission, though the 113th was independent of Merrill's command, despite requests from Sun and Merrill to combine the units. The terms of CAI's command did not allow any American to directly command Chinese units, with the exceptions of Stilwell and Brown.[2]

Galahad was organized along the lines of a Chindit brigade, with three battalions each divided into two teams plus a reconnaissance platoon. A rear detachment stayed behind to look after supplies and other administrative matters for the unit while it was in the field. The force had no artillery, but each team included mortar and machine gun crews. Lieutenant Colonel William L. Osborne commanded the 1st Battalion, divided into Red and White Teams. Lieutenant Colonel George McGee's 2nd Battalion contained Blue and Green Teams, while the Khaki and Orange Teams made up Lieutenant Colonel Charles Beach's 3rd Battalion. Galahad numbered 2,600 when it set out on its first mission.[3]

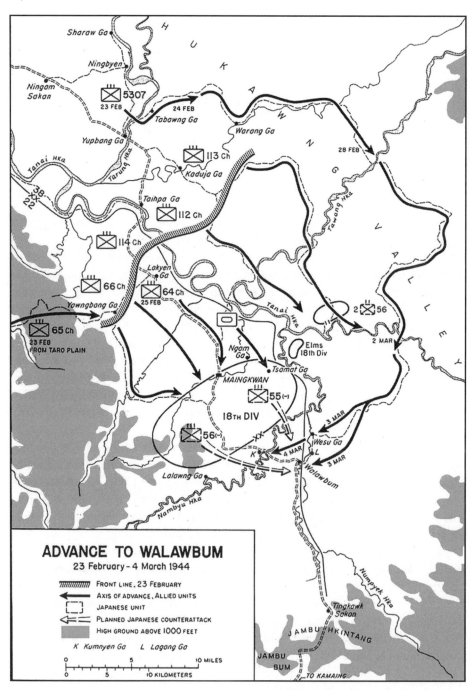

ADVANCE TO WALAWBUM
23 February – 4 March 1944

FRONT LINE, 23 FEBRUARY

AXIS OF ADVANCE, ALLIED UNITS

JAPANESE UNIT

PLANNED JAPANESE COUNTERATTACK

HIGH GROUND ABOVE 1000 FEET

K Kumnyen Ga   L Lagang Ga

0   5   10 MILES

0   5   10 KILOMETERS

NCAC's advance to Walawbum. (U.S. Army)

The unit's two senior commanders were General Merrill and Colonel Charles N. Hunter. Merrill was a popular leader and greatly respected by his men. "He had a down-to-earth, smiling simplicity and a shrewd, politically wise geniality and charm," recalled Ogburn. "He knew what was what and spoke with the authority of the theater." Colonel Hunter, who had brought the unit over to India, presented quite a contrast. "Hunter was a tough, no-nonsense, hard-bitten man of few words," noted Lieutenant Samuel V. Wilson, commanding the 1st Battalion's reconnaissance platoon. "At the same time, he had a cutting dry humor, and beneath the crusty exterior he was one of the most warm-hearted people I had known. That part of himself he kept concealed from those who were not close to him."[4]

On February 24, the offensive began. "Well gentlemen, here's what you have been waiting for," said Merrill to his commanders. The three reconnaissance platoons led the way eastward, in search of the Japanese flank. In the process, Private Robert Landis was killed—the first Galahad casualty. Wilson's platoon found the flank, and led the way southward. As the march progressed, one officer noted "a very definite change in the actions and attitude of the men. The combat veterans understood and others knew that D-Day had passed, and the enemy could be encountered at any time. We were now in a situation where an instant's hesitation or wrong move could mean life or death."[5]

The march was not without its quaint moments. During a rest, Private Benny Silverman of 3rd Battalion asked Sergeant David Hurwitt, "where in the hell are we going?" "Why in hell are you asking me," grunted Hurwitt. "Why don't you ask the general?" Just then Merrill happened to be passing by. "Hey General!" Silverman yelled to him, "Where the fuck are we going?" A mortified Hurwitt expected the worst, but instead Merrill came over, gathered the men around, chatted a bit, and then pulled out a map. "He then started telling us where we were going," remembered Hurwitt. "And the more he related to us the whiter I got … after the general got done with his briefing he got up and said, 'Okay, fellers?' We had about enough strength to nod. You know no general acts like this to a group of enlisted men … I tell you that was the measure of our guy. He was the kind of man you could get to love."[6]

As the Marauders turned south, they encountered Kachin villages and units of the Kachin Rangers. The Kachins had scores to settle with the Japanese, as many of their villages (including Walawbum and Maingkwan) had been subject to Japanese reprisals for Kachin guerrilla activities. The Kachins found common cause with the Marauders, a feeling which was reciprocated. "The Marauders took an immediate and lasting fancy to the Kachins," remembered Ogburn. "The bare-breasted women made quite a hit with the Marauders," noted James E. T. Hopkins, a surgeon with 3rd Battalion, "and the naked little children quickly lost their fear of the soldiers and were soon munching K-ration crackers given by the men." In addition to their pleasant and open dispositions, the Kachins "not only knew the country and the trails," observed Ogburn, "but they also knew better than anyone but the Japanese where the Japanese were."[7]

On February 26, Liao's Chinese troops started a slow advance southward, forcing the Japanese to give way. Two days later, when Stilwell visited the front, he pressed Liao to "speed up." Liao, Stilwell, and Colonel Carleton Smith, Liao's chief advisor, visited a company astride the road only one-and-a-half miles from Maingkwan. Five minutes after the three officers left, three U.S. P-51s strafed the road, killing the company commander and two others, and wounding 5 more.[8]

On March 3, after eight days of marching and skirmishing with Japanese patrols, Merrill sent his men forward in their first attack. The Americans achieved complete surprise. Beach's 3rd Battalion took position along the Nampyak Hka, overlooking Walawbum itself, the Kamaing Road, and the watercourse, fighting several skirmishes with Japanese forces. Osborne's men stood in reserve near the villages of Wesu Ga and Lagang Ga northeast and east of Walawbum.[9]

McGee's 2nd Battalion penetrated five miles west of Walawbum and, on the morning of March 5, took up a position astride the road at its crossing with the Nambyu Hka stream. As the men took position, they discovered Japanese phone lines running alongside the road. One of the battalion's Japanese-Americans (known as *Nisei*), Sergeant Roy H. Matsumoto, climbed a tree and tapped a line. He overheard a sergeant at an ammunition dump nearby asking for help, and McGee arranged a successful airstrike. "I was up in the tree most of the time from morning to evening, and I did not have time to dig my own foxhole," remembered Matsumoto. "But I was able to obtain much valuable intelligence, especially orders regarding enemy troop movements." This information was passed to Merrill and radioed to Stilwell's headquarters.[10]

Tanaka already had troops on the way, in response to an erroneous report of Merrill's appearance on March 1. While elements of the 55th Regiment watched the Chinese, Tanaka sent the balance of that unit and the whole 56th Regiment against Galahad. He aimed for nothing less than the total destruction of the American force. On March 4 and 5, the Japanese made contact with 2nd and 3rd Battalions, starting two major battles on either side of Walawbum.[11]

East of Walawbum, 3rd Battalion deployed the combat teams on the Numpyek Hka's east bank, and Lieutenant Logan Weston's reconnaissance platoon on the west. Weston's men first contacted Japanese troops coming from the north. The Americans held all morning against increasing attacks, helped by one of the platoon's *Nisei*, Sergeant Harry Gosho, who translated the shouts and commands he heard. Colonel Beach recalled the platoon at about midday, and they withdrew under cover of mortar fire and sniping by Chief Janis, a full-blooded Sioux warrior. The wounded men were taken to a makeshift airstrip at Lagang Ga, where light L-4 and L-5 aircraft flew them to the 20th General Hospital at Ledo.[12]

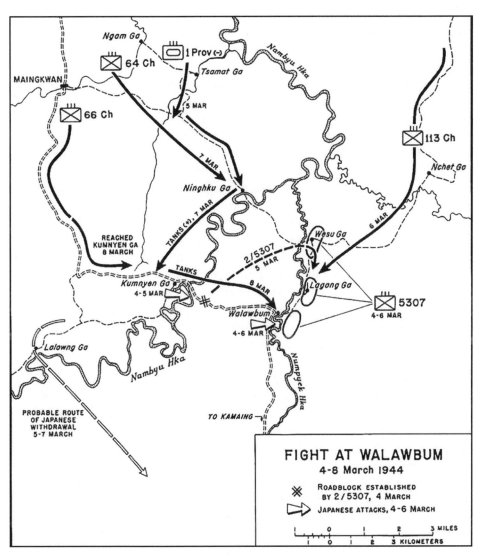

Battles around Walawbum. (U.S. Army)

The 2nd Battalion had been in position just a short time when Blue Combat Team ambushed a Japanese patrol. The men quickly finished digging in, and soon thereafter the first mass Japanese attacks came. McGee's battalion withstood six Japanese attacks that day, interspersed with shelling, repulsing all with massed small-arms fire. At day's end, McGee counted 100 Japanese bodies against losses of one killed and five wounded. That night, concerned about being able to resupply the men, Merrill ordered his troops to retreat and join 1st Battalion, which they did on March 6.[13]

For the next two days, 3rd Battalion withstood repeated Japanese attacks across the river. The Japanese shelled Orange Combat team with mortars and artillery, and attacked several times in increasing numbers, but never less than company strength. "They kept coming—it was classic," recalled a lieutenant. "They just kept coming across the field across from the river, and we kept shooting at them." Both sides taunted each other with cries of "Roosevelt eats shit!" or "Tojo eats shit!" Small Japanese groups made it across the river, but were quickly wiped out. By the evening of March 6, it was obvious that the Japanese were stymied.[14]

Meanwhile on the main front, the Chinese infantry ground forward, assisted by Brown's tanks. Maingkwan fell to the 66th Infantry Regiment of Liao's 22nd Division on March 5. As the Chinese forces pressed in from the north and west, Brown's tanks (supported by a battalion of Chinese infantry) slashed southeast against the Japanese right flank. Communications breakdowns hindered Tanaka's response to these movements, and his division became disorganized; at one point on March 6, Brown's tanks brushed against division headquarters and scattered Tanaka's staff by firing from across a creek. The surprised tankers were unable to press their advantage.[15]

The reports from the division's northern flank, the lack of decisive success against the Americans, and his own near-capture convinced Tanaka to withdraw. Fortunately, his options extended beyond fighting his way past the Marauders at Walawbum. On their initiative, the 18th Division's engineers had cut two trails—one 15 miles long running west of the Jambu Bum, and a second, shorter trail cutting southeast past Walawbum to the Kamaing Road two miles south of the village. Stilwell's forces were not aware of either. Tanaka decided to use the first trail to move the bulk of his men, and gave the order on the afternoon of March 5. He ordered the wounded and supplies to start moving immediately, with the rest of the division to follow the next day. If possible, the Japanese would fight their way past Walawbum and keep the pressure on the Marauders. "Every man," Tanaka directed, "in the next few days must fight hard." Sergeant Matsumoto heard this order and relayed it to Merrill and Stilwell.[16]

On the morning of March 7, the Marauders repelled one final attack along the river. Soon thereafter, firing in the rear was heard; it was Sun's infantry firing three volleys of three rounds, the prearranged signal for their approach. Unfortunately, this resulted in return fire, and a handful of casualties in both American and Chinese units. Once the mess was straightened out, Merrill turned over his positions to the Chinese and withdrew the Marauders for rest and resupply. "The idea [of Merrill's discretionary orders] was not to risk heavy losses," fumed Stilwell in his diary when he found out the next day. "That was the discretion allowed, and not go roaming."[17]

Sensing a victory, Stilwell ordered what he called a "squeeze play," a converging attack by all NCAC units against the 18th Division. Communications difficulties resulted in orders being late to some units, and so the coordinated attack Stilwell had planned for March 8 instead turned into disjointed attacks against Tanaka's rearguard. By March 9, when Walawbum fell for good to Chinese infantry, it was clear the Japanese had escaped the net.[18]

Stilwell's forces paused to regroup. In the past three months, the Chinese had sustained 802 killed, 1,479 wounded, and 530 lost to other causes. The Marauders had lost eight killed and 37 wounded, 70 evacuated to various diseases and injuries, and 109 sick. These losses left Merrill with approximately 2,300 men fit for duty.[19]

Despite Tanaka's escape, his division was in bad shape, with many infantry companies down to just 50 or 60 men each. The 18th Division was slowly withering away. Most importantly, by March 9, NCAC owned all of Burma north of the Jambu Bum. The front had advanced 30 miles in less than two weeks. "Between us and the Chinese," General Merrill explained to the Marauders, "we have forced the Japanese to withdraw farther in the last three days than they have in the last three months of fighting."

Stilwell's forces were now halfway to Mogaung.[20]

* * *

Further south and west, a different drama played out, as Wingate's Chindits prepared to fly into Burma and get Operation Thursday underway in earnest. The Chindit invasion was the largest airborne operation of World War II to date. Slim gave Thursday three objectives: "1. To help the advance of combat troops (Ledo Sector) [NCAC] to the Myitkyina area by drawing off and disorganizing the enemy force opposing them and prevent the reinforcement of these forces. 2. To create a favorable situation for the Chinese [Y Force] advance westwards across the Salween. 3. To inflict the maximum confusion, damage, and loss on the enemy forces in Burma."[21]

Fergusson's 16th Brigade was already on the move, and now Wingate planned to fly in Calvert's 77th and Lentaigne's 111th Brigades to the Indaw area via glider. The other three brigades would stay in reserve for the time being. Cochran's 1st Air Commando would handle air support and glider operations. Planners identified three landing zones in the jungle, all within 40 miles of Indaw and the railroad that served as 18th Division's supply line. The zones were codenamed Broadway, Piccadilly, and Chowringhee; each was large enough to house a C-47 airstrip and offered good access

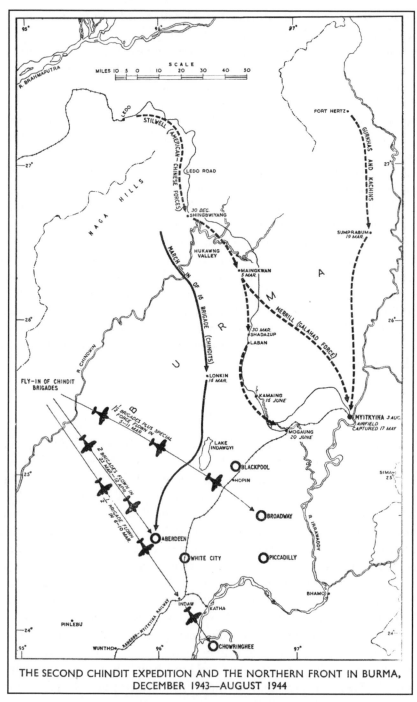

THE SECOND CHINDIT EXPEDITION AND THE NORTHERN FRONT IN BURMA,
DECEMBER 1943—AUGUST 1944

Overview of Operation Thursday. (Royal Air Force)

to Indaw. Piccadilly had been used for air operations before, namely the evacuation of the sick via C-47 during Operation Longcloth in April 1943.[22]

Wingate planned the first fly-in for 6pm on the evening of March 5, to take advantage of a near-full moon. Calvert would lead his 77th Brigade and elements of 111th Brigade to Broadway and Piccadilly, followed a few nights later by the balance of 111th Brigade into Chowringhee. From there, the Chindits would send columns against the railroad near Indaw, while a small detachment called Dahforce headed for the Kachin areas south of Myitkyina.[23]

By March 5, Calvert and his men had assembled at Lalaghat Airfield, in northeast Bengal. Arrayed around the field were the 61 gliders set to take his men in, most double-towed behind C-47s of the 1st Air Commando. Wingate and Tulloch manned Special Force's headquarters nearby. Cochran and Alison were there making final preparations with their 1st Air Commando aircraft; Alison would handle part of the landing operations and go in by glider. Slim, who had briefed Stilwell on Wingate's plans the day before, was also present, as was Air Marshal John Baldwin of Third Tactical Air Force, Stratemeyer of Eastern Air Command, and General Old of Air Transport Command. Everyone felt the electric sense of impending adventure. "We were all so eager," recalled Calvert, "We could never again be keyed up to such a pitch morally, physically, or materially." Cochran put it to his pilots succinctly: "Nothing you've ever done, nothing you're ever going to do, counts now. Only the next few hours. Tonight you are going to find your souls."[24]

Wingate had prohibited aerial flights near the three landing grounds, so as not to tip off the Japanese. Captain Charles Russhon of Cochran's staff suggested an overflight by a lone B-25 just to make sure, and Cochran agreed. At 11am on March 5, Russhon took off in a B-25 piloted by Colonel R. T. Smith, the 1st Air Commando's bomber commander. Two hours later they flew over Broadway. "Everything looked normal," recalled Russhon. "We flew around it in a complete circle, and I made a dozen stills. Then we headed for Piccadilly to the south." What Smith and Russhon saw there shocked them. "Hundreds of teak logs lay in rows across the open space," reported Russhon. "They had been placed since I photographed the clearing weeks before. Anything trying to land among them would have been smashed ... It seemed like a trap."[25]

Russhon and Smith realized the importance of this discovery. Using the radio was out of the question for security reasons, so they flew to Hailikandi Airfield, where Russhon's assistants quickly developed the film. Unable to reach Cochran or Alison by phone, Russhon considered driving the 12 miles to Lalaghat, but found a small scout plane and flew to the field. He jumped out and grabbed a jeep, speeding over to where Calvert's men prepared to embark.[26]

It was 4:30pm, just 90 minutes before the operation was to begin. Russhon handed the photos to Cochran and Alison, who immediately understood their significance. The men found Wingate, and were soon joined by the other senior officers in a huddle around the photos. Wingate demanded to know who had ordered this mission, and Cochran replied that he'd "had a hunch." Wingate smiled and returned to the photo.

Urgent questions followed. Was this an ambush? Nobody was sure, and there was no time to investigate. Postponement was not an option; they had to go that night or cancel. Could the plan be changed that quickly? Wingate hesitated to make a decision, aware he was not going on the mission that night. Calvert, Cochran, and the field commanders indicated they were in favor of going, and preferred to start with Broadway alone.[27]

Slim and Wingate stepped aside for a chat. "The decision is yours," said Wingate to Slim. "I knew it was," recalled Slim. "Not for the first time I felt the weight of decision crushing in on me with an almost physical pressure ... On my answer would depend not only the possibility of a disaster with wide implications on the whole Burma campaign and beyond, but the lives of these splendid men, tense and waiting around their aircraft. At that moment I would have given a great deal if Wingate or anybody else could have relieved me of the duty of decision. But that is a burden the commander himself must bear."

"The operation will go on," Slim directed. Baldwin concurred, and after some discussion Wingate determined to send all of Calvert's forces to Broadway.[28]

"So things began to move again," recalled Tulloch. Cochran jumped on the hood of a jeep in front of the pilots assigned to Piccadilly. "Say fellers," he announced, "We've got a better place to go!" The men absorbed the changed information and then scattered to their planes. Calvert's troops boarded. At 6:12pm, just 12 minutes behind schedule, the first planes rumbled down the runway, gliders in tow. They circled the field and then headed east.[29]

Calvert watched through the window of his glider as India turned into Burma. The moonlight made the terrain relatively easy to discern. He noted it was his fourth crossing of the Chindwin, and his first by air. "Perhaps this was a better way to go back," he mused. After a few hours, they reached Broadway. The glider pilot cut the towline and Calvert recalled a "sudden tremendous silence" after the C-47 banked away. The glider banked in and came down with a bounce and a crash, causing only minor injuries to the occupants. Calvert dismounted and soon found John Alison trying to mark the field with lights for the other landings, while other men set about moving gliders to the side.[30]

The Broadway landings did not go smoothly, as the men soon discovered ruts in the land that were undetectable from the air. At this time, the first large wave of gliders appeared, each silently streaking in. "The first few landed safely, avoiding obstacles," noted Calvert, "but many of them became ditched and immoveable." One glider containing a bulldozer sailed through the field and crashed into the trees beyond, the pilots making a miraculous escape. The second wave was on route, but Calvert needed time and daylight to arrange the field to receive them. He had arranged two code words with Tulloch—"Pork Sausage" meant all was well at Broadway, while "Soya Link" meant trouble and to stop all flights. At 2:30am on March 6, Calvert radioed "Soya Link" to Special Force headquarters, a message that produced gloom in Wingate but not in the other senior officers. At 6:30am, Calvert transmitted "Pork Sausage" and opened the field.[31]

Daylight on March 6 revealed the results of the previous night. "Of the 61 gliders which took off," reported Special Force's staff, "46 reached hostile territory, 8 landed prematurely in friendly territory, and 7 were recalled. Of the 46 gliders which reached hostile territory, 35 safely discharged their loads at Broadway, 2 more crashed on the strip, and 9 were cut loose prematurely over hostile territory. No opposition was encountered at Broadway." About half of the occupants of the nine lost gliders made it back to India safely, while their landings sowed confusion among Mutaguchi's army. Despite the last-minute excitement, Operation Thursday was off to a promising start.[32]

U.S. Army engineers of the 900th Field Unit, who made it in with most of their equipment, began smoothing the field into a usable airstrip. By nightfall, Broadway had a good runway for aircraft; Wingate himself arrived for a look in one of the 64 C-47s to land on the night of March 6/7. Chowringhee opened the same night when 111th Brigade began its fly-in. Over Operation Thursday's first week, relays of C-47s came in to Broadway and Chowringhee while light aircraft flew out casualties. "In a few days," remembered Calvert, "We had 12,000 men, 2,000 mules, masses of equipment, anti-aircraft and field guns all established behind the enemy lines."[33]

"Our first task is fulfilled," Wingate announced in an Order of the Day on March 13. "We have inflicted a complete surprise on the enemy. All our Columns are inside the enemy's guts. The time has come to reap the fruit of the advantage we have gained. The enemy will react with violence. We will oppose him with the resolve to conquer our territory of Northern Burma. Let us thank God for the great success He has vouchsafed us and we must press forward with our sword in the enemy's ribs to expel him from our territory. This is not the moment, when such an advantage has been gained, to count the cost. This is a moment to live in history. It is an enterprise in which every man who takes part may feel proud one day to say 'I WAS THERE.'"[34]

* * *

While these operations were taking place, Mountbatten visited Stilwell. Boatner's mission to Washington, combined with the wrangle over transport planes during the Arakan battles, had produced a near break in relations between Mountbatten and Stilwell at a time when Allied unity was essential. Stories in the press that implied NCAC was the only formation in the theater doing any fighting did not help either. On March 2, General Marshall in Washington ordered Stilwell to meet with Mountbatten and iron out their differences.

On the afternoon of March 6, Stilwell left the front to greet Mountbatten in Taipha Ga. The SEAC commander flew in with an escort of 16 fighters, which Stilwell noted was four times the number of NCAC's support aircraft. Stilwell dressed in a plain U.S. uniform with a Chinese Army cap; Mountbatten looked crisp with full shoulder boards and ribbons. The men talked for 90 minutes, and Stilwell "ate crow," as he informed Marshall. "We are great personal friends." Mountbatten agreed, writing after the meeting that Stilwell "really is a grand old warrior but only the Trinity could carry out his duties which require him to be in Delhi, Chungking, and the Ledo Front simultaneously."[35]

Mountbatten wanted to see the battlefront, and after some attempt to dissuade him, Stilwell took Mountbatten forward to CAI's new headquarters near Maingkwan. The two men traveled 11 miles by jeep over what Mountbatten called "the most appalling jungle track imaginable." That night, they stayed under a makeshift tent consisting of supply parachutes suspended by poles. "We could hear the sound of gunfire all round our headquarters during the night," noted Mountbatten, "and twice had to douse all our lights when a Japanese aircraft flew over."[36]

At dawn the next day, March 7, Mountbatten and Stilwell visited the battlefields around Maingkwan. Liao led the men on a detailed tour of the fighting that occurred just a few days before. The wreckage of the battle was still plain to see. "Plenty of dead Japs, horses and junk. Good killing … Louis much impressed," recalled Stilwell. "Doesn't like corpses." For his part, Mountbatten noted the "particularly unpleasant" smell of the battlefield. The sight of maggot-covered Japanese bodies almost made him ill, a reaction he also noted among some of Liao's staff. "I must confess," Mountbatten told his diary, "I was not sorry when we turned back and made for Stilwell's headquarters, where he left me."[37]

Stilwell loaned his jeep to Mountbatten for the drive back to Taipha Ga, and the admiral started driving north at 9am with two Chinese passengers from Stilwell's staff. They passed some of Pick's work crews on the way, and soon came upon a group cutting bamboo to widen the track. Always reluctant to slow down, Mountbatten continued at speed past the work site. The left front tire caught a piece of bamboo, shooting it up toward Mountbatten's head. The bamboo scored a direct hit on his left eye with such force that it threw him back in the seat and he momentarily lost control of the jeep. Within a few feet he had it stopped and got out.[38]

"It took a certain amount of moral courage to feel and see if my left eyeball was still in its socket, as I could not believe after such a blow that it could still remain there," recalled Mountbatten. "My relief at finding it still in place was tempered by my finding that I was completely blind in the left eye. I put a first-aid dressing on it and drove on." Not far along, he found Gordon Seagrave's Burmese hospital and stopped. Seagrave examined him, and directed him to go to the 20th General Hospital in Ledo. Mountbatten indicated he was planning to drive there anyway, and would arrive that evening. "Young man," countered Seagrave, "This is plenty serious. You must fly there as quick as you can." Thus advised, Mountbatten drove to Taipha Ga and caught a plane to Ledo.[39]

Luckily for him, the 20th General Hospital's staff included one of the foremost eye doctors in the United States, Captain Harold G. Scheie, who was waiting with Colonel Ravdin when Mountbatten was brought straight in from the airstrip near the hospital. At 11:15am, about two hours after the accident, Scheie examined the Supreme Commander. He did not like what he saw—a contusion of the left eyelid and eyeball, deep abrasions in the eyeball, and significant hemorrhage. "You must cancel your tour and go straight to bed," he told Mountbatten. Both Mountbatten's eyes were immediately bandaged; the left one was treated with atropine and both eyes put on a rest program. Nurses undressed the Supreme Commander and led him to bed, ordering him to stay on his back and not move.

"I now found myself completely blind," Mountbatten recalled, "lying in surroundings I couldn't even picture."[40]

* * *

The day after the drama at Lalaghat, Slim flew to Imphal to confer with Scoones and review the strength and dispositions of IV Corps. Gracey's 20th Indian Division stood 44 air miles southeast of Imphal around Moreh and Tamu on the Burma border; the twisting of the road made the distance closer to 65 miles. Cowan's 17th Indian Division held Tiddim, 164 winding road-miles south of Imphal and approximately 40 miles inside Burma. Major General Ouvrey Roberts's 23rd Indian Division was stationed around the Imphal Plain with one brigade in training, another in reserve, and a third holding a hill position near Ukhrul, 40 miles northeast of Imphal. North of there, the locally-raised Assam Regiment guarded key trail junctions at Jessami and Kharasom, east of Kohima. In reserve on the Imphal Plain was the two-regiment 254th Tank Brigade, with U.S.-made Stuarts and Lee-Grant tanks.[41]

Logistically, IV Corps had many units and supplies built up on the Imphal Plain for an offensive. Some of these could be used to sustain a defense, while others would be a liability; Scoones planned to evacuate all unneeded men as quickly as possible if a siege developed. An aggressive airfield construction program had yielded six fields in the Imphal Plain. Two all-weather fields with concrete runways were in operation: one north of Imphal at Imphal Main and another 15 miles southeast at Palel. Four dirt fields, suitable for fair-weather operation only, also were open: Tulihal and Kangla on the southwest and northeast sides of Imphal, respectively, and Wangjing and Sapam along the road to Palel.[42]

It was clear that IV Corps would soon face a Japanese offensive. Slim confirmed with Scoones that Cowan's and Gracey's divisions would withdraw to prepared positions in the hills immediately surrounding the Imphal Plain, luring the Japanese with them. Once both divisions had taken up their final positions, the reserve forces, with the support of RAF planes and the corps artillery, would enter the battle and defeat Mutaguchi's troops. Slim authorized Scoones to order the withdrawal once the IV Corps commander determined the Japanese offensive was fully underway. Gracey and Cowan would start pulling back once receiving the codeword "Moccasin." "I made a mistake," Slim later admitted. "To put the responsibility on local commanders was neither fair nor wise. I was in a better position to judge when a real offensive was coming for I had all their information, and, in addition, intelligence from other sources ... There was thus a real risk, which I did not appreciate, of the withdrawal being started too late."[43]

The March on Delhi got underway on the night of March 7 as Yanagida's 33rd Division started its advance northward. While the division engineers, the division artillery, and a company of tanks guarded the road south of Tiddim around Fort White, three columns of the division snaked their way northward. On the left, the reinforced 215th Regiment moved into the jungle hills west of the Tiddim–Imphal Road with the mission of flanking deep behind Cowan's division and cutting the road around Mileposts 100–109, roughly 60 miles behind the front line and less than 10 miles north of the key bridge over the Manipur River. The division's center column, based upon the reinforced 214th Regiment, sought to swing through the hills past Cowan's east flank and capture the key village of Tongzang and Tuitum Saddle on the road approximately 40 miles behind the 17th Indian Division and south of the bridge. The rightmost force, a large unit of infantry, armor, and artillery known as Yamamoto Force (after its commander, Major General Yamamoto Tsunoru) moved north along the Kabaw Valley to strike Gracey's division and then attack toward Imphal via Palel. INA units accompanied each column, with the bulk assigned to Yamamoto's force.[44]

Cowan's forces were heavily shelled on March 8, and repelled Japanese probing attacks for two days. As the front had generally been quiet over the past weeks, Cowan became suspicious and reported these developments to Scoones. While his two infantry brigades, Brigadier R. T. Cameron's 48th and Brigadier A. E. Cumming's 63rd, started aggressive patrolling, Cowan began moving his supplies and rear-echelon troops northward. He also designated defensive positions along the road at Mileposts 159, 134, 125, and 120, and moved 63rd Brigade northward to cover the flanks and rear.[45]

The British activity alarmed Yanagida, who feared an attack. He reported his concerns to Mutaguchi on March 9. The message arrived at the same time as the first reports of Wingate's operations, and Mutaguchi convened a staff conference. Some of his staff recommended postponing U-Go, but Mutaguchi dismissed their concerns and ordered the operation to proceed. General Kawabe was not so sanguine, and ordered detachments from all over Burma to hunt the Chindits. This included two battalions from the 15th Division—20% of its infantry strength—which were just arriving to join the U-Go offensive. "My resolution remained unchanged,"

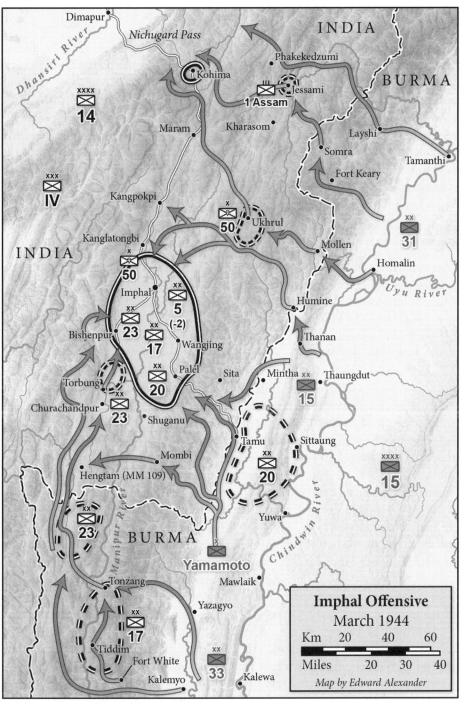

The attack on Imphal and Kohima. (Edward Alexander)

recalled Mutaguchi, although the troop diversions were "a matter of great regret and concern to me."[46]

Sharp skirmishing continued as Yanagida's men advanced into the 17th Indian Division's rear. Still no order came from Scoones. Over the next days, Cowan's troops continued to move supplies and set defenses along the road, including at Tongzang and the key Manipur River bridge nearby. Because of the winding nature of the road through the mountains, a few key positions could command large stretches of the route. Finally, Cowan's reports, plus those of V Force scouts in the hills, convinced Scoones. On the evening of March 13, he called Cowan and issued the codeword: "Moccasin". After a short conversation, Scoones rang off with a "Good luck, Punch." A few hours later Japanese troops reached the road and cut the phone line. The 17th Indian Division was isolated.[47]

* * *

Meanwhile, Mountbatten endured darkness at Ledo. His left eye healed slowly and steadily. Dr Scheie's regimen of rest and atropine seemed to be working, and by March 11 almost all the blood was gone from the eye. The nurses started applying hot compresses. On March 13, Mountbatten's vision had improved to 20/30 in his left eye from just seeing "hand movements" six days before.[48]

For Mountbatten, the week of hospitalization "was the longest week of my life." He was surprised to find his American nurses were originally from Italy, Poland, the Netherlands, Germany, and Lithuania. "Although these five girls came from five different nationalities it was very clear they were all enthusiastic U.S. citizens," he noted. They took care of him 24 hours a day, in shifts. "My nurses fed me like a baby, they washed me, they tended to all my most intimate and embarrassing wants, they cared for me and I began to know them by their touch and by their voices." Mountbatten became quite friendly with the nurses and Captain Scheie, as "there was nothing else to do except talk."[49]

Despite his condition, Mountbatten stayed in command. His Assistant Chief of Staff, Major General Godfrey E. Wildman-Lushington, kept him informed of developments on the battlefront. General Pownall ran the headquarters in Delhi and forwarded all pertinent information and correspondence. Mountbatten attempted to transact business orally, having staff read him telegrams and dictating responses, and tried to follow situation maps by description. It became clear as the days passed that the expected major Japanese invasion of India was getting underway. "The situation was obviously becoming very critical," recalled Mountbatten, "I found it increasingly difficult to deal with it by hearing reports without being able to see the maps and by having to dictate signals without being able to see what they looked like."

By the morning of March 14, one week to the day since his injury, Mountbatten had had enough. He asked Scheie to "kindly take the bandages off my eyes and release me from the hospital so I could go and take charge of the battle." Dr Scheie requested 10 minutes to think the matter over and left the room.

Twelve years later, Scheie admitted to Mountbatten why he needed those 10 minutes. "I thought your eye had been so seriously damaged that if after a week you got up and moved about with the bandage off there was every chance that you would lose the sight of your left eye," he said. "On the other hand from what you had told me there appeared to be every chance that you might lose an entire Army Corps if you didn't take charge of the battle. I wanted the ten minutes to balance the value of your eye against the value of a battle."

Dr Scheie made his decision. "He would ordinarily be kept longer to allow the eye to quiet," wrote Scheie in his case notes, "but due to his position he must leave." Scheie returned to Mountbatten's room, and told the Supreme Commander it was "quite safe for you to go. I will take your bandages off and you can do what you like but if you don't mind, I'd like to come with you." Mountbatten gratefully agreed.

Later that morning, the men boarded Mountbatten's plane for Comilla and a meeting with Slim, after which they flew on to Delhi and SEAC headquarters. Scheie continued observing and treating the eye, and for 10 days limited Mountbatten in his reading. By early April, Mountbatten had made a full recovery.[50]

Mountbatten's instincts were correct, and his departure from the hospital could not have come at a better time. When he left Ledo, he flew into a cascading crisis caused by the three offensives— Stilwell's renewed campaign, Operation Thursday, and U-Go— which started in the last week of February and first fortnight of March. After weeks of relatively localized fighting, the Burma–India front had now erupted into a massive series of battles covering a triangular area between Ledo, Indaw, and Imphal.[51] The next two weeks would be dramatic, as both sides tried to bend events to their advantage.

CHAPTER 6

The Critical Weeks

Mountbatten's plane landed at Fourteenth Army headquarters at 10am on March 14. The Supreme Commander immediately went into conference with Slim and Baldwin to review the situation. It was grim. With 17th Indian Division isolated, Scoones would have to commit 23rd Indian Division, his only reserve, to its relief. This meant that IV Corps would be short of troops to meet any other emergencies, and more Japanese attacks were expected shortly. Slim had anticipated Imphal might need reinforcements, and had arranged for Briggs's 5th Indian Division to be prepared to move by land or air to Imphal from the Arakan on short notice.[1]

Slim explained the situation, and stated his plan to fly 5th Indian Division into Imphal. He noted the need to move it sooner than anticipated, to give Scoones some reserves. Transport aircraft were in short supply, however, as most available C-47s were tied up supporting NCAC, the Chindits, and Cowan's surrounded troops. Slim pressed for Mountbatten to again pull transports from the Hump airlift, this time to fly in Briggs's soldiers. Mountbatten asked Slim to give him an estimate of how many planes were needed. At 12:30, Mountbatten took off for Delhi, landing in the early evening.[2]

Upon arrival in Delhi, Mountbatten summoned Giffard. Up to this point, the 11th Army Group Commander had come across to fellow officers as "complacent" about the Japanese movements, telling Chief of Staff Pownall that "Slim had plenty of troops and could move them as he wanted." Pownall did not share this sanguine view, "for it is quite clear to everyone else that the situation was just on the point of boiling up." Giffard had alerted Lieutenant General Montagu G. N. Stopford's XXXIII Corps headquarters and Major General John M. L. Grover's 2nd British Division, then undergoing amphibious training in southern India, to prepare to move to Assam. Mountbatten castigated Giffard for doing so little, and pressed him to act more decisively. Giffard now realized how critical Slim's situation was becoming, and ordered Stopford and Grover to get their formations moving.

Slim's estimate arrived that night via telegram, stating that 260 sorties would be necessary to move each of the division's three brigades. "Press most urgently for these aircraft," Slim appealed, "in view of the present situation." The next day, Mountbatten decided to stretch his emergency authorization for transport aircraft from February. He signaled Washington that under those emergency terms he would divert 30 C-47s (or their equivalent) from the Hump for 30 days. The Joint Chiefs replied by releasing 20 C-46s for SEAC's use. They would be available from March 18 to April 20.[3]

* * *

As Mountbatten flew away from Comilla, the rest of Mutaguchi's army crossed the Chindwin and entered India. "Everybody is in extremely high spirits," noted one soldier. Like the 33rd Division, the 15th and 31st Divisions also grouped their troops into right, center, and left units. Yamauchi's 15th Division moved with the 51st and 60th Regiments on the right and center, led by a battalion of the 67th Regiment in the Honda Raiding Force. The reinforced 1st Battalion from the 60th Regiment, comprising the division's left column, angled southward to join the battle against Gracey's 20th Indian Division. Meanwhile, Sato's 31st Division crossed near Homalin and started west. The division formed three columns, centered on each of its three component regiments: 58th on the left, 124th in the center, and 138th on the right.[4]

Almost immediately, problems developed among the bullocks that were intended to be used both as transport and food. They were not well-conditioned for the hills of eastern India and struggled on the march. Some of them fell ill within days of starting out, while the Chindwin's waters swallowed both healthy and sick animals. Others died in the weeks after crossing due to disease, malnourishment, or exhaustion. By April 1, it was clear that Mutaguchi's supply arrangements had broken down.[5]

British planes spotted the Japanese crossings, and on March 16 Scoones ordered Gracey to retreat toward Imphal. Gracey wanted to hold at Moreh, but Yamamoto's advance, which made contact on the 15th and 16th, threatened to cut off his division from Imphal. Instead, Gracey pulled his three brigades (Brigadier D. A. L. Mackenzie's 32nd, Brigadier S. Greeves's 80th, and Brigadier W. A. L. James's 100th) back in stages to Shenam Saddle, 40 road-miles west of Moreh. Armor from the 254th Brigade helped cover the withdrawal, winning a major tank battle on the 16th. Within 10 days, the bulk of Gracey's division was in place at Shenam and meeting the first tentative Japanese pursuit. The last elements left Moreh on April 1 and quickly joined their comrades.[6]

Among the elements moving back was a unique unit: Elephant Company, under the command of Lieutenant Colonel James Howard Williams, a former Burma timberman known affectionately as "Elephant Bill." He had 79 elephants assisting with construction and jungle clearing in the area around Moreh. Gracey ordered Williams to pull out, and on the morning of March 17, Elephant Company started its retreat to Imphal in two groups. The Japanese advance caught one group of 33, scattering them, but the other group of 45 arrived in Imphal on March 22 after an epic odyssey through the jungle, moving by night to avoid patrols from Yamamoto Force. One elephant from this group had been lost along the way.[7]

Meanwhile, the critical situation on the Tiddim Road continued. The 37th Brigade of Roberts's 23rd Indian Division headed south, passing throngs of rear-area personnel who were heading north in some confusion. Led by two battalions of Gurkhas, the brigade reached Milepost 98 on March 15 and immediately attacked the Japanese forces in the area. Roberts's troops made some progress against fierce resistance, but the advance stalled after two miles. During the fighting, the Gurkhas recovered stragglers from the 17th Indian Division's supply dump at Milepost 109, which had been overrun on March 14.[8]

At Tiddim, Cowan issued formal withdrawal orders early on March 14. The 17th Indian Division's 16,000 men, 2,500 vehicles, and 3,000 mules became a 7–10-mile-long snake; 63rd Brigade stood at the head, 48th Brigade at the tail, and in between wound a column of cars and trucks carrying the division's supplies and wounded. All excess vehicles had their engines disabled and were pushed into nearby ravines. The plainspoken Cowan made no bold pronouncements about the situation, but the austere language of his orders conveyed a serious message all the same.[9]

Cowan's division started north at 5pm that evening, advancing 20 miles. The next day, Cumming's 63rd Brigade attacked Tuitum Saddle and Tongzang, clearing it on March 17 and pushing to the Manipur River bridge, which fell intact. Cowan paused to regroup and receive supplies by air from the RAF. He switched the 48th and 63rd Brigades for the next attack, which would be on the supply dump at Milepost 109.[10]

Meanwhile, Roberts's men struggled southward. The 49th Brigade also arrived and attacked into the hills west of the road. The Japanese commander, Colonel Sasahara Masahiko of the 215th Regiment, sent units around the British west flank, some reaching the road in Roberts's rear. The result was an interlocking sandwich of British and Japanese units along the Tiddim Road between Mileposts 96 and 100. Roberts's men went on air supply and set about clearing the Japanese roadblocks behind them. All thought of further attack south was temporarily abandoned. "It was not easy," commented a colonel on Roberts's staff, "to be more than the anvil on which the hammer of 17 Div. fell."[11]

Further south, Cowan's division attacked northward toward the supply dump at Milepost 109. While a battalion of the 48th Brigade cleared the hills east of the Tiddim Road, the balance of the brigade fought for five days to reach the supply dump. Late on March 23, they were literally within sight of their objective.[12]

As the divisions compressed the 215th Regiment, Colonel Sasahara radioed Yanagida of his intent to attack and destroy Roberts's forces. At the end of his message, he indicated that in any event he would "hold roadblocks ... to the last.

The codebooks will be burned, if necessary." Communications difficulties meant that the message's conclusion arrived first. Yanagida, deeply concerned that the 215th Regiment was on the verge of annihilation, on March 24 ordered Sasahara to withdraw westward immediately. By the time Yanagida discovered the true situation, it was too late to stop Sasahara's pull-back. "Compliance with this order," noted a staff report laconically, "caused the 33rd Division to lose the opportunity of completely destroying the 17th Division."[13]

Cowan pushed his men forward as Japanese resistance slackened. The division recovered the supply dump on March 25, and Cowan's staff were surprised to find it nearly intact. On March 28. Cowan's and Roberts's troops met at Milepost 102. Cowan took command of the combined force and turned north. After pushing aside a roadblock at Milepost 82, the 17th Indian Division reached Imphal on April 4, detaching 23rd Indian Division to cover Imphal's southern approach at Torbung, near Milepost 20. Cowan's division was almost intact, though exhausted, but after six days of rest was ready to return to action.[14]

Yanagida considered the results of the last two weeks, and made a drastic decision. The offensive had to be stopped. On the night of March 26, he radioed Mutaguchi that his "combat situation … is not developing satisfactorily." Yanagida went further. "In the future," he predicted, "the offensive will encounter such extreme difficulties that the occupation of Imphal within the scheduled three weeks is an impossibility. In addition, the advent of the rainy season and difficulties of supply will eventually result in tragedy." Cowan's and Roberts's troops had impressed him; he told Mutaguchi that Japanese "organization and equipment are inferior to that of the enemy" and claimed "the strategic value of Imphal has been exaggerated."[15]

This signal, extraordinary in any army but especially in the Imperial Japanese Army, stunned Mutaguchi. "The suggestion of General Yanagida was considered inappropriate," noted a staff report, "and he was directed to execute the Army's orders." Mutaguchi now lost confidence in Yanagida, and started bypassing him and communicating directly with the 33rd Division's chief of staff.[16]

Further north, the 15th and 31st Divisions wound their way into India. Their advance crossed several parallel mountain ranges northeast of Imphal, each over 5,000 feet in elevation. "The spine-like ridges rise and fall precipitously in rapid succession," noted a British officer of Roberts's division, "and their sides are densely covered with mixed jungle, including an unpleasant prickly bamboo which grips all that comes within its clutches." The British nicknamed the area "New Guinea" because its terrain and remoteness reminded them of scenes from newsreels about the fighting on that island. Few trails led westward, and the Japanese advance cut across the north–south orientation of the landscape. "In general, the advance of the Division was relatively smooth," noted a Japanese staff report, "but the transportation of supplies through the rugged mountain ranges was extremely difficult … The men also suffered from exhaustion and malnutrition."[17]

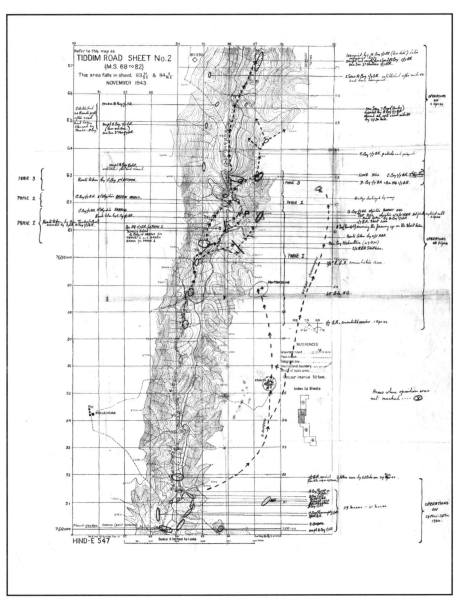

A sketch map of the fighting along the Tiddim Road from March 28 to April 3, 1944, from the 17th Indian Division's War Diary. (U.K. National Archives)

Scoones's commitment of 23rd Indian Division on the Tiddim Road meant that most of the division's units northeast of Imphal needed to be withdrawn. They were replaced by the two-battalion 50th Parachute Brigade under Brigadier M. R. J. Hope-Thomson, reinforced by 4/5 Mahrattas left behind by Roberts. Sato's left column brushed up against Hope-Thomson's paratroopers at Sangshak, near Ukhrul. Although outside his zone of operations, column commander Major General Miyazaki Shigesaburo diverted southward and attacked Sangshak on March 22. Elements of the 15th Division also joined the battle. Over four days, the Japanese stormed successive hill positions while the paratroopers tenaciously held on. Supply airdrops were partially successful, but the defenders grew progressively more exhausted. "Troops very tired," signaled Hope-Thomson shortly after 5pm on March 26. "Doubt ability to resist further sustained attack. Send help." This message crossed a signal from Imphal: "Fight your way out. Go south then west. Air and transport on the look-out." At 10:30pm, Hope-Thomson's men cut their way out to Imphal. Scattered parties moved through the hills, many appearing at Imphal after three or five days. The defenders lost 652 casualties, including 100 prisoners; the battle cost the Japanese 500 casualties. Most importantly, the Japanese advance had been held up for five precious days.[18]

The defenders of Sangshak traded their lives for the time to get reinforcements to Imphal and Kohima. As they stood and died, Briggs's 5th Indian Division started its fly-in. Some units came off the firing line in the Arakan, moved to the airfield, packed and loaded, flew to Imphal, and unloaded—all in the span of three days. Fortunately, Fourteenth Army logisticians had provided detailed loading tables that guided and speeded the process. Leading was Brigadier Evans's 123rd Brigade, which flew in on March 20 and 21, followed by General Briggs on the 22nd when weather and the need for pilot rest slowed operations, then the divisional artillery, and lastly Salomons's 9th Brigade. By March 26, 531 aeroplane sorties had brought in 5,924 men, 129 jeeps, 313 mules, 36 motor-carriers, and 40 guns into Imphal, Palel, and Tulihal.[19]

For Briggs's men, it was quite an adventure. "It was the first and only time," recalled a staff officer, "that a division was transported by air out of action on one battle front to immediate action on another front several hundred miles distant." Most of the soldiers had never been on a plane before. The American pilots, the first Americans many men had ever seen, merely added to the exotic flair of the trip.[20]

The 5th Indian Division's arrival would help stabilize the crisis north and northeast of Imphal. Yet Slim understood what the battles in that area showed of Japanese intentions toward Kohima and Dimapur. "Within a week of the start of the Japanese offensive," he recalled, "it became clear that the situation in the Kohima area was likely to be even more dangerous than that at Imphal. Not only were the enemy columns closing in on Kohima at much greater speed than I had expected, but they were obviously in much greater strength." A captured Japanese order from Sangshak confirmed his worst fears. Slim had expected a strike toward Kohima by a Japanese regiment, but the enemy correspondence revealed that the entire 31st Division was on its way. "We were not prepared for so heavy a thrust," Slim admitted. "Kohima with its rather scratch garrison and, what was worse, Dimapur with no garrison at all, were in deadly peril."[21]

Faced with this crisis, Slim diverted the 5th Indian Division's last brigade—Warren's 161st—to Dimapur and Kohima. They would have to hold until more help arrived.[22]

* * *

As these dramas played out in India, both Stilwell and Wingate embarked on the next stages of their campaigns in northern Burma. By March 10, the Chindits had three brigades ready to start operations.

Already, Wingate's plans were changing. On March 8, he decided to close Chowringhee on the 10th, and fly in the last elements of 111th Brigade to Broadway, which would then become the main base for all Chindit operations in Burma. Herring's British-trained Kachin Levies, known as Dahforce, were intended to fly into a small landing zone east of Broadway called Templecombe; instead, they would come into Broadway on the night of March 11 and then march east to energize guerrilla operations in the hills.[23]

At Chowringhee, Lentaigne's 111th Brigade set off on its various missions on the morning of March 10. Lieutenant Colonel J. R. Morris took 49 and 94 Columns, designated Morrisforce, eastward to cut roads south of Myitkyina and operate with Dahforce. Meanwhile, Lentaigne marched west with the brigade headquarters, 30 Column, and 40 Column to cross the Irrawaddy and link up with the remainder of his brigade, coming down from Broadway, and wreak havoc near Indaw.[24]

Japanese opposition had been nonexistent thus far, but that afternoon the first reactions came. Nine Zeros passed over Lentaigne's men and struck Chowringhee. They found a few disabled gliders and shot them up. The Chindits had left petrol cans in the gliders, which exploded, giving the false impression that major damage had been done. In reality, the Japanese had wasted an airstrike on a worthless target. "Joe and I were laughing together," recalled Masters, "and every face down the column was grinning ... We continued our march."[25]

The next day, Lentaigne's men encountered their first enemy on the ground, four Japanese-loyal Burmese police officers, who were captured as the brigade prepared to cross the Irrawaddy on boats flown in by glider. C-47s were scheduled to return and pick up the gliders for re-use. The prisoners were tied up and put on a glider along with two sick Gurkhas. The six passengers went for a wild ride when the glider shot into the air as it was grabbed by a towrope from an Air Commando C-47 and flown to India. Meanwhile, the river crossing proceeded slowly, and by March 12, only two-thirds of the force was across. Lentaigne ordered 40 Column, still on the Irrawaddy's east side, to join Morris, while 30 Column and the headquarters proceeded with the original plan.[26]

The Japanese came for Broadway on March 13, with a force of 30 bombers and fighters. Six RAF Spitfires based on the field rose up the meet them, assisted by anti-air and artillery units flown in. Between air and ground action, the British shot down five attackers. This response also ruined the Japanese attack, which caused little damage. Four days later, 11 Zeros came in low and made a surprise strafing run on the airfield, damaging many installations. They destroyed five Spitfires on the ground, and shot the sixth out of the sky. Cochran's Air Commando avenged the raid with strikes on the Japanese airdromes, and maintained air superiority in the skies over Burma.[27]

Significantly, these strikes demonstrated that the Japanese had committed virtually all of their remaining air assets in Burma against the Chindits. The attacks also occurred during the week Mutaguchi's Fifteenth Army started the invasion of India, and just before Briggs's division started its flight to Imphal. "The fact that we had no alternative but to use our feeble air force against these airborne forces [the Chindits]," observed Mutaguchi, "was a very great obstacle to the execution of the Imphal campaign."[28]

Calvert meanwhile assembled his 77th Brigade and set off from Broadway on March 9, leaving elements behind as a garrison and patrol ("floater") force. His columns fanned out as they struck westward toward the main railroad running up to Mogaung and Myitkyina. Calvert sought to establish what he later termed "a semi-permanent block between Hopin and Mawlu where the road and railway to the north run side by side." On March 16, he found the desired spot along a group of wooded hills outside the village of Henu, two miles north of Mawlu and 20 miles north of Indaw. The hills overlooked the road and railway, and commanded the dry paddyland to the south and west.[29]

To establish a perimeter, it was necessary to clear the hills of the Japanese troops who had come up from Henu to patrol the area. Japanese infiltrators had taken position on a key hill to the southwest topped with a small pagoda, ever after known to the British as Pagoda Hill. Calvert needed to clear the hill to make it part of his block. He gathered the nearest unit, part of the South Staffords, and explained his plan of attack. The men took position, Calvert shouted "Charge!" in what he called "the approved Victorian manner," and the South Staffords went up the hill. "There," recalled Calvert, "at the top of the hill, about fifty yards square, an extraordinary melee took place, everyone shooting, bayoneting, kicking at everyone else." Lieutenant George A. Cairns engaged a Japanese officer, who cut off his left arm; Cairns shot the officer, retrieved his sword, and started hacking and stabbing other Japanese before collapsing from loss of blood. The Japanese broke and ran southward, leaving the hill in British hands.[30]

Captured documents identified the Japanese as a scratch force of rear-area troops, but more would certainly be on the way. The British set up their defenses and beat back nightly Japanese reconnaissance patrols. Supplies and equipment were dropped in, and by March 21, Calvert had a working airstrip and a well-fortified position. The parachutes in the trees gave the block its name: White City. He kept the two columns (36 and 63) of 3/6 Gurkhas and the two (38 and 80) from the South Staffords in the perimeter, while the Lancashire Fusiliers acted as floater units with 20 and 50 Columns.[31]

On the evening of March 21, Japanese infantry attacked White City from the north. "Very savage fighting took place for eight hours," noted a staff officer, "during which the enemy penetrated into the Stronghold and were flung out again. A final [counter] attack, preceded by direct air support, saw the enemy break and run." Captured maps, a captured battalion flag, and prisoners identified the attackers as coming from 3rd Battalion, 114th Regiment, 18th Division, which had hurried from a rest area into the battle. Interrogations revealed the Japanese still underestimated the Chindits' strength, believing they faced only a small raiding force, as in 1943.[32]

At the same time, Fergusson's 16th Brigade approached Indaw. The men had been constantly on the move since February 5. Two columns had successfully attacked Lonkin, disrupting Tanaka's left flank and earning Stilwell's gratitude. On March 19, Fergusson set up a Stronghold at Mahnton, a village 16 miles west of White City. Wingate named it Aberdeen, after his wife's hometown. On March 20, Wingate visited and personally sited the airstrip. He also ordered Fergusson to attack Indaw immediately, despite the latter's request for his men to have three days of rest.[33]

Wingate pressed for speed because he knew that Slim was about to take his reserves and possibly some of his transport planes to meet the threat posed by U-Go. The Chindit commander changed his plans and decided to commit his reserve units weeks earlier than planned. Slim released 14th and 3rd West African Brigades to Wingate, and the troops started flying in to Aberdeen and Broadway on March 21. The last brigade, 23rd Brigade, went to XXXIII Corps. Wingate protested to Slim, threatening resignation, and ultimately radioed London asking for more transport aircraft. "Give Special Force four transport squadrons now," Wingate said, "and you will have all Burma north of the 24th parallel plus a decisive Japanese defeat." Slim supported this request for planes: "I regard them as a necessity for a major success and an insurance against any situation demanding air maintenance on a large scale." The Combined Chiefs dispatched 79 U.S. and British C-47s from the Mediterranean.[34]

Wingate was not the only general with forces in north Burma worried about logistics. Further north, General Tanaka viewed the Chindits' operations with great alarm—their arrival had cut his division's supply line. Tanaka's men had been living on accumulated food and ammunition stocks since January, as the buildup for Mutaguchi's India invasion received all supply priority. For the same reason, the division had also been unable to replace losses, and by mid-March numbered just

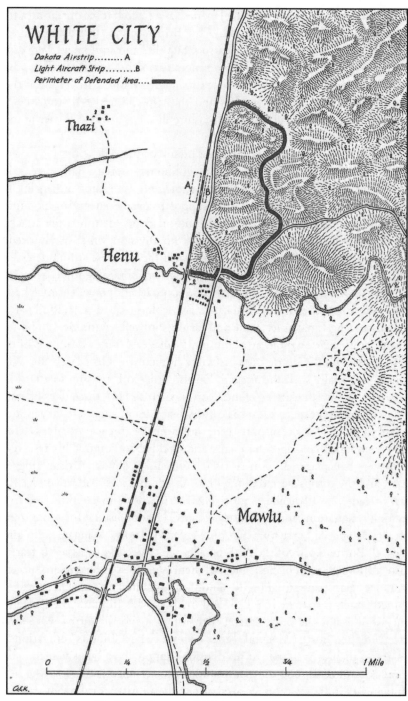

The White City area. (U.K. Ministry of Defence)

6,300 effective strength (out of a regulation 14,000) among the two infantry, one artillery, and one engineer regiments facing NCAC. Operation Thursday commenced just as supply and replacement shipments to the 18th Division were about to resume. "Tanaka's supply position," noted a later analysis, "was fundamentally compromised by the Chindit fighting along the railway to North Burma." Kawabe's chief of staff believed this development made Tanaka's mission "impossible."[35]

On March 24, General Wingate flew to Broadway in a B-25 provided by the 1st Air Commando. He then traveled by small plane to visit Calvert at White City. After an inspection, Wingate pointedly stood along the railroad and gloated about how he was astride the 18th Division's line of communications. "Be of good heart," he told Calvert as they parted. After a short visit to Aberdeen, Wingate flew back to Broadway.[36]

At Broadway, Wingate and his aide, Captain George Borrow, took off in the B-25 for Imphal. According to Colonel Claude Rome, who watched it go, the plane was having engine difficulties and took off awkwardly. It reached Imphal Main safely, where Wingate conferred with Baldwin about RAF support for the Chindits. Just after 5pm Wingate climbed into the B-25 and sat in the co-pilot's seat for the flight back to Lalaghat. Baldwin waved goodbye and headed for his own plane. The American pilot, First Lieutenant Brian F. Hodges, powered up the B-25's engines and took off, flying westward into the twilight.[37]

The plane never made it. "The night was fairly clear," recalled Tulloch, "An RAF pilot crossing the mountains west of Imphal reported having seen a bright flash a long way to the north." Two of Cochran's pilots, including Alison, made similar reports. The next morning, Air Commandos flew over the area and sighted a wrecked aircraft. Two days later, a ground expedition reached the site and found the B-25's charred remains. The crash, explosion, and fire had consumed most of the plane and its occupants. Nobody could have survived the impact. Scattered papers and the pith helmet confirmed that it was Wingate's plane.[38]

Wingate's sudden loss made a profound impression. "Wingate's death did not seem entirely real," wrote John Masters. "but then nor had Wingate. He had come to represent an attitude rather than a man, or even an idea." The loss shook Calvert and his men at White City. "We were still numb from the shock," Calvert recalled upon hearing the news. "It was like going smoothly along in an aeroplane when the navigator comes in and says, 'The pilot has died of heart failure. There is no co-pilot and none of us knows that to do.' You may realize from this a little of what we felt. So much was locked away in him." Slim announced Wingate's death to Fourteenth Army, calling him "truly dynamic" and "irreplaceable" with "sparks of genius."[39]

In Maymyo, Mutaguchi digested the news. "I realized what a loss this was to the British Army," he recalled, "and said a prayer for the soul of this man in whom I had found my match."[40]

Slim appointed Brigadier Lentaigne to succeed Wingate as Special Force commander, with Tulloch as his deputy. As 111th Brigade was divided by the Irrawaddy, Lentaigne designated two successors. Colonel Morris, who by seniority would have taken charge if the brigade was united, was promoted to Brigadier and retained command of the three columns in Morrisforce east of the river. The five columns on the Irrawaddy's west side came under Major Masters.

Lentaigne flew from the field to his new headquarters on March 30. "We pledged ourselves to Brigadier Lentaigne," recalled Cochran. "He said he needed our help. He was a man of broad vision and generous mind."[41]

The defeats at White City and elsewhere made the Japanese realize the scale of the Chindit operation. Burma Area Army dispatched its reserves to the Indaw area, and Kawabe ordered the Major General Hayashi Yoshihide to take command of all ground operations against the Chindits. Hayashi would have 5,000 men in his 24th Independent Mixed Brigade along with three battalions from the 2nd Division. Lieutenant General Takeda Kaoru's 53rd Division, just arriving in Burma, was ordered to assist as soon as it could get its troops on the scene.[42]

The Chindits immediately felt the presence of Hayashi and his men.

* * *

During this period, the NCAC front had been anything but quiet. General Tanaka's troops were digging in on the Jambu Bum, although wet weather slowed their progress. Tanaka deployed most of his infantry in the pass, with one battalion covering the mountain trails to the east. Tanaka had received orders to hold the Mogaung Valley as along as possible, at least until the successful conclusion of U-Go, if necessary to the destruction of his division.[43]

As his forces regrouped, Stilwell considered the next stage in his campaign. Anxious to not give Tanaka a break, Stilwell came up with a plan similar to the operation just concluded. He decided to rest the 38th Division and send Liao's 22nd Division and Brown's tanks against Japanese positions at the Jambu Bum. At the same time, Merrill's men and the Chinese 113th Regiment would swing into the Japanese rear and block the road near Shaduzup, a village at the top of the Mogaung Valley just a few miles south of the Jambu Bum.[44]

This plan produced a strong reaction among NCAC's commanders. A teary-eyed Sun protested his division being left out of the attack, feeling a loss of face. "Told him he'd get plenty to do further south," Stilwell recalled, and that seemed to satisfy Sun. Merrill felt the flank march was too shallow, and sent Hunter to propose a deeper penetration closer to Kamaing. Stilwell decided to compromise, sending 1st Battalion and the Chinese to Shaduzup. Merrill would take 2nd and 3rd Battalions to Inkangahtawng, roughly 10 miles south of Shaduzup and 12 miles north of Kamaing. Both roadblocks would be set by March 24.[45]

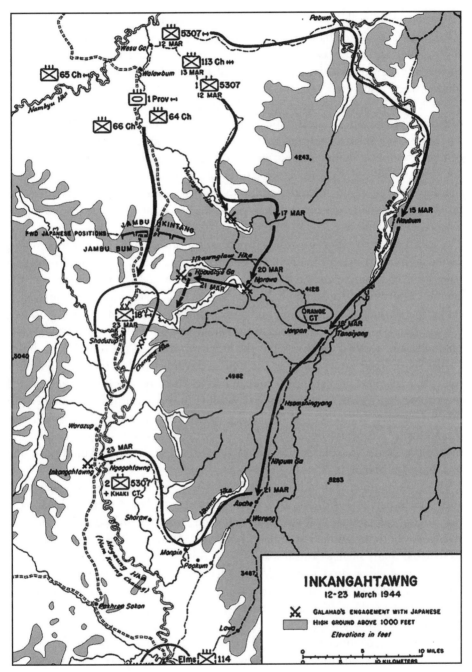

The NCAC advance against the Jambu Bum and the Kamaing Road. (U.S. Army)

Curiously, Stilwell did not brief Merrill or Hunter about Detachment 101 or the Kachin Rangers, which had several units operating in the areas to which the 5307th was headed. These men knew the area intimately, and had developed great success against the Japanese. This omission caused great consternation among Merrill's officers when discovered.[46]

On March 12, the movement began. The Marauders left the Hukawng Valley after one day and entered the steep mountains to the east and southeast. "The country we had to cross in bypassing the Japanese," recalled Ogburn, "was a conglomeration of hills resembling the patternless jumble of waves in a tide rip and often so steep your feet would go our form under you while you were climbing ... Sometimes the slopes were too much for the mules; the packs would have to be unloaded and broken up and the pieces carried up or passed up from hand to hand." Some ridges reached over 4,000 feet.[47]

Osborne's 1st Battalion used the only major southward trail into the mountains. Two days into the march, Lieutenant Wilson's reconnaissance platoon discovered a large force of Japanese astride the route. After futilely trying to push through the enemy, Osborne made the difficult decision to turn east and cut a path around it. Men took turns slashing at virgin jungle and thick bamboo, in some cases cutting tunnels through bamboo clumps. "The head of the column sounded like a spike-driving crew on a railroad," recalled Ogburn, "but the jungle imprisoned the sound, as it did us ... We were twelve hours a day on the trail, as a rule—whether there was a trail or not." This pace meant that the 30-mile march to Shaduzup took two weeks, aided toward the end by the Kachin Rangers. Weather, missed airdrops, and the need to prevent Japanese ambushes also impeded progress. Not much could be done about the first two factors, but better coordination with the Kachin Rangers would have helped the third. Nonetheless, it was soon clear that 1st Battalion would not reach Shaduzup by March 24.[48]

At the same time, 2nd and 3rd Battalions swung further east and followed trails and watercourses into the hills. The elevation changes told on the men, sparking the first widespread cases of sickness and exhaustion. "The terrain was indeed proving terrible for both the animals and men," recalled a Marauder, "but the route allowed us to avoid many small skirmishes and the sacrifice of many of our men." Merrill's group made good progress, and, on March 15, encountered their first Kachin Rangers and OSS personnel, who immediately assisted as guides and scouts. In return, the Marauders gave them food and cigarettes, and offered medical treatment to the Kachin villages they passed.[49]

The weather continued wet, with near-daily rain over the first six days of the advance. "God is mad at me," raged Stilwell to his diary. The news from Imphal also caused additional concern. "This ties a can to us and finishes up the glorious spring 1944 campaign." Nevertheless, Stilwell found room for optimism. His mood improved when his staff presented him a birthday cake on March 19 for his 61st birthday.[50]

The Chinese-American assault on the Jambu Bum started two days after Merrill got underway. As the 66th Regiment pushed against the Japanese in a frontal assault, the 64th Regiment swung east in an attempt to flank. Brown's tankers supported the 66th's advance, but their effectiveness was hampered by the inability of the tankers to always tell Chinese and Japanese troops apart. On March 14, the Chinese took the Japanese outpost positions, and in two days of rainy and sharp fighting secured the Jambu Bum's crest and north side. "The 66th acquitted itself," noted one of Stilwell's staff, "with distinction both for aggressive action and fighting spirit."[51]

The Japanese retreated southward, leaving a mile of felled trees and mines blocking the road. Two days of steady work by Chinese engineers finally cleared the road, and, on March 20, Brown's tanks spearheaded an attack southward, pushing seven miles to the Hkawnglaw Hka stream. However, the infantry only pushed half of the distance, and would not follow further. Brown found the stream undefended, but dared not advance across without infantry support. The next day the advance resumed, and found the Japanese dug in along the stream. The Chinese attack failed, and the tanks withdrew. "During this engagement," noted Brown, sadly, "the tanks unfortunately fired into Chinese troops who had in some places moved up within 50 yards of the Japanese positions."[52]

The infantry advance remained stalled at the stream. A platoon of tanks returned to try and break the stalemate. The Chinese agreed to mark their positions and troops with white flags and sheets. The tank commander led his five tanks forward to the lead infantry platoon, then crossed the stream. Fifty yards on, he spotted some troops also showing a white flag. As the armor drew near, the flag dropped—the troops were Japanese. The enemy opened fire and "threw a magnetic mine on the rear of each of the five tanks," reported Brown. "All five tanks were immediately set on fire and had to be abandoned. Every tank crew member of the platoon was wounded, but, due to the close proximity of the Chinese line, all of them were able to get back to safety and only three men died later of their wounds." Brown's tanks withdrew shortly thereafter to refit.[53]

Further south, Merrill's two battalions reached the village of Janpan on March 19 and 20. They held a medical clinic for the local Kachin people and met up with more OSS officers and Kachin guerrillas, who provided intelligence and agreed to act as guides. Planes brought in supplies and orders from Stilwell. Merrill divided his force, sending Colonel Hunter with 2nd Battalion and Khaki Combat Team of 3rd Battalion to march the last 40 miles to Inkangahtawng. The 3rd Battalion's Orange Combat Team and the headquarters group would patrol around Janpan and secure the rear communications. As these operations proceeded in the coming days, the Marauders recovered two downed American pilots whom the Kachins had rescued and brought to safety.[54]

Hunter's force started southward and quickly found the terrain changing. "The march of ten miles to the southwest would take the unit from an elevation of three thousand feet to six hundred feet," recalled a Marauder. "The first two miles of the march followed a very steep, ill-defined trail through bamboo and other jungle growth to descend a thousand feet to the Hkum Hka." The Marauders followed the river for eight miles, crossing it over 25 times before arriving near Manpin on the Mogaung Valley's eastern edge on the afternoon of March 22. A supply drop came down, and Hunter changed his location to Sharaw, a little further west. There, he ordered McGee's 2nd Battalion to move the last 20 miles to the road the next day, March 23. Khaki Combat Team would follow behind as a reserve and to guard supplies and the route back into the hills.[55]

On the morning of March 23, the Marauders moved out. By late afternoon, they were close to the road and had seen no Japanese. The 2nd Battalion was at Ngagahtawng, a village less than five miles east of Kamaing Road and separated from it by the north–south-flowing Mogaung Hka. McGee prepared to bivouac and rest, when at 4:30pm an American patrol encountered a Japanese patrol along the Mogaung Hka. With the element of surprise now lost, McGee needed to act quickly. He immediately crossed the 2nd Battalion, leaving Khaki Combat team on the river's east side with the mules and mortars. As dusk fell, the Marauders dug in along the road north of Inkangahtawng. "We were on the eastern side of an open field about 175 yards across," recalled Private George Rose. "It had been previously burned off and cleared all around ... Our perimeter was formed in a half circle leading back to the river on each end." It was "a miserable night, due to anxiety, discomfort, and intermittent rifle shots by the Japanese," recalled an officer. "During much of the night the Marauders heard truck motors and tail gates slamming as enemy reinforcements arrived ... As dawn came, all men of Blue, Green, and Khaki knew the small skirmishes were over and that a major battle was imminent."[56]

McGee's appearance in his rear prompted a strong reaction from General Tanaka. The block at Inkangahtawng was astride his line of supply and only 12 miles north of his supply base at Kamaing. Indeed, American patrols had been reported within five miles of Kamaing. The block had to be eliminated. Tanaka pulled together some rear-area troops and sent them south from Shaduzup, while also calling up 250 men from the 114th Regiment in Myitkyina, who arrived during the night. The 114th's commander, Colonel Maruyama Fusayasu, also received orders to follow that detachment with a further 800 men in two battalions.[57]

The increased Japanese presence became clear on the morning of March 24. A reconnaissance by two American platoons showed the enemy present in force. At 7am, the first Japanese probes came against the Marauder perimeter, followed by an artillery barrage. Soon, massed attacks started from the north, south, and west, totaling sixteen attacks in all during the day. "The Japanese came pouring out of the woods, charging across the open field toward our position," said a Marauder. "All day

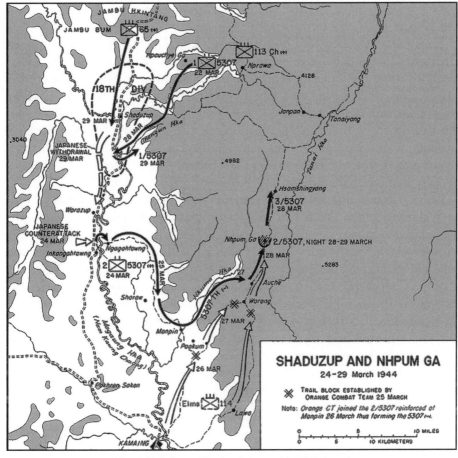

The NCAC front, March 24–29, 1944. (U.S. Army)

long they came in wave after wave." Curiously, the Japanese never seemed to attack with more than 40 men; "If they had charged with their men all at once they would have overrun us," said Rose. One of the earliest attacks penetrated the American lines, but was quickly wiped out. All others were repelled by disciplined American fire assisted by mortars from across the river.[58]

McGee called for support, but radio issues made it difficult to get any help. Late in the afternoon, P-51s flew over and strafed the Japanese. At Sharaw, a frustrated Hunter realized that his radio would only receive, not transmit. He was helpless. Fortunately, Merrill could transmit and, at 4:30pm, he ordered McGee to retire eastward. That night, the Marauders pulled back to Ngagahtawng. Kachins reported Maruyama's infantry moving northeast from Kamaing into the American rear, and

Merrill ordered Hunter to retrace his steps northward toward the villages of Auche and Nhpum Ga.[59]

Shortly after McGee pulled back, Osborne's force finally arrived near Shaduzup. On March 25, the battalion moved down a streambed toward the Mogaung Hka, just across from the Kamaing Road. Osborne feinted toward Shaduzup itself with a small force, while aiming for a spot five miles south of town. At dawn on March 28, the battalion attacked across the river, scattering a Japanese camp and gleefully shooting up traffic and marching men on the road itself. The Americans enjoyed Japanese rations and appropriated some equipment for their use. The surprised Japanese countered with heavy artillery fire, but only feeble infantry attacks during the day. That night, the Chinese 113th Infantry relieved Osborne's men.[60]

Faced with this new threat to his rear, and with sizeable Chinese forces pressing on his front, Tanaka decided to withdraw southward 10 miles to Warazup and regroup. Liao's pursuers entered Shaduzup on March 30, linking up the same day with the 113th Regiment. NCAC was now across the last serious terrain obstacle before Mogaung, and the master of the northern third of the Mogaung Valley.[61]

Stilwell judged the situation well in hand. He felt it was an opportune time to leave the front and see Chiang Kai-shek in Chungking. Earlier in the month, Chiang had messaged Stilwell, advising caution and asking about future plans. Stilwell decided to reply in person, both to discuss strategy but also try to get reinforcements so NCAC's campaign could continue. "If I can't move Peanut," he wrote in his diary, "[the] jig is up for the season." On March 28, he landed in Chungking.[62]

CHAPTER 7

"I Believe It Will Be Difficult to Hold"

On the afternoon of March 28, Stilwell met with Chiang. They reviewed the situation in Burma, and Stilwell explained the progress of NCAC over the last several weeks. He also noted that irregular forces operating from Fort Hertz had secured Sumprabum, thus removing any threat to the flank of either NCAC or the 175,000 troops of Y Force massing along the Salween. Stilwell requested reinforcements for his operations in northern Burma, and Chiang agreed to dispatch troops across the Hump, to be equipped in India and used by NCAC. The next day, Chiang specifically committed two divisions, 14th and 50th, to this effort. Despite this good news, Stilwell detected a disinterested attitude among most of the Chinese leadership: "*Nobody* particularly interested in the campaign!" he vented to his diary.[1]

Stilwell desired a Y Force attack across the Salween, but Chiang had so far proved reluctant to issue the necessary orders. A mid-March exchange of messages between Chiang and Roosevelt on the subject failed to move Chiang to action. On March 29, Stilwell wired General Marshall an appreciation of the situation on the Burma–India front, which Marshall took to President Roosevelt. He asked the president to again intercede with Chiang, as one of head of state to another. On April 3, Roosevelt wrote to Chiang that Y Force "should not be held back on the grounds that an amphibious operation against the South Burma coast is necessary prior to their advance. Present developments negate such a requirement ... I do hope you can act." Chiang made no direct reply, but on April 14, Y Force received orders to finalize preparations for an advance. To save face, the Chinese informed General Marshall via Hearn that the move "was made on initiative of Chinese without undue influence of outside pressure."[2]

On March 30, Stilwell flew back to Burma and found the Marauders in a difficult battle. McGee's men had continued their retreat under close Japanese pursuit, covered by Lieutenant Weston's reconnaissance platoon. Sensing danger, Merrill ordered 1st Battalion to join him, and called for Chinese reinforcements. The earliest any fresh units would arrive would be in five days—around April 3. As the lines passed Auche and started northward, Merrill sought a place to make a stand. He needed to protect the five-acre clearing at Hsamshingyang, 1,500 feet above sea level and the headwaters of the Tanai Hka. It was perfect as a supply drop zone, light plane airfield, and concentration point. Overlooking the clearing was a 2,779-foot elevation topped by Nhpum Ga, a settlement of two huts on the north end of a razorback ridge running 15 miles south. Nhpum Ga "measured about three hundred yards from north to south and one to two hundred yards from east to west," recalled an officer. The trail from Auche ran right past Nhpum Ga.[3]

On March 28, Merrill visited McGee and ordered him to hold Nhpum Ga with the 900 men in 2nd Battalion, while 3rd Battalion would cover the key supply dropping zone at Hsamshingyang. Patrols would link the two units. McGee acknowledged the orders and the men parted, Merrill hiking four miles back to Hsamshingyang. The Marauder commander took ill on the trail and had to be helped back to the clearing. He immediately was taken to a field hospital, where the 5307th's doctors diagnosed a heart attack. A small plane was called, arriving on March 29. "General Merrill," recalled James Hopkins, one of the doctors, "refused evacuation until he was assured that all men who needed urgent evacuation had been sent out." By the evening of March 29, Merrill was in 20th General Hospital at Ledo. Colonel Hunter assumed command of the Marauders in his place.[4]

As he was transported to the hospital, Merrill remained determined to do what he could for his men. He reported the situation to NCAC headquarters and requested 75mm pack howitzers be dropped to the Marauders at Hsamshingyang. Merrill knew that some of his volunteers were trained artillerymen, and could quickly make use of the guns in the battle now starting. Two guns were parachuted in on April 2, and almost immediately went into action. "Morale picked up all over the area," noted Hopkins.[5]

Meanwhile, McGee had set up his defense at Nhpum Ga. It was shaped in a rough oval, with protrusions to the west and northeast to cover key heights. The northeast sector also included the area's lone spring. The Marauders spread their 13 machine guns across key points, while the battalion's 17 mortars took position in the center to provide fire in all directions. Mules and hospitals also congregated in a depression in the perimeter's center. By late morning of March 28, the men had dug in rudimentary positions.[6]

The 2nd Battalion completed its preparations none too soon, as the Japanese launched their first attacks just before noon. They probed the southern part of the perimeter before falling back. Mortar and artillery fire harassed the Americans into the night, with the American response muted due to ammunition shortages. The next morning, a C-47 dropped rations and ammunition to a grateful 2nd Battalion. Japanese attacks on March 29 and 30 were met by fierce American fire. McGee realized the Japanese were no longer attacking from the south, but were working around the perimeter's east end; this movement threatened to sever his link with 3rd Battalion, but neither Marauder battalion could spare men to counter

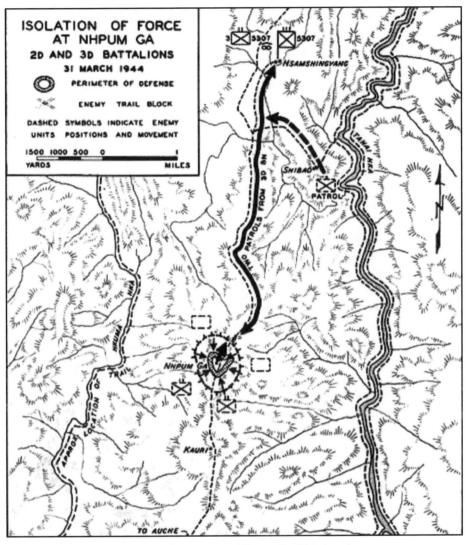

The Marauder position at Nhpum Ga. (U.S. Army)

it. On the morning of March 31, 3rd Battalion confirmed McGee's worst fears: the Japanese had cut the trail between Nhpum Ga and Hsamshingyang. McGee and his men were isolated.[7]

* * *

The Chindits also faced a strong Japanese reaction, which made itself felt on all three Strongholds.

Broadway was held by 3/9 Gurkha Rifles of Calvert's brigade, assisted by floater units from 82 Column, all under the command of Claude Rome, the man who observed the difficult take-off of Wingate's B-25. Rome aggressively patrolled the surrounding area, and on March 26, friendly Kachins reported the approach of a significant Japanese force, later determined to be a battalion. That afternoon, 82 Column ambushed 150 Japanese near the clearing, killing 31 and driving the rest away. The next day, March 27, the Chindits successfully ambushed another Japanese patrol near the perimeter. These actions represented what one officer later called "the first warnings of danger [to Broadway] from enemy ground forces."[8]

Rome digested these developments, put Broadway's garrison on high alert for the night. The nightly C-47 supply landing took place without incident, bringing needed barbed wire and other supplies to strengthen Broadway's defenses. Fifteen minutes after the last C-47 departed, Japanese forces attacked the Gurkha positions west of Broadway, touching off a fierce firefight that lasted 90 minutes. Other Japanese infiltrators entered the clearing, crossed the airstrip, and started harassing Rome's garrison from the rear as other Japanese troops sought to break in. "The attack then flowed all around the perimeter until dawn," recalled Calvert, when at that point the Japanese withdrew. Gurkhas charged with drawn *kukri* knives, driving the Japanese further into the jungle. Daylight revealed that the light planes based there had suffered heavy losses. Broadway's airstrip was also temporarily out of action.[9]

For the next two days, both sides mortared each other and traded attacks. The Japanese repeatedly crept up to the wire to try and cut it, or distract the defenders by yelling "Hey, Joe!" before throwing grenades and attacking. The Gurkha defenders used their guns and knives to repel all these efforts. On March 31, 82 Column and a Gurkha company attacked northward into the Japanese main body of 250 men. A bombing run by 1st Air Commando B-25s preceded the ground attack, and proved so effective that "when our troops reached the enemy they found only minor opposition," reported Calvert, "the main body retreating in disorder and leaving much equipment behind." Captured documents identified the Japanese as coming from the 18th Division, sent from the north. The Japanese had lost over 150 killed in what would be their only ground attack against Broadway, while the Chindits lost 67 killed and 14 wounded. By April 2, the airfield was back in operation.[10]

A different drama played out 40 miles to the southwest. On March 24, Fergusson's brigade moved to execute Wingate's order to attack Indaw. Fergusson had only six of his eight columns with him; the two diverted to Lonkin had not yet caught up. He decided to use the two columns of the 2nd Leicesters to attack Indaw from the north and northeast, supported by the 45th Reconnaissance Regiment's two columns. The columns of 2nd Queen's would set up blocking positions south and west to try and isolate the town. "The main assault upon Indaw," noted Fergusson, "was therefore carried out by four columns, amounting to 1,800 men, who had just completed an arduous march of four hundred miles without so much as a day's rest."

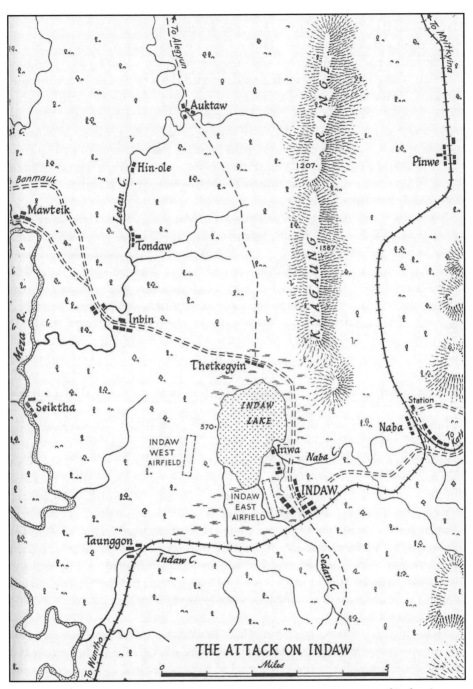

The Indaw area. Aberdeen is off the map, to the northwest. (U.K. Ministry of Defence)

Wingate had estimated up to 3,000 defenders in Indaw—an accurate estimate, as Hayashi had just arrived with four battalions of infantry.[11]

Fergusson's march ran into problems. First, his men discovered that a Chindit column had just passed through the area a few days before, announcing their intention to attack Indaw from the north. It later developed this was part of 111th Brigade, spreading a false story to cover a movement west and southwest toward Pinlebu. "What was an admirable cover plan for them," commented Fergusson, "was the worst possible from the point of view of my own task." A bigger issue soon reared its head, as it was discovered that the land north of Indaw was almost completely dry. "I reckoned I was faced with an advance of no less than fourteen miles without water," said Fergusson, "with the prospect of having to fight for it at the end of that time; and I didn't like it a bit."[12]

Nonetheless, Fergusson's troops pressed on. On March 25, the Leicesters skirmished with a group of Burmese loyal to the Japanese. Firing broke out as Fergusson prepared a final conference with his commanders. Instead, he sent his men on their missions with a hasty "Off you go!" The Leicesters moved around Indaw and struck the airfield on the eastern end of town, next to the village of Inwa. They quickly discovered that Hayashi concentrated all five of his battalions around Indaw and wanted to make a hard fight. The Leicesters held off Japanese attacks over the next two days, subsisting on captured rations. "I couldn't exploit their presence there without reinforcements," said Fergusson. The 45th moved southward to try and reach the Leicesters, but ran into stiff resistance and made no progress after two days of fighting with dry canteens. To make matters worse, radio communications became spotty due to the terrain and atmospherics. "Those days were of unrelieved gloom," said Fergusson.[13]

In addition, the news from the Queen's was decidedly mixed. The force swinging south of Indaw, 21 Column, had been surprised in bivouac and forced to retreat in disorder. However, 22 Column had enjoyed some success along the road west of Indaw, ambushing a convoy of six trucks full of Japanese troops. One truck got away, but the occupants of the other five were killed to a man after a night of fighting.[14]

Fergusson appealed for Brodie's 14th Brigade, which had assembled at Aberdeen. Wingate had assured Fergusson that Brodie and his men were destined for Indaw, but instead they had moved off on another mission. On the evening of March 27, a frustrated Fergusson ordered his men to retire northward. B-25s from the 1st Air Commando struck Indaw, blocking Japanese pursuit. Once all of the 16th Brigade's columns were determined to be safely away, Fergusson directed everyone to Aberdeen for a rest.[15]

Meanwhile, at White City, Calvert "had decided that it was time to impose his will on the enemy by sallying forth from the block and taking Mawlu," reported a staff officer, "in which the enemy claimed to be concentrated in readiness for the extermination of our troops." Calvert committed 50 and 63 Columns to the attack, and personally accompanied the troops.[16]

At dawn on March 27, the columns attacked Mawlu from northeast, southeast, and northwest, and routed the Japanese in sharp fighting. Some of the defenders fled south, where the Chindits shot many down. Others, who retreated into the town, were burned out by flamethrowers or hunted down by the Gurkhas of 63 Column. The Gurkhas worked "with kukri and bayonet," according to an officer. "At this juncture the enemy broke and ran, not for the first time in the campaign." Over 50 Japanese bodies were counted, against a loss of 45 Chindits killed and wounded.[17]

After the victory, the Chindits discovered the extent of Japanese bluster. "The defenders appeared to be a company of a battalion of the 113th Regiment," recalled Calvert. "There were a few of the 3rd Battalion, 114th Regiment, also among the dead. Those running away were clerks, railway operators, administrative personnel, etc." They left behind an intelligence bonanza. "The Gurkhas, who can ferret out anything," said Calvert, "probed a few filled-in foxholes, and found masses of buried documents ... Among the documents was a complete record of the Indian (Traitor) National Army, and of other agents trained in Burma for India."[18]

Thus victorious, Calvert's men marched back to White City. But this move had attracted Hayashi's attention—now that Indaw was secure, he determined to neutralize White City.

* * *

Meanwhile, Mutaguchi's invasion of India appeared to be progressing well. Despite its failure to destroy the 17th Indian Division, Yanagida's 33rd Division was closing in on Imphal from the south and southwest. Yamamoto's force was making good progress against 20th Indian Division, and threatened to break into the Imphal Plain itself. On March 28, the 15th Division's leading elements cut the Imphal–Kohima Road, isolating IV Corps.[19]

East of Kohima, the 138th Regiment of 31st Division encountered Lieutenant Colonel William F. "Bruno" Brown's 1st Assam Regiment. Brown's main body held Jessami, with Lieutenant John "Jock" Young's A Company defending an outpost at Kharasom. Brown and Young had orders to fight "to the last man and the last round." Both places were attacked on March 26, and over the next five days, both units held their own against repeated charges. Unfortunately, they had lost communication with Kohima, and recall orders could not be issued. A U.S. colonel repeatedly flew a Piper Cub to airdrop orders written in the clear, but Brown had moved his men to a wooded hill away from Jessami proper; the Japanese received the messages instead. On the night of March 31, an intrepid lieutenant snuck into Brown's perimeter and relayed the retreat order. Brown ordered his exhausted men to withdraw on the night of April 1, but a Japanese attack late that afternoon scattered the defenders. The 1st Assam Regiment had to make its way out in small parties. Ultimately, 280 of 500 men—including Brown—turned up in Kohima.[20]

At Kharasom, Lieutenant Young never received the withdrawal orders. On the afternoon of March 31, Young gathered his surviving officers and NCOs and ordered them to take the company westward and then northward to Kohima. He would stay behind with the dead and wounded who could not be moved. When asked why, Young stated, "My orders were to fight to the last man. I shall obey those orders and I shall be the last man." Young refused all offers to stay with him, and with difficulty got his company moving toward Kohima. His men last saw Young stacking grenades and ammunition around his bunker. He died at the hands of the Japanese the next morning; his body was never identified. His company managed to join the rest of the regiment at Kohima. These stands by the 1st Assam Regiment delayed the Japanese advance by another five critical days.[21]

* * *

Stilwell had been following the situation in India closely. "Very serious now," he wrote in his diary on April 1. "Slim wants help." The Japanese advances toward Kohima and Dimapur threatened to sever Stilwell's lifeline on the Bengal–Assam Railway. Cutting that railroad would strangle supplies for both NCAC and the Hump airlift to China, with impacts felt from Manchuria to Assam. Stilwell requested a meeting of SEAC's senior leadership to discuss the situation. On April 3, Mountbatten, Stilwell, Slim, Lentaigne, Stopford, Baldwin, Tulloch, and Wildman-Lushington convened in a building next to the airfield in Jorhat.[22]

Slim and Stilwell arrived early and met privately. This was their first face-to-face meeting in a month, since their talk on March 4 at Stilwell's headquarters. At that time, Stilwell told Slim of a secret plan to strike across the mountains to Myitkyina before the monsoon, and Slim had agreed to keep the plan in confidence. Now, Stilwell offered to assign Sun's 38th Division to Fourteenth Army to help hold the railway. The American warned "it would mean stopping his advance, probably withdrawing, and certainly not getting Myitkyina before the monsoon," recalled Slim. "I was sure this was Stilwell's great opportunity. I, therefore, told him to retain the 38th Division ... and to push on to Myitkyina as hard as he could go." Stilwell then said that he expected to execute his Myitkyina movement, codenamed End Run, by May 20.[23]

In the plenary session, the attendees reviewed the situation. Slim said the critical period would last until April 9, but expressed confidence in victory. He outlined Fourteenth Army's plans and reviewed his orders to secure Kohima and relieve Imphal. Stilwell agreed to divert some of his newly-arriving Chinese troops to protect the Hump airfields and the nearby rail lines, while continuing his offensive southward. The Chindits received orders to both disrupt Fifteenth Army's communications and dispatch forces northward to meet Stilwell's southward advance. Mountbatten ratified all plans, and the leaders returned to their battles.[24]

"Conference at Jorhat yesterday," cabled Stilwell to General Marshall. "Much to my surprise no repeat no call on us for help." He reported Slim's remarks and noted with some alarm that "they expect to lose Kohima repeat Kohima," and that much of the Japanese 31st Division was approaching that place. "I do not share in this optimistic British outlook," Stilwell concluded. "If the Japs move fast, I believe it will be difficult to hold Dimapur. In any event the railway will probably be interrupted for a considerable period."[25]

* * *

General Stilwell correctly sensed the confusion that reigned in Dimapur and Kohima at the time. News of the Japanese advance had thrown the rear-area troops stationed in both places into disorder. Few combat soldiers were available, and most of those that were had been detached from their units. One such person was Lieutenant M. A. Rahman, returning from leave. Normally in Cowan's 17th Indian Division, Rahman reached Dimapur and found the road to Imphal blocked. "Dimapur was like a disturbed anthill," he recalled. "Everyone seemed to be moving somewhere. Non-fighting troops were being evacuated and reinforcements were being grouped together to form units to defend Dimapur. I was given an adhoc company to defend the main approach from Kohima ... I am glad the Japanese did not come on to Dimapur."[26]

Kohima was scarcely better prepared. On March 22, Colonel Hugh Richards arrived from Delhi to take command of the garrison at Kohima. He quickly appreciated that the town and its Kohima Ridge occupied a key geographic position, as a focal point of roads and trails. The key ground was the Ridge itself, as it overlooked a main intersection and dominated the road to Imphal. The ridge was really a series of hills running north–south, with gently sloping saddles connecting each feature. Since their development as a supply base a year earlier, the various hills were known by their function. From south to north, they were: GPT (General Purpose Transport) Ridge, Jail Hill, DIS (Detail Issue Store), FSD (Field Supply Depot), Kuki Picquet, and Garrison Hill. A northwest extension of Garrison Hill housed a hospital and was known as IGH (Indian General Hospital) Spur. Most of these hills were covered by thick woods interspersed with the structures of both the town and the base. Garrison Hill was terraced and landscaped, and was home (complete with clubhouse and tennis court) to the Deputy Commissioner for the area, Charles Pawsey. The Imphal–Dimapur Road skirted the ridge to the east before turning west past Garrison Hill. Treasury Hill and the Naga Village settlement overlooked the ridge from the northeast; those heights also extended north to the hamlet of Merema. Southward loomed the imposing Pulebadze mountain, while three miles to the west rose a knoll topped by the village of Jotsoma. Kohima Ridge was thus overlooked by surrounding

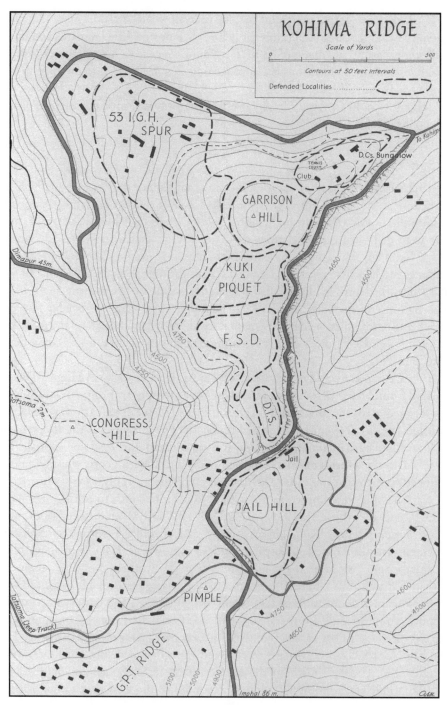

Kohima Ridge. (U.K. Ministry of Defence)

Geoffrey Scoones. (Imperial War Museum)

General Wingate after Operation Longcloth, in the uniform he wore to Quebec. (Imperial War Museum)

General Chennault. (U.S. Army)

The military conferees at Quebec. Left to right: Lord Louis Mountbatten, Admiral of the Fleet Sir Dudley Pound, General Sir Alan Brooke, Air Chief Marshal Sir Charles Portal, Air Marshal L. S. Breadner, Lieutenant General Sir Hastings Ismay, Field Marshal Sir John Dill, Admiral Ernest J. King, General Henry H. Arnold, Admiral William D. Leahy, Lieutenant General Kenneth Stuart, Vice Admiral Percy W. Nelles, and General George C. Marshall. (Imperial War Museum)

General Kawabe. (U.K. Ministry of Defence)

General Slim, seen in 1945 in London. (Imperial War Museum)

General Giffard. (Courtesy of Arabella Birdperson)

Chiang Kai-shek and Madame Chiang with General Stilwell in 1942. (U.S. Army)

Philip Cochran (left) and John Alison. (U.S. Air Force)

General Mutaguchi with his senior leaders and staff in 1943. Front row, left to right: Lieutenant General Genzo Yanagida, 33rd Division; Lieutenant General Tanaka Shinichi, 18th Division; Mutaguchi; Lieutenant General Matsuyama Sukezo, 56th Division, and Lieutenant General Sato Kotoku, 31st Division. (U.S. Army)

Stilwell inspecting Chinese troops at Ramgarh. To his right are Generals Lo Cho-ying and Sun Li-jen. (U.S. Army)

General Pick (with pipe) and a staff officer on the Ledo Road. (U.S. National Archives)

A C-46 transport flies the Hump. (U.S. Army)

Bose (right) with Gandhi in the 1930s. (Author's collection)

A column of General Wei's Y Force troops on the march. (Library of Congress)

General Boatner. (U.S. Army)

General Stratemeyer. (U.S. Air Force)

General Sakurai. (U.K. Ministry of Defence)

General William Old, who led the air transport forces supporting Fourteenth Army. (U.S. Air Force)

Tankers of Colonel Brown's 1st Provisional Tank Group. (U.S. Army)

A formation of Kachin Rangers. (U.S. Army)

General Messervy. (U.K. Ministry of Defence)

General Evans. (Author's collection)

A C-47 parachuting supplies to ground troops. (U.S. Air Force)

Japanese troops massing along the Burma–India border. (U.S. Air Force)

Building a bridge on the Ledo Road route, February 1944. (U.S. Army)

General Stilwell (center) confers with Sun (left) and Liao (right), 1944. (U.S. Army)

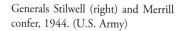

Generals Stilwell (right) and Merrill confer, 1944. (U.S. Army)

Wingate (in pith helmet) briefing American pilots before the start of Operation Thursday. Philip Cochran is to Wingate's left. (Imperial War Museum)

Operation Thursday's first planes and gliders head for Burma. Each C-47 pulled two gliders in what was called a "double tow." (Imperial War Museum)

Charles Russhon with actress Claudine Auger, seen after the war on the set of the James Bond film *Thunderball*, on which he served as technical advisor. (U.S. Air Force)

Wingate and company at Broadway, the night of March 6/7, 1944. Left to right are Colonel Francis G. Brink, John Alison, Mike Calvert, Captain George Borrow (Wingate's aide), Wingate, Lieutenant Colonel Walter Scott, Major Francis Stewart. (Imperial War Museum)

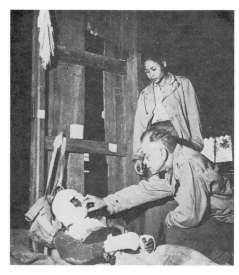

Stilwell (left) and Mountbatten during the latter's visit to the NCAC front, March 1944. (U.S. Army)

Gordon Seagrave examines a patient in the field. (U.S. Army)

General Stopford. (Imperial War Museum)

General Grover. (National Portrait Gallery, London)

Joe Lentaigne. (Imperial War Museum)

The northern side of the Imphal Plain, looking north from an aircraft over the town of Imphal. Imphal Main is in the foreground, with the Imphal–Kohima Road extending in a straight line past the runway. The hills in the top and right of the image were scenes of fierce fighting between April and June 1944. (Imperial War Museum)

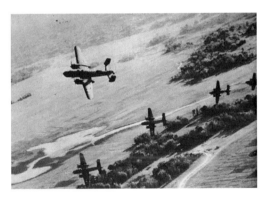

B-25s of the 1st Air Commando over Burma. (U.S. Air Force)

P-47s of the 1st Air Commando take off on a mission. (U.S. Air Force)

A view of White City. The airstrip is in the foreground, with the Chindit positions on the overlooking hill. (Imperial War Museum)

Marauders on the march. (U.S. Army)

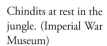
Chindits at rest in the jungle. (Imperial War Museum)

General Warren. (Imperial War Museum)

Lieutenant John Young. (Kohima Educational Trust)

Evacuating Chindit wounded via American light plane. (Imperial War Museum)

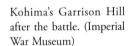

Kohima's Garrison Hill after the battle. (Imperial War Museum)

Charles Pawsey's bungalow after the battle, looking up the hill. (Imperial War Museum)

West African troops boarding a C-47. (Imperial War Museum)

Looking northeast over the Kohima battleground of late April and May. The Imphal–Kohima Road runs across the image. Jail Hill is in the center, with D.I.S. directly across the road and Treasury Hill behind it. To the right of Treasury is the Gun Spur area. (Imperial War Museum)

General Dorn (right) with General Wei (left) and General Ho Ying-chin (center). (U.S. Army)

A C-47 drops supplies low over Allied positions at Myitkyina. (U.S. National Archives)

Troops of the 5th Indian Division fight their way northward along the Imphal–Kohima Road. (Imperial War Museum)

A command conference on the Imphal Road between Generals Grover (left, in helmet), Salomons (center) and Stopford (right). (Imperial War Museum)

Chinese troops fighting their way toward Mogaung and Myitkyina. (Imperial War Museum)

Mike Calvert (left) giving instructions to two of his commanders during the fighting for Mogaung. At right is Major James Lumley, father of actress Joanna Lumley. (Imperial War Museum)

A 75mm pack howitzer in action at Myitkyina. (U.S. Army)

heights: Pulebadze to the south, Jotsoma to the west, and Naga Village/Merema to the east and northeast.[27]

Richards needed to organize a defense of this area, and quickly determined to concentrate his limited forces on Kohima Ridge itself. He sent away most of the logistical troops stationed nearby, evacuated the hospitals, and organized the men in the replacement depot into platoons to be assigned to combat units. Richards also recalled Brown's Assam Regiment, and unsuccessfully sought to keep a battalion of the West Yorkshire Regiment that had orders for Imphal.[28]

Stopford added to the confusion when he arrived on March 23. His headquarters wouldn't formally open until April 3, but he took charge anyway. Slim gave him several missions, starting with protecting Dimapur and the railroad. Once Dimapur was secured, XXXIII Corps was under orders to reopen the road to Imphal. Grover's 2nd British Division was on the way, moving much faster by rail than anyone thought possible; many British commanders now had cause to thank the American railroaders, whose improvements to the Bengal–Assam Railway had occurred just in time. For the moment, however, Stopford's only field force was Warren's 161st Brigade, which was just arriving at Kohima. Stopford believed the key point to deploy his defense was Dimapur itself, and judged Kohima to be a lower priority. Despite protests from Richards, Stopford ordered Warren's men to retrace their steps. On March 31, Warren's brigade retired to Nichugard Pass, 10 miles east of Dimapur. Over the following days, elements of 2nd British Division arrived, and on April 4, 161st Brigade was ordered back to Kohima.[29]

Meanwhile, Richards prepared his defense as best he could. On April 3, Brown's survivors reached Kohima. The local Naga people kept Richards informed of Japanese movements via Charles Pawsey, a World War I veteran who had spent years among the Nagas as Deputy Commissioner. Pawsey could have left, but did not want to abandon those who he regarded as his people. He also understood that, if he left, the British would lose face forever. The Nagas recognized his importance; "Charles Pawsey," affirmed one, "was one of the reasons the Nagas remained loyal to the British … His action at a critical time improved the image for the British administration." Pawsey remained at Richards's side through the battle, and the Nagas assisted the British as guides, porters, and spies.[30]

Sato planned a three-pronged advance on Kohima. Miyazaki and the 58th Regiment would drive straight up the Imphal Road, while the 138th Regiment secured Naga Village and swung around behind Kohima to cut the road to Dimapur. The 124th Regiment would be in reserve to support either advance. Mutaguchi hoped to reach Dimapur, and asked his superior, General Kawabe at Burma Area Army, for air support to assist Sato's offensive. Kawabe replied that no extra aircraft were available, and pointedly reminded Mutaguchi that Dimapur was "not within the strategic objectives" of U-Go. Except for a few small patrols, no Japanese soldier would get closer than 32 miles to Dimapur.[31]

On April 4, Richards's outposts made first contact with the Japanese. Warren's lead battalion, 4th Royal West Kents, plus a company from 4/7 Rajput, arrived with artillery on the late afternoon of April 5, shortly before the Japanese closed the road to Dimapur after dark. This left Richards with 2,500 men, 1,000 of whom were noncombatants. The garrison's combat strength centered on the West Kents, assisted by the Assam Regiment, five detached companies of Indian infantry, a battalion of the paramilitary Assam Rifles, and the half-trained Nepalese Shere Regiment. There was enough ammunition and food to last for weeks, although water was short.[32]

Warren found Japanese shellfire already striking around Garrison Hill. He quickly realized his entire brigade could not fit into the perimeter; he took position at Jotsoma and formed an all-around defense. His artillery would assist the defense of both Jotsoma and Kohima.[33]

Kohima faced its first test on the evening of April 5, when Miyazaki's men attacked GPT Ridge and Jail Hill. The latter held out, while the troops defending the former gave way and retired toward Dimapur. The Japanese swung east and repeatedly attacked Jail Hill on the April 6, forcing its evacuation. That night, a West Kent company wiped out a Japanese penetration into the structures between FSD and DIS; an exploding ammunition dump flushed many Japanese into the open where the British gunned them down. Daylight on April 7 revealed 44 Japanese bodies in the defile between the hills. Other Japanese had sheltered in the ovens of a bakery, and Lance Corporal John Harman went in with grenades, dropping one into each oven. Two men, including an officer, survived and were captured by Harman, who carried them back to British lines over his shoulder like logs. The officer was found to have a map of Japanese artillery positions around Kohima.[34]

The siege soon settled into a routine of sorts. The Japanese would fire furiously at dusk in what the defenders called the "evening hate." Repeated night attacks denied anything but the most fitful sleep, while during the day snipers, machine guns, artillery, and mortars harassed Kohima's defenders. British artillery from Jotsoma, aided by spotters in Kohima's perimeter, engaged the enemy as needed. The loss of GPT also meant the loss of most of the garrison's water access except for a small spring on Garrison Hill; Richards's defenders were limited to one pint of water per man, per day.

Japanese attention next shifted to Garrison Hill. Elements of two Japanese battalions attacked up the terraced slopes from Naga Village against the reinforced company holding the terraces. Mortar fire blanketed the British positions as the Japanese pressed upward. Indian Bren gunners defended to the last as the tide washed over them. Pawsey's bungalow fell, and the defenders, reinforced by A Company of the West Kents, took position at the tennis court. Supporting fire came from the clubhouse, with Bren guns mounted on a pool table and other furniture. There, the Japanese surge stopped, leaving the width of the tennis court between the two sides. These lines would not move for weeks.[35]

Further south, the Japanese had placed a machine gun overlooking DIS that threatened to make the British position untenable. Harman single-handedly attacked the position and killed the crew in broad daylight. He hoisted the gun over his shoulder and started back to the lines, seemingly unconcerned about the danger. A heretofore hidden Japanese machine gun shot him dead. This action, plus the one at the bakery the day before, earned Harman a posthumous Victoria Cross.[36]

Meanwhile, Grover's 2nd Division struggled to open the road. On April 8, Sato's 138th Regiment had reached Zubza, 32 miles from Dimapur, and set up several defended roadblocks in the 10 miles between Zubza and Jotsoma. Warren tried to break out westward, but found the defenses too strong; Grover's British troops would have to fight their way in.

Despite Stopford's encouragement to take risks, Grover was torn between the imperative of relieving Kohima and protecting the road to Dimapur with only two of his three brigades on the scene. He posted Brigadier J. D. Shapland's 6th Brigade along the road and sent his lead brigade, the 5th under Brigadier Victor Hawkins, forward. With tank support from M3 Grants, the infantry slowly advanced toward Jotsoma.[37]

Richards and Laverty tracked these movements via radio's link between the West Kents' headquarters and Warren. Laverty was somewhat jealous of his prerogatives regarding his battalion, and maintained control of this connection to the outside throughout the siege. The tension between the two senior officers did not matter much, as Captain Tom Coates of the West Kents explained. "The siege was primarily a privates' battle," he recalled, "and our success was due mainly to the very high morale and steadiness of the NCOs and men."[38]

* * *

Imphal also found itself under siege when Japanese attacks started against Scoones's new position around the Imphal Plain. Yamauchi's 15th Division swung southward along the Imphal–Kohima Road and through the hills and tracks to the east. If his troops broke out into the Imphal Plain, the Japanese would be only a few miles from Imphal Main airfield and IV Corps headquarters.

Briggs's 5th Indian Division blocked the advance with Brigadier Salomons's 9th and Brigadier Evans's 123rd Brigades; they had arrived just in time. Evans's 123rd Brigade covered the area northeast and east of Imphal, including the approaches from Ukhrul and Sangshak. Evans set his men to intense patrolling, and on April 4, his men wiped out a Japanese company pressing westward toward Kameng.[39]

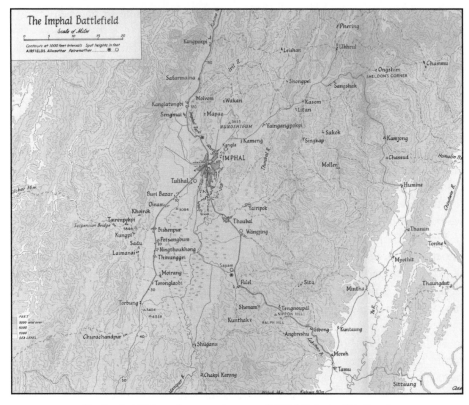

The Imphal Plain and surrounding area. (U.K. Ministry of Defence)

On the Imphal–Kohima Road, IV Corps had a major supply dump at Kanglatongbi, known as Lion Box. Most of its 12,000 defenders were not trained infantry, so Salomons's 9th Brigade moved northward to assist. South of Lion Box was the village of Sengmai, and a few miles past Sengmai was IV Corps headquarters itself, in an area known as the Keep. A mile beyond the Keep was Imphal Main airfield.[40]

Yamauchi sent his main effort toward Lion Box, but also sought to flank the position to the east. He sent the 60th Regiment to attack toward Kanglatongbi through the hills east of the road. On the night of April 4, the Japanese first broke into Lion Box, but could advance no further on account of Salomons's troops at Sengmai. "On April 5 and 6," reported an officer, "[2nd] West Yorkshire platoons, accompanied by tanks, patrolled forward to Lion Box … and mopped up all resistance that remained before returning to Sengmai at dusk." The next morning, the order was given to evacuate Lion Box, and the 2nd West Yorkshire protected the support troops as they emptied the depots of what supplies they could get. In the late afternoon, the defenders fell back to Sengmai. The Japanese captured very few supplies, while losing 68 killed in action. Yamauchi paused to regroup and consolidate before resuming the attack.[41]

Further east, elements of the 51st Regiment attacked the hills around Nungshigum. On April 6, a patrol of 3/9 Jats were thrown off a hill just north of the Nungshigum heights. Jemedar (Lieutenant) Abdul Hafiz led two sections of his platoon in a counterattack, preceded by a Jat war cry. Shot in the leg, he continued up the hill and seized a Japanese machine gun before killing more Japanese. Despite being wounded in the chest, Hafiz grabbed a Bren gun and, with his dying breath, told his men, "Reorganize! I will give you covering fire." The ferocity of this assault caused the Japanese to flee, and ever after the hill has been known as Runaway Hill. Hafiz earned the Victoria Cross for his leadership—the first Muslim in World War II to do so.[42]

The Japanese regrouped and attacked again. The battle lines rolled back and forth over Nungshigum and Runaway Hill until finally, on April 11, the Japanese held both places. Yamauchi's men were at the edge of the Imphal Plain and stood six miles from Imphal Main, four miles from IV Corps headquarters, and 14 miles from the center of Imphal. The Japanese could see aircraft taking off from Imphal Main; it would be only a matter of time before observers from Nungshigum would direct artillery and airstrikes on Scoones's most important airfield. The Japanese needed to be ejected.

On April 12, artillery shelled Nungshigum and a company of 1/17 Dogras attacked with support of half a squadron of Lee tanks from 3rd Dragoon Guards. They got nowhere, and had to pull back. The next morning, the British returned with a full squadron of tanks and two companies of Dogras, supported by shelling from the divisional artillery of 5th Indian Division and an artillery regiment from IV Corps Artillery. Hurricane and Vengeance fighter-bombers opened the battle with repeated bombing and strafing runs.[43]

As the smoke cleared, the tanks and infantry started up Nungshigum's sides. "The tanks ... climbed up like big, slow, black beetles," stated an observer, "balanced themselves on knife-edge ridges and pumped bullets and shells into every Japanese man and bunker that could be seen, the agile Dogras protected the tanks from interference. And under the armored cover they assaulted the Japanese trenches and bunkers. The struggle flickered from bunker to bunker." The tank officers exposed themselves to navigate and direct, and every officer in the attack was killed or wounded. The Dogra infantry also lost every officer to death or wounds. But the attack continued, and the Japanese retreated. A few defenders tried suicide attacks to stop the tanks without success, and their elimination ended the battle. Dusk found Nungshigum and the surrounding area back in British hands, where it would stay for the rest of the siege.[44]

After regrouping, Yamauchi sent the 60th and 67th Regiments against Sengmai on April 13 and again on April 18. Both times, the attacks failed in the face of stiff resistance. "The failure to breach the enemy's defenses at Sengmai," noted a Japanese staff report, "marked the turning point in the operation."[45]

By April 19, the lines north of Imphal had stabilized. The defeats had depleted Yamauchi's already weak division, and gave him reason to regret the diversion of some of his units to fight the Chindits. Worse still, disease ravaged the 15th Division's ranks, affecting General Yamauchi himself. The division was forced to go over to the defensive, pending the receipt of any reinforcements.[46]

Fighting also continued south and southwest of Imphal, as the 33rd Division and Yamamoto Force fought to break into the Imphal Plain. In the first week of April, 33rd Division assembled opposite Torbung, south of Imphal. Japanese attacks on April 8 and 9 met with limited success, and Roberts realized he would soon be outflanked. His troops retreated northward to Bishenpur, where the Silchar Track and the Tiddim Road intersected 20 miles south of Imphal. Bishenpur also stood in a narrow defile between mountains on the west and Loktak Lake to the east. There, the 17th Indian Division, plus 32nd Indian Brigade of Gracey's division, relieved Roberts's men and took position to defend.[47]

On April 14, behind the 33rd Division's positions at Moirang, something happened that would have repercussions for many years to come. The INA forces that had accompanied Mutaguchi's invaders so far had been disappointed in their rear-area assignments, but the excitement of returning to India as potential liberators sustained them. That day, their morale soared when Colonel Shaukat Malik raised the Azad Hind flag over Moirang, marking the first time Bose's government asserted control over a part of India's mainland.[48]

Further to the east, Gracey's men organized their positions at Shenam. They occupied a series of hills along the road, running west-northwest toward Palel. From east to west, they were named: Nippon Hill, Cyprus, Crete East, Crete West, Lynch Pimple, Scraggy, Malta, Gibraltar, Recce Hill, and Patiala Ridge. Steep drop-offs south of the road channeled the Japanese attack up the road and into the hills.

As Yamamoto Force was slow to deploy, Gracey's men were able to dig in. A British patrol discovered Japanese advance units had already occupied Nippon Hill. On April 11, the 1st Devonshires successfully assaulted Nippon Hill. They held it for five days until the Japanese threw them back to Crete East. Further Japanese attacks on April 20 and 21 captured Crete East, forcing the evacuation of Cyprus and the assumption of new positions at Crete West and Scraggy. Both sides paused to regroup; the next round of fighting would come soon enough.[49]

As the battle intensified, Scoones authorized "Elephant Bill" Williams to get out with his charges as best he could. Williams decided to go through the trackless hills directly west from Imphal in an effort to reach Silchar, 120 miles away on the other side. On April 5, he set off from near IV Corps headquarters with 15 days' rations, 53 elephants, 90 attendants, 40 armed Karen escorts, four officers, and 63

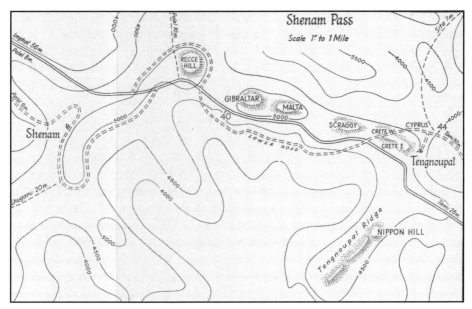

The Shenam Saddle area. (U.K. Ministry of Defence)

Gurkha camp-followers as evacuees. Three weeks later, the party emerged from the wilderness and found safety in the tea plantations east of Silchar.[50]

Scoones's quartermasters were also assessing the supply situation. The Imphal–Kohima Road was cut, and the Silchar Track was incapable of carrying large vehicles, so IV Corps was essentially isolated from overland transport and supply. Heavy Japanese attacks were occurring all around the Imphal Plain, with the expectation of more to come. At the present rate of consumption, IV Corps had supply reserves for about 30 days of operations. Scoones cut rations to his men and animals by one-third, and also directed economy of movement to save fuel. "Fresh supplies will be issued to maximum availability," directed Brigadier L. T. Loup, IV Corps' chief quartermaster, on April 2. "Continuous and energetic steps will be taken to ensure maximum economy."[51]

It was clear that IV Corps could only survive on air supply. The first planes landed on April 8, bringing in supplies and artillery, and evacuating the wounded. Scoones planned to fly out non-combat units as planes came in to reduce his ration strength and get them out of the way. The local population had scattered into the hills west of Imphal and were left to their own devices.[52]

Loup provided Fourteenth Army with a weekly list of "demands" for supplies and transport priorities, and would continue to do so until the siege was lifted. His first one, delivered April 10/11, quietly laid the situation on the line. "It is not at present known what tonnage can be expected by air daily or whether it is possible to give any indication as to whether a regular allotment of so many sorties a day can be made to 4 Corps," Loup wrote. "Equally, it is realized that weather and/or other operational commitments make it difficult to forecast any definite daily allotment. It is, however, suggested that an attempt be made ... as it is most important from every point of view that units and formations [of IV Corps] be kept up to strength." He then outlined IV Corps' key needs in order of priority—personnel to replace losses, arms, ammunition, equipment to fortify defensive positions, food, other supplies, and stationery. "May early information be sent as to approximately what rate of sorties may be expected?" he asked.[53]

On April 17, in response to Loup's message, Baldwin's and Slim's staffs met at Comilla to plan a long-term airlift into Imphal. The garrison in Imphal, numbering about 155,000 men and 11,000 animals, needed an estimated 540 tons per day to sustain it in fighting condition through the end of June. The conferees decided to start an organized lift from the Bengal airfields into Imphal under the codename Operation Stamina. The planes just arriving from the Mediterranean would be employed, along with several squadrons on hand and planes diverted from the Hump, making an Anglo-American force of 232 C-47s. Stamina would begin the next day, April 18.[54]

* * *

Meanwhile, in Burma, the Chindit operations had prompted a Japanese reorganization. On April 8, Burma Area Army activated Thirty-Third Army under Lieutenant General Honda Masaki. The 18th and 56th Divisions came under Honda's command, as did Hayashi's 24th Independent Mixed Brigade and all forces fighting the Chindits. Kawabe also attached the 53rd Division, which would arrive in early May. Honda's mission was to hold north Burma and coordinate all operations against NCAC, Y Force, and the Chindits.[55]

In Indaw, Hayashi turned his attention toward White City. He released the 2nd Battalion 51st Regiment to rejoin the 15th Division at Imphal, and marched the rest of his forces toward Mawlu and White City. Hayashi ordered White City to be "annihilated" in a mass attack from the south and east.[56]

Calvert's garrison, reinforced with part of 3rd West African Brigade and Fergusson's 16th Brigade, was ready. Hayashi thought the Chindits were occupying Mawlu, and tipped his hand by attacking the empty town on the evening of April 6. Hayashi's artillery and mortars shelled both Mawlu and White City relentlessly, to which Calvert's 25-pounders and mortars answered. "As night fell, with the usual wild cries the attack started," recalled Calvert. "On reaching our extensive wire, the attackers were lit up by our 2-inch mortar star shells, and mown down by Vickers machine guns, Bren guns, rifle fire, and Mills grenades ... After an hour or two, they withdrew." Just after dawn, 1st Air Commando planes bombed Hayashi's positions.[57]

Hayashi tried again and again to crush White City, but "the strong, closely integrated honeycomb defenses withstood even the most desperate efforts," noted a staff report. "The sequence of attack was the same practically every night and only varied in intensity," said Calvert. "The Jap would start shelling at about 5pm, continuing until dusk. He would then attack, just after last light, the east and southeast perimeter through the jungle." The Chindits saturated the approaches with mortar fire, while booby-traps and mines further disrupted the Japanese advance. The attacks almost all foundered on the wire, in the face of determined fire from the defenders. Two tanks joined the battle on the evening of the April 11, but British fire disabled one and drove the other away. "Having done his best," Calvert said of his opponent, "fighting would die down. Sometimes he would make a further attempt at midnight" or try to recover bodies. The battle was intense, but the Chindits fought with confidence.[58]

On April 11, Calvert led eight columns (four battalions) out of White City to launch spoiling attacks against the Japanese. After pushing into Hayashi's rear at Sepein, Calvert swung around and attacked the Japanese from the east, assisted by Air Commando aircraft. Over 190 Japanese were killed, and Calvert pushed to within a half-mile of the White City perimeter before withdrawing. "This virtually ended the battle," reported a staff officer. "The enemy had suffered far too many casualties carry on, and, after some firing by artillery on 17 April," they withdrew. "The garrison of the block was able to sally forth and count bodies at their leisure." The Chindits tallied over 1,000 enemy dead, including a colonel—over 50% of Hayashi's total force.[59]

White City was secure, but the concentrated death and destruction of the battle—combined with the heat and humidity—made the block an unpleasant place to be. Quicklime was flown in and helped some, but flies and odors proliferated, clinging to everyone and everything. "We can always find White City now," commented a pilot to Calvert. "We navigate by smell."[60]

The aftermath of Calvert's victory also made military history. Calvert dispatched his wounded men via light plane to Aberdeen, where they would catch a C-47 flight to India. On April 21, one of these flights, carrying three casualties and an American pilot, went down 15 miles west of Mawlu. Planes could not get in to rescue the men, so an overland rescue expedition started from White City. "Send the egg-beater in," commanded Cochran from 1st Air Commando headquarters. The Commandos' lone operational Sikorsky YR-4B helicopter flew to Aberdeen in stages, arriving April 25. The helicopter pilot, U.S. Lieutenant Carter Harmon, learned that Chindits had secured an airstrip in a riverbed not far from the stranded men. He flew to the stream bed, landed and refueled, got his bearings, and took off again. Harmon knew the Sikorsky would struggle to carry himself and one passenger, and that four trips would be needed. On April 25, he picked up two casualties before the engine overheated and needed a rest. The next day, he made two trips to pick up the final casualty and the pilot, taking off as troops (which turned out the be the rescue party) swarmed the landing zone. Harmon flew back to Aberdeen, having accomplished the first battlefield helicopter rescue in military history.[61]

"During the big and decisive battle at White City fortified block," noted a staff officer, "the other brigades had not been idle." Brodie's 14th Brigade cut the railroad southwest of Indaw, and raided the now-vacant Japanese base at Indaw with Fergusson's 16th Brigade. Masters's 111th Brigade ambushed Japanese trucks on the roads west of Indaw before turning toward Aberdeen. East of the Irrawaddy, Morrisforce and Dahforce each successfully raided the Bhamo–Lashio Road, assisted by friendly Kachins. Worried about overreach, Lentaigne vetoed any plans to push south or east into the hills along the Burma–China border.[62]

Lentaigne's decision frustrated Herring, but resulted from developments elsewhere that had limited further Chindit operations. "The future plan of the Force had now crystallized," wrote a staff officer. "The expectation held by General Wingate that further troops up to a division in strength would be available for flying in if the Force could capture Indaw West airfield had come to nothing, due mainly to the employment of all available resources to hold up the Japanese offensive on the Imphal front ... Also the Force had [just] been relieved of the responsibility of assisting 4 Corps in any way." Lentaigne needed to look northward to help Stilwell's advance. Some Chindit units were worn, and a period of reorganization was needed to meet the new mission.[63]

* * *

Further north, McGee's battalion held its hilltop at Nhpum Ga. Nightly attacks kept the defenders on alert, while during the day, harassing fire of all types kept the defenders from getting rest. Every position—even the hospitals—was in the line of fire. The increasing amount of dead men and animals attracted flies and created a severe stench. Airdrops on April 2, 5, and 6 brought much-needed food and ammunition. Water remained scarce for most men, as what amount was received went to the 2nd Battalion's wounded. Still, the defenders battled on.[64]

The garrison's morale stayed high thanks to the artillery fire from Hsamshingyang. The air activity also helped, as P-51s arrived to bomb and strafe Japanese positions every day. The men also saw the unarmored C-47s fly through ground fire to drop supplies. "Despite the fire," noted Captain H. L. Greengus of the 2nd Troop Carrier Squadron, USAAF, "the ships flew in at stalling speed, only a few hundred feet above the ground, to make sure the water and ammunition were received by our Allies instead of the Japanese. In the pattern over the dropping target, the Second Troop Carrier Squadron constantly was under machine gun fire." Five C-47s were damaged on April 2, two seriously enough to be put out of commission. "We don't give a damn if the weather's bad or the Japs are raising hell," commented a pilot, "those fellows on the ground need the stuff and we're going to get it to them regardless of consequence."[65]

One advantage that McGee enjoyed was the presence of several *Nisei* in his perimeter, most notably Sergeants Matsumoto and Gosho. The Japanese-Americans crawled around the perimeter and translated what they heard from the enemy. McGee therefore could anticipate Japanese attacks and prepare accordingly. On April 5, Matsumoto overheard a Japanese plan to assault Lieutenant Edward McLogan's position on a shelf (known as McLogan Hill) along the perimeter's west side, below the ridge crest. The night of April 4, a machine gun had been overrun there, but the Japanese had pulled back; they decided to try again in force at dawn the next day, April 6. The Americans retired to the top of the ridge and booby-trapped their former positions. At dawn the next day, the Japanese attacked. "We held our fire until the enemy charged into the line of foxholes," recalled Matsumoto. "We then opened with some fifty automatic weapons— heavy and light machine guns, BARs, Thompson submachineguns, and M-1 rifles—as well as carbines and grenades. The second wave of the enemy troops hesitated in confusion. At that moment, I stood up and gave the order to attack in Japanese. The troops obeyed my order and they were mowed down." After the fighting, the Americans reoccupied their former positions. McLogan Hill was not tested again.[66]

Meanwhile, Hunter decided to commit the entire 3rd Battalion to a relief attack. "Gentlemen," Hunter told the battalion's officers on April 3, "in the morning we start an attack that will drive through to the Second Battalion. It may take two or three days, but we will get through." The next morning, Orange Combat Team attacked down the trail, but were quickly held up by camouflaged Japanese bunkers. The pack 75s came forward to engage them point-blank; Khaki Combat team swung eastward, but soon found itself sucked into the battle along the trail. Each day brought a little progress, measured in scores of yards advanced against fierce opposition. By April 7, the exhausted 3rd Battalion had stalled 500 yards short of breaking through.[67]

That afternoon, the 1st Battalion erupted from the jungle into the Hsamshingyang clearing after six days of marching. Osborne's men arrived with empty packs, having cancelled a supply drop and marched part of the previous night. Eight-hundred tired but exhilarated men arrived at Hunter's headquarters. "It was a happy reunion," recalled Lieutenant Ogburn. "We brought reinforcements and they had food."[68]

Hunter detailed 250 men under Major Thomas Senff to swing west of the battle and try to force a Japanese retreat by threatening their line of communications. The rest of 1st Battalion would guard Hsamshingyang and provide reinforcements for 3rd Battalion. Senff set off the next day, April 8, and by evening was in position southwest of Nhpum Ga, near the trail leading southward. He was almost astride the Japanese supply route and in a position to turn the besiegers into the besieged. On April 9, the Japanese broke off the action, Tanaka directing the survivors to Myitkyina. Shortly after noon, the 3rd Battalion and 2nd Battalion joined hands, followed soon after by Senff's force. The siege of Nhpum Ga was over.[69]

Lieutenant Ogburn went forward to see the field. The men of 2nd Battalion were exhausted but happy to be alive. "Where there were trees," he recalled, "a tornado seemed to have struck. All around, dead Japanese were sprawled as if they had dropped haphazard from the sky, and along the trial were limbs and torsos thrust helter-skelter out of smashed-in bunkers." Dead horses and mules looked like "a field of giant melons." Hunter ordered flamethrowers and quicklime to be used to clean up the bodies.[70]

* * *

Kohima continued to hold out, despite the best efforts of Sato's division. But casualties mounted, and Richards was forced to abandon DIS. Meanwhile, more wounded crowded into IGH Spur, filling the area behind the sector held by Brown's Assam Regiment. There, a group of doctors led by the indefatigable Lieutenant Colonel John Young did what they could, despite short water and enemy activity. Supplies were running low, and Japanese shelling was making the situation at the hospital worse. Young appealed to Richards, who, on the evening of April 12, asked for an airdrop of medical supplies, to which Laverty added mortar ammunition and grenades.[71]

That night, the garrison repelled another attack. On the morning of April 13, the Japanese deliberately shelled IGH Spur, inflicting over 50 casualties on already wounded men and killing three doctors. In the afternoon, three U.S. C-47s parachuted water and the requested supplies, but almost all of it drifted into Japanese lines. The Japanese used some of the captured mortars to shell Kohima's defenders. A little later, RAF transports successfully dropped ammunition and medical supplies to the garrison, but the ammunition was found to have been meant for the artillery at Jotsoma and was the wrong caliber for any of Kohima's guns.

These developments, plus the constant week-long strain of siege, sapped the garrison's morale. The West Kent War Diary called this day "The Black Thirteenth." Richards sensed the mood and issued an Order of the Day. "The relief force is on its way," Richards told his men, "and all that is necessary for the Garrison now is to stand firm, hold its fire and beat off any attempt to infiltrate among us. By your acts you have shown what you can do …. I congratulate you on your magnificent effort and am confident that it will be sustained."[72]

That night the Japanese attacked the garrison from north and south. They penetrated within the trenches on FSD, held by two understrength West Kent companies. In close-quarters combat, which involved one soldier strangling a Japanese officer with his bare hands, the defenders drove off the attackers. At the tennis court, B Company of the West Kents endured repeated attacks. A Bren gun jammed, and some Japanese rushed the position; the gunner died but another soldier beat off the attackers with a shovel. The Assam Regiment reinforced the sector the next day.

For Kohima's defenders, the next few days were a blur of shelling, sniping, and attacks from Japanese troops. Artillery from Jotsoma and RAF Hurricane fighter-bombers supported the defense when possible. Thirst increased despite rain coming on April 14, as there were few ways to catch the water. Blasted trees no longer gave shelter from the weather or concealment from the enemy, and many snared supply parachutes. But the garrison stood firm because of the sights and sounds to the west.[73]

While Kohima endured, Hawkins's brigade fought to open the road. Rain slowed operations and limited the use of tanks. On April 14, Warren promised Laverty and Richards: "I'm doing my best, but intend to make a proper job of it." The next morning brought good news, as at 11am on April 15, the 5th Brigade and 161st Brigade joined hands.[74]

Warren signaled this development to Kohima, and promised relief would come the next day. He immediately sent 1/1 Punjab attacking eastward to make good on his word. But Grover arrived in the afternoon and postponed the final relief attack for one day, citing lack of "time for recce … and lack of adequate provision for the security of the right flank of the brigade." Warren regarded these as acceptable risks in view of the garrison's condition, but had to acquiesce to a postponement until April 17. Japanese attacks on the road were defeated on April 16, but the threat of Jotsoma again being cut off remained. On the morning of April 17, despite only a mile or so remaining between the troops and Garrison Hill, Warren postponed his relief effort yet another day.[75]

The garrison's morale wavered at these repeated delays of rescue. Grim jokes circulated about help never arriving, while both officers and men began to lose confidence that they would get out of Kohima alive. In the hospital, wounded officers asked for their sidearms back—they wanted a quick end when the Japanese came.[76]

On the night of April 17, the Japanese launched a mass charge against FSD, preceded by heavy artillery fire. "We couldn't do a thing sir," reported a West Kent soldier to an officer on Garrison Hill. "The Japs were simply all over us." The exhausted defenders reeled backward off both FSD and Kuki Piquet in the early hours of April 18.

This defeat left Richards and his garrison with a perimeter roughly 350 yards wide by 350 yards deep, centered on Garrison Hill. There was no further retreat possible: it was do or die. Every man who could, including the wounded and Richards himself, took a weapon and went to the line. The defenders peered into the darkness and braced for an assault. Dawn would save them, but hours of darkness stretched ahead.

As they waited, a young soldier turned to Richards. "Sir, can I ask you a question?"

"Of course," Richards replied. "What is it?"

"When we die, sir, is that the end or do we go on?"[77]

* * *

As these battles raged, Mountbatten moved SEAC's headquarters 1,300 miles from Delhi to Kandy, on Ceylon. On April 15, Mountbatten flew to Kandy, where, over the previous week, various staff sections had transferred operations. This long-discussed movement took him out of India's capital, which Mountbatten groused was "a somewhat negative atmosphere," to a fresher and cooler hill station in Ceylon's center. Mountbatten pronounced his new location "a delightful place to work." It also had the advantage of being actually in SEAC's area of responsibility, in contrast to Delhi, which fell under India Command.[78]

The move to Kandy did raise some questions, however. First, it was 500 miles further from the Burma battlefront than Delhi; this meant more and longer plane rides for SEAC's ground and air staff when they needed to conduct business with India Command or the fighting units. Admiral Somerville was the only one of Mountbatten's commanders to welcome the move, as it put him close to his fleet at Colombo. The volume of people moved also seemed extravagant. SEAC's staff size, first estimated at 4,100 but later increased to over 10,000, attracted criticism from India and London alike. The many newcomers overwhelmed SEAC's new home, so much so that SEAC "has become the principal, one might say the only, industry of Kandy," as Mountbatten observed.

SEAC's new accommodations were quite luxurious, and the atmosphere relaxing. Mountbatten sited Supreme Headquarters in the Peradeniya Botanical Gardens, with Giffard's and Peirse's headquarters nearby, while Somerville set up in Kandy itself. Most officers quartered in the Suisse Hotel or the Queen's Hotel in town. Mountbatten took the King's Pavilion for his residence, with his personal staff in the out-buildings. "It certainly makes the whole difference having such a lovely house to live in," mused Mountbatten. Stilwell spent three weeks in Kandy in August 1944, and called SEAC's location "a paradise ... Everything trim and clean, waterfalls everywhere, deep and distant views. The air took me back to 1906 in Yellowstone, clean and bracing."[79]

General Pownall hoped the move would be a positive thing, as Delhi had been "a hurly-burly of detail" that entangled everyone. "We ought to be able to work here more happily and as a family party," he mused to his diary. "Whether we shall remains to be seen."[80]

* * *

At Imphal, the latter half of April marked the end of a month of movement and crisis for the British, as the battle lines stabilized in the hills around Imphal. To the north, stalemate settled in as Briggs's 5th Indian Division regrouped after its repulsion of Yamauchi's 15th Division. In Shenam, the Japanese 213th Regiment tried unsuccessfully to push back Gracey's 20th Indian Division. Elsewhere, British patrols frustrated Japanese attempts to infiltrate from the north, while RAF planes hampered the deployment of Yamamoto Force's artillery.[81]

Near Bishenpur, the 33rd Division sought once again to flank Cowan's 17th Indian Division. While the rest of the division held at Potsangbam, south of Bishenpur, the 214th and 215th Regiments marched into the steep hills to the west and turned north toward the Silchar Track and Cowan's rear. Key objectives along the track included the hills Point 5846, Wooded Hill, and Wireless Hill.[82]

British scouts detected the movement, and Cowan dispatched the 32nd Brigade to block the Japanese. The 1st Northamptonshire led the march. "The weather then I recall," wrote Private Denis Short, "was hot and humid, a 'lull before the storm' … The march was very slow as we trekked along the Silchar Track" into "the steeply rising jungle-covered hills, they looked quite menacing." The battalion reached the top of Point 5846 on April 15 and started digging in. "Our attention was suddenly distracted by some heavy rifle and machine-gun fire—accompanied then by loud screams and shouting," recalled Short. "We were under Jap attack!" British fire repulsed this initial assault, followed by several more over the next week. Other Japanese units attacked Wooded and Wireless Hills without success, while flanking movements also failed. By the last week of April, a temporary stalemate set in along both the Tiddim Road and Silchar Track.[83]

Mutaguchi realized that Briggs's defense had closed the northern door to Imphal. Yet Imphal loomed tantalizingly close, and the Japanese commander determined to try again with stronger units. He signaled Sato to detach an infantry regimental group, about one-third of his division, to move south and attack Imphal in conjunction with Yamauchi's division. Mutaguchi also visited 33rd Division on April 22 "to spur the division to greater efforts," recalled a staff officer. His disdain for Yanagida, who the army commander viewed as defeatist, was plain to see. "During his visit, Mutaguchi virtually ignored Yanagida and devoted his time to working with Colonel Tanaka, the Chief of Staff." The 33rd Division planned to renew its offensive in May.[84]

Meanwhile, Operation Stamina started on April 18 with 75 flights into Imphal—a significant jump over the previous high of 46 on April 11. The next day, over 100 planes landed for the first time, and landings ranged between 106 on April 19 and 166 on April 23. On April 28, only 87 planes arrived. The cargoes included requested supplies, personnel, mail, and stationery. Bithess paving material also came in, and was immediately put down on some of the dirt airfields to help them drain during the monsoon. After the bithess delivery, 20 C-46s were returned to Hump, as they were too heavy for the runways at Imphal.[85]

Even so, it was not enough. The airlift delivered 1,250 tons less than needed in its first 12 days. Some planes arrived empty, while others had problems navigating weather and clouds over the mountain ranges between Bengal and Imphal. To simplify loading, Bengal's airfields became single-commodity loading points, while all fields in Imphal were used for deliveries. Still, the Allied air supremacy over eastern India, coupled with the Japanese commitment of their aircraft against the Chindits, ensured the transports could fly with little interference from Japanese planes.[86]

Scoones and his staff understood the implications of Stamina's performance thus far. On April 30, Scoones sent Slim an appreciation of the situation at Imphal. "The initial enemy plans on all fronts have been frustrated," Scoones wrote. "The enemy is likely to continue his operation for the capture of Imphal." Scoones promised to mount the best defense he could, including counterattacks where possible against 15th and 33rd Divisions. As for supply, Scoones and Loup assumed the monsoon would start on or about May 21; when that happened, only half of the daily sorties were likely to come in, as four of Imphal Plain's six airfields would be largely unusable due to mud and wet. "Against a total tonnage demand of 37,360 tons up to 31 July," Loup warned, "it will only be possible to fly in 21,995 tons, i.e. *a deficiency of 15,365 tons.*" Unless the Imphal–Kohima Road was reopened by June 15, "when resources will be eaten down, then about two divisions and a proportion of Corps troops must be flown out of the area." The implication of Loup's calculation was stark: Imphal could hold for the time being, but IV Corps would soon start to wither for lack of sufficient supplies. Without victory at Kohima and a link-up with XXXIII Corps, IV Corps would start folding within six weeks.[87]

* * *

On April 18, dawn broke over Kohima without a Japanese attack. Instead, British artillery and airstrikes hammered Japanese positions in the surrounding hills. Richards and his men saw tanks and infantry advancing from the west. The relief force cleared a final roadblock and, shortly before noon, 1/1 Punjab of Warren's brigade reached IGH. The siege was broken.[88]

Immediately after the linkup, Young began evacuating the wounded into waiting trucks, which sped them to Dimapur. Over the next two days, Kohima's weary and exhausted defenders were replaced by fresh troops from Shapland's 6th Brigade. The Japanese made half-hearted attempts to attack, but the relief went on without interruption. Richards finally left Kohima Ridge on April 20, after handing over to Shapland.[89]

Garrison Hill's appearance shocked Shapland's troops. "The place stank," recalled Major John Nettlefield. "The ground everywhere was ploughed up with shell-fire and human remains lay rotting as the battle raged over them … Men retched as they dug in." The amount of wreckage impressed others. "It was possible to pick up anything from a Tommy-gun to a pair of ladies' shoes," noted Lieutenant Colonel Wilbur Bickford, commanding the 1st Royal Berkshire. "The place was a veritable paradise for flies."[90]

Kohima's relief came at a bad time for Sato. Not only had he failed to fully capture Kohima Ridge, he had now received the orders from Mutaguchi to detach three battalions of infantry and one of artillery under Miyazaki to Imphal. Sato assembled the force, two battalions of the 124th, one of the 138th, and 3rd Battalion of the 31st Mountain Regiment, south of Pulebadze near the village of Aradura. Meanwhile, the rest of the 138th and 124th, bloodied in battles along the road, fell back to defensive positions at Merema and Kohima. The 58th held its ground on Kohima Ridge, and Sato resolved to use its ebbing strength to attack Garrison Hill one more time.[91]

General Grover also took this time to deploy his division and decide his next move. Captured documents revealed both Mutaguchi's orders for the detachment and Sato's plans to comply. Prodded by Slim and Stopford, who were in turn pushed by messages from Washington and London, Grover decided to attack with his entire division. Hawkins would move first to Merema and then south of Kohima, while Shapland would attack outward from Garrison Hill. Brigadier Willie Goschen's 4th Brigade (minus one battalion left to protect the road) would march from Jotsoma to Pulebadze in an effort to flank Sato's troops to the south. Warren's tired force would help protect the road to Dimapur.[92]

Sato's men attacked Garrison Hill, now held by the 1st Royal Berkshires and 2nd Durham Light Infantry, on April 23. The Royal Berkshires at the tennis court held firm, while the Durhams fought a back-and-forth action that ended with the defenders back in their positions after hours of heavy fighting. Four of the seven attacking companies were virtually wiped out, and those losses were irreplaceable. Sato realized that if he detached the forces Mutaguchi wanted, his division would likely be unable to hold its positions around Kohima, which was essential to preventing Imphal's relief. He cancelled Miyazaki's marching orders and ordered all of his units to the defensive. The entire 31st Division would fight it out with Grover's British on Kohima Ridge.[93]

* * *

On the NCAC front, operations paused because of the need to bring forward supplies and to let the road construction progress into the newly-liberated area. It rained daily, making mud an ever-present obstacle. Sun's division returned to the battle and took position on the eastern flank. Stilwell repeatedly went forward to Sun and Liao's divisions, but failed to induce them to move faster. "The piled-up inertia is terrible," he mused to his diary on April 11. "Nobody will do anything." Two days later, Stilwell told Marshall that "in the locker we have a couple of shots left in spite of slow progress lately ... Keeping the stiffness in the division commanders' backbones is our hardest job, on their unexpected success they would be glad to rest." Happily, Stilwell detected "no change in the attitude of Chinese rank and file. They can keep going ... Fine job is being done by all American personnel."[94]

The Chinese forces ground slowly forward, reaching the vicinity of Warazup by April 23. Stilwell ordered Liao to advance on Inkangahtawng, but instead of moving his division, Liao simply moved his headquarters and kept his troops in place. This was repeated for several days, and finally Colonel Brown reported to Stilwell that the Chinese would not move without permission from Chiang. For his part, the Generalissimo was warning Stilwell to "be judicious" in employing the Chinese under his command.[95]

Stilwell's spirits were not unduly low. "We are still plugging our way down the rathole," Stilwell wrote his wife. "we had tough going the first ten days this month, but a lot of Japs assumed horizontal positions and we are on the move again."[96]

CHAPTER 8

"A Brilliant Feat of Arms"

Toward the end of April, developments on the battlefront caused the senior leaders on both sides to reassess and adjust their strategies. It was the eve of the monsoon, and the ongoing campaigns showed every sign of extending well into the rainy period. The Allies in particular had successfully weathered the crises of March and April, and needed to establish a favorable situation in the theater before the rains arrived.

Affecting the Allied strategy for Burma and India was the deteriorating situation in China. In mid-April, the Japanese launched Operation Ichi-Go, a major offensive southward intended to secure southeastern China's rail lines and air bases, many of which hosted Chennault's Fourteenth Air Force planes. Chennault reported the attack to Stilwell, and received an order to defend Chengtu—the major base where the B-29s would be arriving—above all else. Chennault replied that defending Chengtu would be "child's play" and asked for greater freedom of action.

Chennault's reply startled both Stilwell and Stratemeyer, the senior American air officer in the China–Burma–India Theater. Stratemeyer drafted a sarcastic reply for Stilwell to send to Chennault. "I am glad to hear that the defense of Chengtu is child's play," Stratemeyer wrote. "I had gathered from your letter of April eight that the security of China as a base for Matterhorn [codename for the B-29 offensive from Chengtu] and other military operations against Japan might be in doubt. It is a relief to know that we have no problem at Chengtu and under these circumstances of course the question of action in emergency will not arise. Until it does, there is no intention of limiting the scope of your operations in any way." Stilwell read this and heartily approved. He sent the unchanged text forward over his name.[1]

The Chindits needed new directives after nearly two months of active operations behind Japanese lines. Stilwell, Slim, and Lentaigne were worried about the approaching monsoon, but did not want to give up the tactical advantages of Special Force's presence in the Japanese rear. "For lack of an all-weather [air]strip," commented one of Lentaigne's staff members, "it was vital to get physical touch with CAI for the evacuation of sick and wounded." It was decided that the Chindits would operate in support of NCAC's southward advance toward Mogaung. Accordingly, on April 27, Lentaigne ordered his troops to shift northward. Masters's 111th Brigade would take the Aberdeen garrison and march north to set up a new block (first named Clydeside, but changed to Blackpool when the original codename was compromised) 30 miles southwest of Mogaung, at Hopin. Brodie's 14th and Calvert's 77th Brigades, with elements of 3rd West African Brigade attached, would close down Broadway and White City and move north to cover Blackpool's western and eastern flanks, respectively. Fergusson's exhausted 16th Brigade would be flown out from Broadway and Aberdeen before the Strongholds closed. "It was visualized," said a staff officer, "that when Clydeside had been established and Jap efforts to break it had been overcome by the four brigades of the Force, it would then be possible to release two brigades to cooperate with CAI in the capture of Mogaung." At that time, Stilwell's headquarters would take direct command of the Chindits, although the exact date would be determined later.[2]

Meanwhile, Mountbatten renewed his efforts to short-circuit the north Burma advance. He requested the halting and pull-back of NCAC to free transport aircraft for the Imphal-Kohima emergency several times during the month of April. "My conclusion," Mountbatten stated on April 14, "is that the conquest of Northern Burma ... is impossible to carry out by the given dates [late 1944], and even by later dates it is unsound and should not be attempted." The Combined Chiefs of Staff were divided on these proposals. In a series of messages starting April 16, General Marshall (via his direct channel through CBI Theater) shared the U.S. views with Stilwell: possession of Myitkyina was essential to enhancing communications with China, and would facilitate land and air operations in China in support of the Pacific offensives.[3]

On May 3, these views turned into a directive from Marshall, setting these goals for U.S. forces in the CBI Theater. Stilwell received the order in the field the next day. "We must employ every means at our disposal to neutralize action by enemy that would hinder" the westward advance to the Philippines and Formosa area, Stilwell read. "Planes based on China land airdromes must augment our carrier-based aircraft. The responsibility is yours for air support from China by air forces under your command ... this is to be done without prejudice to the Formosa support or to other operations of greater immediate strategic importance. Examples of such operations are your present move to secure Myitkyina and Operation Matterhorn."[4]

This message was the clearest break between the British and American strategies in Burma. It gave Stilwell and his commanders a degree of independence that Mountbatten could never counter or control. From this point on, the Allies in CBI would be moving on diverging courses.

* * *

Marshall's order suited Stilwell perfectly, as he was already in the process of executing it. As soon as General Merrill had sufficiently recovered from his heart attack to return to duty, Stilwell started coordinating Operation End Run to take Myitkyina. British and American scouts, assisted by Kachins, had reported a little-known trail over the rugged Kumon Range that connected the Shaduzup area with Myitkyina; it involved climbing a 6,000-foot mountain pass at Naura Hkyet and a total march of 100 miles from the Nhpum Ga area. The trail was insufficient for a supply route, but a sizeable force could use it for movement, and the Japanese appeared be only lightly patrolling the area. Stilwell decided this would be the best route for his forces to move.[5]

The key to End Run's success would be the condition of the Marauders. They had just won a great victory at Nhpum Ga against the Japanese, which was the longest single battle fought by American infantry on the Asian mainland since the Boxer Rebellion. "There is nothing new in what we have learned from this fight," noted Hunter, a former Infantry School instructor, with pride, "it is just a repetition of principles as set forth in the Infantry Field Manuals." However, the loss of 364 men killed and wounded had reduced the 5307th to 1,400 men—less than 50% of its starting strength.[6]

In the days following the battle, the Marauders had consolidated in the area of Hsamshingyang and Nhpum Ga. There, they replenished food and ammunition, and regrouped. Mail and changes of clothes were delivered for the first time in months. There was little contact with the Japanese, except for patrols and periodic long-range shelling. To pass the time, Hunter ran close-order drills and had a mule race. Most Marauders were aware that the 90-day limit for their mission was approaching, and many anticipated a good and long period of rest. The doctors in particular wanted the respite, because during the recent battles they had seen the first cases of complete physical collapse among the men. Among those still on duty, virtually everyone was suffering from malaria, dysentery, rashes, infections, malaise, or a combination of the above, not to mention weight loss. "Depleted by five hundred miles of marching in packaged rations," noted Lieutenant James H. Stone, a doctor attached to the unit at this time, "the Marauders were sorely stricken ... Many remaining in the regiment were more or less ill, and their physical condition was too poor to respond quickly to medicines and rest."[7]

These problems went largely unnoticed by Stilwell and his staff. Stilwell had sent staff officers to have a look at the Marauders, and they failed to appreciate the exhaustion and disease hidden among the new uniforms and exhilaration of a break from operations. "Galahad is OK," mused Stilwell in his diary. "No worry there." Perhaps he saw what he wanted to see, as about this time he also noted "Lesson: Get a dependable American, spear-head [sic].[8]

The plan for End Run, developed with Hunter and Merrill's assistance, called for the creation of three task forces totaling 7,000 American, Chinese, and Kachin soldiers. H Force under Hunter would contain the 5307th's 1st Battalion, the 150th Regiment of the Chinese 50th Division, and a Chinese artillery battery.

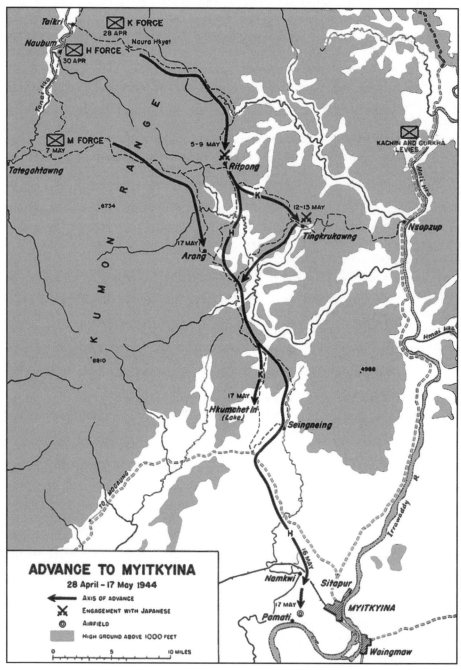

The advance to Myitkyina (Operation End Run). (U.S. Army)

Colonel Henry L. Kinnison's K Force comprised the 5307th's 3rd Battalion and the 88th Regiment of the Chinese 30th Division. Both of these forces would number about 2,700 men each and would march on Myitkyina. The third force, M Force under McGee, made up of 300 Kachins plus the 500 survivors of the 5307th's 2nd Battalion, would provide flank protection to H and K Forces by ranging along the trails to the south and west of their route. Code words would be used to indicate progress: *Cafeteria Lunch* meant 48 hours to go prior to attacking the Myitkyina airfield, *Strawberry Sundae* meant 24 hours to go, *In the Ring* meant the attack had started, and *Merchant of Venice* meant the airfield was captured and ready for use.[9]

The Marauders greeted this operation with what Lieutenant Sam Wilson described as "a kind of dull anger ... there was some outrage and some resentment, but we also had a favorite saying: 'Well, you volunteered for this.'" Stilwell admitted to Merrill that he was asking a lot of the Marauders, but felt he had no choice. He ordered Merrill to begin evacuating the Marauders from Myitkyina "if everything worked out as expected." Merrill let it be known among the Marauders that Myitkyina was to be the last mission, after which the men would be flown to India for rest and a celebration.[10]

On April 28, the End Run Forces got moving. "We set off with that what-the-hell-did-you-expect-anyway spirit that served the 5307th in place of morale," noted Ogburn, "and I dare say served it better." They would needed this determination. As the men reached the Kumon Range and started up the steep slopes to the pass heavy rain set in. "I remember the worst experience of my life," said Sergeant Bernard Martin in 3rd Battalion, "and that was that climb ... the grueling climb that we made and the way the animals suffered." In some places, the mules had to be unloaded, led forward, and then men carried their loads up and reloaded them. In other places, mules lost their footing and slipped over the steep sides. "Our battalion lost twenty-three mules over cliffs on that climb," recalled Lieutenant Weston. "Our best radio equipment, guns, medical supplies, emergency food, and ammunition also tumbled over the edges. We could do nothing but ... watch our valuable possessions as they crashed on the jagged rocks hundreds of feet below."[11]

On the other side of the mountains, K Force ran into a company-sized Japanese detachment at Ritpong. Kinnison decided to envelop the town. On May 6, his Marauders cut a trail flanking the village and took up position to the south of Ritpong, enabling Hunter's H Force to bypass the fighting and regain the trail to Myitkyina. K Force's Chinese attacked and routed the Japanese in three days of fighting and maneuvering. Kinnison then marched east. On May 12, K Force encountered more Japanese at Tingkrukawng; after a two-day battle, Merrill radioed Kinnison to disengage and follow Hunter's path.[12]

Meanwhile, Stilwell waited anxiously for news from Merrill. "Depression days," he wrote in his diary on 1 May. "Commander's worries ... The die is cast, and it's sink or swim. But the nervous wear and tear is terrible." On May 14, Merrill visited

H Force via light plane and confirmed the plan with Hunter. The Myitkyina airstrip was the objective, and Myitkyina itself would be left alone for the moment. "I'll be the first man on the field" after its capture, said Merrill, and he would issue orders for subsequent movement at that time.

"Can stop this show up to noon tomorrow, when the die is cast," Merrill radioed Stilwell, "if you think it too much of a gamble. Personal opinion is that we have a fair chance and that we should try." Stilwell ordered Merrill to "Roll on in and swing on 'em."[13]

That evening, Hunter transmitted "Cafeteria Lunch."[14]

* * *

Simultaneously with End Run's jump-off, while the End Run forces moved south, the Chindits undertook their move northward in compliance with their new orders. Fergusson's exhausted men were flown out of Broadway and Aberdeen to rest camps in India during the first week of May. "There was a slight feeling of anti-climax," recalled Fergusson. "We had walked a hell of a long way, but we hadn't much to show for it … a lot of trudging and pioneering, and not much honor and glory." On May 9, after a last skirmish with the Japanese, White City closed down, followed by Broadway on the morning of May 13. Brodie's 14th Brigade and 3rd West African Brigade (now commanded by Brigadier A. H. G. Ricketts) marched toward Indawgyi Lake, intending to set up a seaplane base there to receive supplies and evacuate casualties to India. Brodie also had the mission of protecting Blackpool's western flank. Calvert's 77th Brigade sought a position to perform the same mission on Blackpool's eastern flank.[15]

On May 7 the 2,500 men in Masters's 111th Brigade set up the Blackpool Block near Hopin, on a hill overlooking the road and railroad leading north to Mogaung. They marked out an airstrip along the hill's south side. Japanese patrols started probing the block's defenses almost immediately. That night, a Japanese platoon attacked the brigade's eastern perimeter, but was repulsed. Engineers came in by glider to smooth out the airstrip. Soon, C-47s flew over equipment and artillery from Broadway. Intermittent shelling and sniping kept the defenders on edge.[16]

The Japanese refused to give Blackpool any respite. Two battalions of infantry and one of artillery from Tanaka's division arrived to eliminate the block if possible. For five days, they hammered Blackpool's east side. "The actions … defy description or reasonable analysis," wrote Masters later. Each night "a furious battle raged from dusk till an hour or two before dawn, fought at ten yards' range with Brens, grenades, rifles, tommy guns, two-inch and three-inch mortars and some machine-guns." The Japanese usually came to grief along the wire perimeter, while swift counterattacks quickly wiped out any penetrations. During the fighting, C-47s landed at the airstrip 300 yards south, in full view of the battle.

Calvert had taken position a few miles away, overlooking Blackpool and the surrounding area. The Namyin Hka ran between Calvert's position and the railroad, which soon became a problem because of the "appalling" weather that settled in. "Thunderstorms [were] roaring and flashing all around us in this hills with very heavy rain," recalled Calvert. The river turned into a raging torrent, which hampered 77th Brigade's attempts to cross and strike the rear of the Japanese force attacking Blackpool. "The flooding of the Namyin nullified our efforts to help 111 Brigade," Calvert noted sadly.[17]

Rain caused a temporary halt in operations, and hampered flights into Blackpool. It also slowed Brodie's advance to the point that he and his brigade could not play their role in supporting Blackpool. On May 14, 15, and 16, the Japanese attacked Blackpool again. One time they penetrated the perimeter, but were thrown back. "When they launched their final assault to recover their bodies," recalled Masters, "we had defeated them."

* * *

In Imphal, early rains washed the plain and the surrounding hills, a harbinger of the heavier storms coming just a few weeks hence with the monsoon. For his part, General Mutaguchi planned new offensives. His initial timeframe of capturing Imphal was out the window, but he remained determined and confident of eventual victory. He ordered Yamamoto Force and the 33rd Division to renew their efforts to break through to Imphal.[18]

For his part, Scoones sought to build up supply reserves and regroup. Yamauchi's weakened division had gone to the defensive on the northern front, and operations in early May meant skirmishing in the hills north of Imphal, while dispersed columns raided toward Ukhrul to disrupt Yamauchi's rear areas. These raids tried and failed to capture Yamauchi himself, but did force his headquarters to move several times. The 89th Brigade of 7th Indian Division also arrived, falling under command of 5th Indian Division to replace its missing 161st Brigade at Kohima.[19]

On the Tiddim Road, Cowan's 17th Indian Division and the 32nd Brigade endured repeated attacks on Point 5846 and Potsangbam, as the 33rd Division sought to break through and reach Bishenpur. The 63rd Brigade fought a back-and forth action in Potsangbam that kept the Japanese at bay. The 32nd Brigade faced the main Japanese effort at Point 5846, weathering successive assaults. The attacks would be preceded by mortar fire, and then be pressed home at the point of the bayonet. For the Northampton soldiers in the hills, it was "a very frightening experience in facing one's enemy at so close-up a range," recalled Private Short. "Even after many times of being involved in such barbaric of conflicts, we could not help being fraught." After several days, the Japanese pulled back to regroup. For Short and his comrades, the battle atop Point 5846 "was to become unforgettable for us all."[20]

Spirited fighting raged in the Shenam area,. Supported by Japanese units, 250 men of the INA's Gandhi Brigade under Major Pritam Singh tried to infiltrate through the hills north of Scraggy to attack the Palel airfield. Prisoners captured by Gracey's men revealed the attack, and Gurkha patrols combined with British shelling to scatter the INA forces and inflict 250 casualties.[21]

Meanwhile, Yamamoto's forces attacked the front of Crete West. After repeated charges failed to capture the hill, a flanking force moved around its north side and captured Lynch Pimple, isolating Crete West's garrison. The garrison fought its way west to Scraggy, which represented the last hill before the final ridge east of the Imphal Plain. The Japanese pursued and captured Scraggy's base in heavy fighting on May 10 and 11, but could advance no further against a tenacious defense. Despite being pushed back, Gracey's men gave better than they got: against 2,500 British casualties in the first two weeks of May, the Japanese and INA forces lost over 4,000, 3,100 of whom were killed in action.[22]

Scoones knew that Gracey's men, while having so far successfully held out, were exhausted. As soon as the fighting at Scraggy died down, he ordered Roberts's 23rd Indian Division to relieve Gracey's forces. As the 20th Indian Division was close to the enemy, the relief occurred over 12 days, battalion by battalion, ending May 25. Gracey's division retired to the Palel area for a short and welcome rest.[23]

In the midst of these battles, and as Operation Stamina was finally getting into high gear, Slim was facing a serious crisis over transport aircraft. The Combined Chiefs requested return of the 79 transport aircraft to the Mediterranean by May 8. They were specifically trained and equipped for airborne operations, and were needed to support Allied offensives in that theater. However, these 79 planes and their crews represented 29% of the available airlift capacity into Imphal.[24]

Mountbatten remonstrated to the Combined Chiefs, but received no reply. On May 4, Peirse was forced to notify Giffard and Slim that, in four days, the transports would be removed from the Imphal airlift. Giffard immediately protested, with Slim's concurrence; both men knew the fate of IV Corps hung on the availability of those transports. Stanley Woodburn Kirby, the British official historian of the campaign, summarized Giffard's response as stating that "if the aircraft were withdrawn without replacement, [Giffard] could not hold himself responsible for the consequences." On his own authority, Mountbatten ordered Peirse to keep the transports flying on the airlift until specifically directed otherwise, and immediately informed the Combined Chiefs of his decision.

Churchill replied directly to Mountbatten. "Let nothing go from the battle that you need for victory," the Prime Minister commanded. "I will not accept denial of this from any quarter, and will back you to the full." In a further exchange of messages, the Combined Chiefs agreed that Mountbatten could keep the 79 loaned aircraft until June 15, by which time replacements would have arrived and worked up into operational status.[25]

* * *

The logistical issues of Imphal spurred on the forces at Kohima, where Grover deployed his division for a counteroffensive. He decided to envelop the Japanese with Hawkins's brigade attacking from the north, Goschen's brigade attacking the southern flank around Aradura, and Shapland's infantry clearing the bungalow area in the center. Grover planned to start on April 24, and predicted victory within six days.[26]

Encouraged by Stopford, Grover sent his men forward two days early. After trying and failing to get tanks up the back side of Garrison Hill, Shapland's infantry secured positions overlooking the intersection below Pawsey's bungalow. Although the Japanese still held the terrace itself, tanks could now round the bend and advance up Pawsey's driveway—albeit not immediately, as it took several days under fire for engineers to regrade a curve in the driveway to fit a Grant tank.

Further north, Hawkins's brigade started at dusk, moving in single file. Rain held up the column, forcing repeated halts. The men reached Merema on the April 26 and began to probe southward toward Naga Village.[27]

Goschen's infantrymen encountered little opposition to the south, but the terrain slowed their pace to a crawl. "It was a case of up one steep khud [ridge] and down the other side, then up a steeper and down again," recalled an officer. "To anyone who hasn't soldiered in Assam the physical hammering one takes is difficult to understand. The heat, the humidity, the altitude, and the slope of almost every foot of ground, combine to knock hell out of the stoutest constitution." Rain, intermittent to this point, began in earnest on April 28; it rained at least once every day for the rest of the battle.[28]

The slow pace of operations forced Grover to recast his plans. On May 4—the earliest 4th Brigade could be ready—he sent his entire division forward. Hawkins's 5th Brigade, every man wearing gym shoes for stealth, infiltrated Naga Village during the night and occupied the northwest portion early on May 5. The brigade repelled repeated ferocious counterattacks. In the center, Shapland's infantry failed to dislodge Kuki Picquet's defenders, though the Durham Light Infantry managed to get atop FSD for a short time.[29]

Grover called up 4/7 Rajput of Warren's brigade and tanks, and on May 5 renewed the attack. Many tanks bogged down or were disabled, one slipping off the crest of Kuki Picquet into a gully. The 1st Queen's, a part of 33rd Brigade of General Messervy's 7th Indian Division, came forward and launched an attack that cleared all but the eastern slopes of Kuki Picquet and FSD by dusk on May 7.[30]

Further south, Goschen's men ran into the Japanese 124th Regiment, posted by Sato to GPT to prevent just such a flanking move. The 2nd Royal Norfolks, in the lead of the column, encountered several Japanese bunkers whose fire held up the advance. Captain John Niel Randle, in command of the battalion's B Company, attacked and destroyed a bunker, using his dying body to block the firing slit so his company could advance. He received a posthumous Victoria Cross, the second of two awarded for actions at Kohima. By May 7, GPT's crest was in British hands.[31]

To the east, Brigadier Perowne's Chindit 23rd Brigade advanced into Sato's rear. The Chindits found hard going in the steep mountains, but discovered friends among the local Nagas. On orders from Stopford, the Chindits raised a levy of over 2,000 Nagas to support their operations. Members of the Naga Hills Police Force also provided intelligence and fighting power. By late May, these forces were gnawing on Sato's line of communication back to India.[32]

At this point, Grover's advance paused to consolidate. More reinforcements arrived, and the independent 268th Lorried Infantry Brigade relieved some of Grover's units for a short rest. General Messervy's 7th Indian Division headquarters, the division artillery, and 33rd and 114th Indian Infantry Brigades also began arriving on the scene. The 33rd Brigade reinforced the area around FSD.[33]

Sato, on the other hand, had received nothing in the way of supplies or replacements for his mounting casualties. Several of his infantry units had sustained 50 percent losses or greater, and all of his men were malnourished. By mid-May, "only a small amount of ammunition remained, reserves of provisions as well as forage were dangerously low, and local stocks of food were practically exhausted," noted a staff report. "The Division was, in fact, rapidly losing its offensive ability."[34]

"The enemy are superior in weapons and firepower," Sato told his troops in an Order of the Day. "You will fight to the death. When you are killed you will fight with your spirit."[35]

* * *

Meanwhile, on May 11, Y Force finally lurched forward against the Japanese 56th Division. General "Hundred Victories" Wei Li-huang had under his command two corps-size Group Armies: XI Group Army under Sung Hsi-len with 2nd, 6th, and 71st Armies, and Hou Kuei-chang's XX Group Army with 53rd and 54th Armies. The 200th Division was in reserve, and 8th Army was on its way to join.[36]

Wei planned to cross the Salween River and push forward on two fronts. XX Group Army would aim for the key bastion at Tengchung, 125 miles east of Myitkyina and connected to it by a rough trail. XI Group Army would strike down the Burma Road through Sungshan to Lungling, capture the city, and push into Burma.

Assisting Wei would be Y Force Operations Staff (Y-FOS) under Brigadier General Frank Dorn. As with Stilwell's Chinese forces in Burma, the Americans were limited to advising, coordinating airstrikes, and providing supplies and medical support. Dorn and his team had, over the past several months, trained Wei's troops, provided them equipment, and developed with them a very close and warm relationship. Dorn found many commanders' "tactical conceptions" were "antiquated and timid." Much of this perceived caution came from the top. "If we had a real commander," mused

Dorn to Stilwell in May, "there is no reason why the Y Force should not be south of Lashio, but it is advisable to be conservative when Wei Li-huang is involved." Another attitude was at work, however, expressed by one of Wei's division commanders: "We have a second war to fight, and will not fight now."[37]

Wei's Chinese rowed across the Salween River on May 11 without opposition. It became clear over the next few days that the Japanese had set up a defense line 10 miles west, holding key passes in the Kaoli-Kung Mountains. For the rest of May and into June, Wei's forces brought up supplies and artillery and repeatedly attacked the passes, finally clearing them in savage and costly fighting. By the end of June, the Chinese were laying siege to Tengchung, Sungshan, and Lungling. This effective stalemate lasted throughout the monsoon.

* * *

On the morning of May 15, Colonel Hunter's H Force started south on the final leg to Myitkyina. Despite heavy rain, they made good progress, and by 2pm Hunter broadcast "Strawberry Sundae," the signal that the force was 24 hours from attacking. The next day, Hunter's troops reached Namkwi, a village four miles from the airfield. As it was late in the day, Hunter postponed his attack until the morning. Aware that they had left friendly Kachin territory, and that the Burmese were more friendly to the Japanese, Hunter had his men round up all the Burmese in the area and hold them until the attack was over.[38]

Hunter reviewed the maps and aerial photo of Myitkyina that Merrill had given him. The airfield was a half-mile north of the Irrawaddy River and the village of Pamati. One mile east of the airfield was Myitkyina town itself, with small outlying hamlets of Charpate, Radhapur, Sitapur, and Mankrin. The Irrawaddy ran southward past Myitkyina, before turning west at Waingmaw, just southeast of Myitkyina and across the river. The road and railroad to Mogaung, 30 miles away west by southwest, ran roughly parallel to the river.

That night, Hunter sent scouts to the airfield. They found it empty—so empty that one sergeant walked upright along the runway to check its condition. The field was usable, except for oil drums on the runway itself. The Marauders also heard a train chugging on the Mogaung–Myitkyina railway. It was clear that the Japanese had no idea that H Force was there.[39]

Hunter had his men moving shortly after dawn on May 17. At 10:30 that morning, Stilwell's headquarters received "In the Ring" about the time that H Force debouched from the jungle into the valley beside the river. As Osborne's 1st Battalion swung west to take the village of Pamati and its ferry across the Irrawaddy, the Chinese 150th Regiment turned east and swarmed the airfield. One of the 1st Battalion combat teams swept the riverbank eastward, while the Chinese consolidated and OSS officers directed the runway's clearing. They had achieved complete surprise and had captured their objectives without loss. By 12:30pm, Hunter had his radio team transmitting "Merchant of Venice."[40]

Stilwell received the news three hours later. "Enormous relief to get Merrill's report," he recalled. "At once ordered machinery and reinforcements started ... told them to keep going all night." Vinegar Joe also permitted himself a moment of exultation for accomplishing something that Mountbatten and his staff thought was impossible. "WILL THIS BURN UP THE LIMIES!" he crowed in his diary.[41]

The news of Stilwell's achievement quickly shot around the world. Churchill demanded that Mountbatten explain how "the Americans by a brilliant feat of arms have landed us in Myitkyina." Mountbatten concealed his irritation at being left out of knowing Stilwell's plans. "Isn't the news of the capture of Myitkyina airfield great?" he asked his daughter. "It is one of my most interesting fronts, commanded by my deputy, General Stilwell."[42]

Unfortunately, things began to go wrong at this point. Merrill flew in shortly after the airfield's capture, but on the 19th had to be evacuated with another heart attack. A battalion of the Chinese 89th Regiment arrived on May 17, but the supplies and ammunition Merrill and Hunter were counting on were delayed until May 19. General Stratemeyer, fearful of the security of the airfield, had dispatched antiaircraft and engineer units to protect and operate the field on his own initiative. Stilwell flew in on the 18th with war correspondents to see the situation for himself, and stayed two hours. "Hunter knows what he is about," noted Stilwell in his diary.[43]

Hunter, meanwhile, tried to do what he could. On the afternoon of May 17, he sent two battalions of the 150th Regiment toward Myitkyina. The battalions took the wrong road, ending up north of town at Sitapur. There they ran into Japanese snipers, which in turn confused the Chinese units and caused them to fire in all directions, including into each other, before withdrawing in confusion. The battalions tried again on May 18, reaching the center of Myitkyina and its railroad station before Japanese infantry attacked them and produced the same result. Out of ammunition, the Chinese refused to attack on May 19 until more supplies arrived.[44]

These two failures cost the 150th a total of 758 casualties, lost to both enemy and friendly fire. "In considering the unfortunate experiences of the Chinese troops," noted a Marauder officer later, "it is to be remembered that, at a distance of fifty yards, neither they nor the Japs can distinguish each other. It is also well known that the Japanese frequently assumed both Chinese and American uniforms."[45]

These failures to capture Myitkyina itself influenced the Japanese reaction. On May 17, Myitkyina contained 700 men of Colonel Maruyama's 114th Regiment, veterans of Nhpum Ga. They had supplies and ammunition for three months, and had lightly fortified the town. Even so, Maruyama and his officers told the locals they would be pulling out soon. After the victories over the Chinese, General Honda dispatched units from the 56th Division to reinforce the garrison to 4,000 men. On May 20, Maruyama's defenders said they would be staying.[46]

The capture of Myitkyina airfield on May 17 was a triumph for General Stilwell and NCAC. But without possession of the town, that victory would remain partially won.

* * *

The Chindits continued to struggle in Burma. The base at Indawgyi Lake was set up, but rain hampered all other major movements. On May 20, the 1st Air Commando ceased operations for the monsoon period, turning over their support mission to the U.S. and British units operating with NCAC.[47]

The same day, Masters left Blackpool to confer with Lentaigne in his new headquarters at Shaduzup. Three days earlier, Stilwell had assumed operational command of Special Force. Lentaigne confided his concerns and conflicts with Stilwell to Masters, and predicted "trouble ahead." The men visited Stilwell, who asked incisive questions about the situation around Blackpool and predicted Myitkyina would fall "soon." Masters returned to his command that evening.[48]

The Blackpool garrison enjoyed a few days of rest before renewed Japanese activity signaled the arrival of enemy reinforcements. On May 23, a regiment-sized battle group from the 53rd Division reinforced the Japanese forces around the block. The battle group contained three battalions of infantry, one battalion of artillery, and, most significantly, a company of antiaircraft artillery. The infantry attacked repeatedly through a rainstorm that precluded any Allied airstrikes, while antiaircraft fire disrupted C-47 landings and supply drops to the garrison. These developments left 111th Brigade to defend the block on its own.

Nonetheless, Masters's Chindits repelled all attacks until the morning of the 25th, when a small group of Japanese penetrated the block and could not be dislodged. The defenders' mortar ammunition was depleted, and the Chindits were exhausted with no hope of relief in sight. Lentaigne had authorized Masters to withdraw from Blackpool if necessary, and, on the morning of May 25, Masters directed his brigade to retire westward toward Indawgyi Lake. The 1st Cameronians would cover the retreat with 26 and 90 Columns.

"The orders given, men began to drift back past me almost at once," recalled Masters, "Men trudged in a thickening stream down the muddy, slippery path past my command post." The Chindits were exhausted, bedraggled, and many wore expressions of exhaustion. "We did our best, didn't we, sir?" asked a private.

Those wounded who could be moved walked themselves or were carried by stretcher, but some serious cases remained behind. One, a Cameronian on the firing line, addressed his lieutenant. "Gi' me a Bren," he said in his Scottish brogue. "Leave me. I'll take a dozen wi' me."

Just as the last fighting elements were about to withdraw, the brigade's chief surgeon led Masters to a low spot on the path westward. Nineteen men lay on stretchers, all with grievous wounds and in varying degrees of unconsciousness. "I've got another thirty on ahead, who can be saved, if we can carry them," said the doctor. "These men have no chance. They're full of morphia … None can last another two hours, at the outside." The unspoken question hung in the air.

Masters thought for a moment as rain fell and the thunder of shelling resounded in the background. He weighed these men's fate against the brigade as a whole. "Very well," Masters said. "I don't want them to see any Japanese." The doctor refused to do it himself. "Get the stretcher bearers on it at once," replied Masters. "Five minutes."

"I went back up on the ridge, for the last time," recalled Masters. "One by one, the carbine shots exploded curtly behind me. I put my hands to my ears but nothing could shut out the sound." Passing by a few minutes later, just in front of his rearguard, Masters found the bodies hidden from view in the jungle by the path. "I'm sorry," he said, "Forgive me." As rain cascaded down, Masters joined the westward retreat.

The day Blackpool fell, Stilwell and Lentaigne met to discuss future Chindit operations. It was a contentious meeting, as Stilwell expressed his unhappiness at Blackpool's abandonment. Lentaigne protested that the Chindits "can't hold a place where [enemy] artillery can be brought in." Both men agreed the "overriding" priority was, as Lentaigne put it in a message to his commanders, "the necessity of gaining ground contact with CAI before … the rains really set in." That meant the Chindits needed to attack Mogaung. Calvert's 77th Brigade drew the assignment.[49]

* * *

The capture of Myitkyina's airfield injected new energy into the NCAC front, which for weeks had been slowly grinding forward through the rain and mud. Now, suddenly the advance sped up, and reached out toward Kamaing and Mogaung. On May 20, General Sun announced, "We go to take Kamaing now." While Liao's 22nd Division (reinforced with part of 50th Division) kept Tanaka's Japanese occupied in front and on the left, Sun sent his 38th Division around the Japanese right flank. The 112th Regiment headed for Seton, a settlement seven miles south of Kamaing along the road to Mogaung, while the 114th Regiment struck for Mogaung and the 113th Regiment followed behind, in reserve for the moment. The 112th reached Seton on May 25, capturing vast quantities of Tanaka's food and transportation.[50]

Sun's advance to Seton caught the Japanese by surprise. In late April, Tanaka had received parts of the 2nd Division's 4th Regiment and the 56th Division's 146th Regiment, both of which promptly lost one-third of their men during the fighting in early May. Prodded by Kawabe at Burma Area Army Headquarters, Tanaka was looking to counterattack the Chinese. Now Sun's latest movement left the 18th Division effectively surrounded. Tanaka desperately needed to reopen the road if he had any chance of holding for much longer. He threw the 4th and 146th, plus

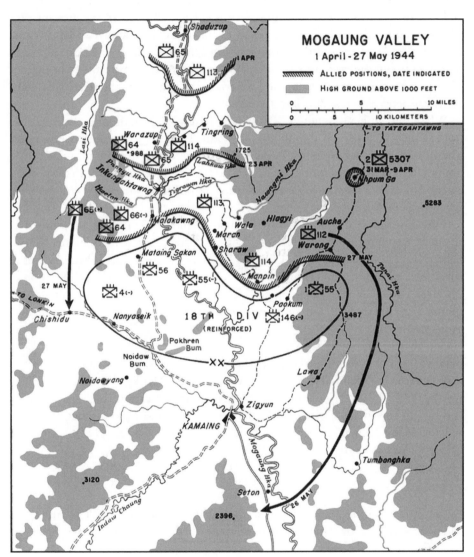

The NCAC front, April–May 1944. (U.S. Army)

his division's rear troops, at the Seton position, but the Chinese held on in bitter fighting. With about 5,000 effective troops remaining, Tanaka was in a difficult spot.[51]

Meanwhile, the Allies at Myitkyina regrouped. British antiaircraft gunners watched the skies above while American and Chinese infantry extended their perimeter and sought to invest the town. Stilwell consolidated all units in the area into the Myitkyina Task Force, and gave the command to Colonel John E. McCammon. Stilwell considered committing Festing's 36th Division, which had been placed at his disposal, but preferred to keep it fresh to exploit what he expected to be a quick victory. Instead, Chinese infantry and American combat engineers, plus half-trained American replacements, flew into the battle.[52]

While the Chinese assaulted Myitkyina's western and southern ends, American forces from Galahad and the 209th and 236th Engineer Battalions swung north toward Charpate and Namkwi, respectively. Skirmishing with the Japanese stalled both units, while enemy counterattacks caused the engineers to break and run. After a period of re-training, the engineers returned to the line to prepare for a new attack, eager to atone for the previous failures.

The same could not be said for the men of the 5307th, most of whom had reached the point of physical collapse. During battle on May 27, Colonel McGee fainted three times at his post. "Galahad is just shot," confessed Stilwell. Scores of Marauders each day were evacuated to Ledo because of illness, fatigue, or wounds. The Task Force Commander, Colonel McCammon, joined them at the end of the month. As May turned into June, General Boatner took charge, determined to avoid a stalemate.[53]

Fortunately, Maruyama's Japanese did not detect the Allied weaknesses. Maruyama planned a counteroffensive to capture the airfield on May 30, but Honda cancelled it after receiving estimates of 30,000 Allies outside Myitkyina; the real number was 10,000–12,000. Honda ordered Maruyama to hold until the 53rd Division, coming up toward Mogaung, could fight its way in and raise the siege. He also ordered Major General Mizukami Genzo of the 56th Division to take command of Myitkyina's defenders.[54]

* * *

At Imphal, Scoones's besieged corps continued to hold out. Both Scoones and Mutaguchi undertook a period of regrouping to prepare fresh offensives for the latter part of May.

Scoones faced a significant problem, as Operation Stamina was not living up to its promises. Against a daily requirement of 189 supply landings, on most days between 90 and 110 flights would come in, bringing all kinds of supplies; returning flights took out casualties, prisoners, and so-called "useless mouths"—administrative units of no fighting value. Weather was the biggest issue: on May 22 it kept all but

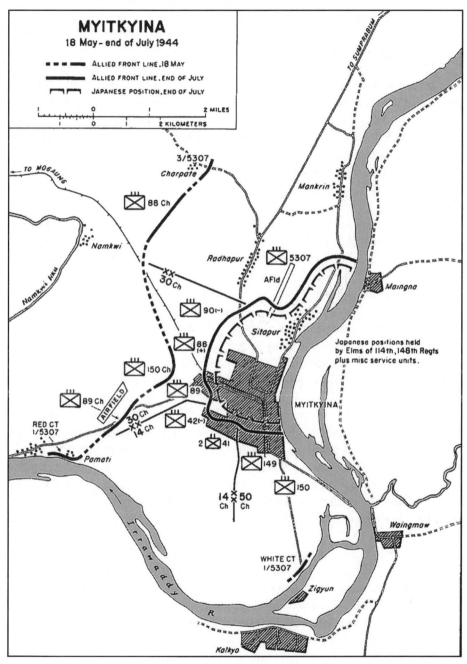

The Siege of Myitkyina. (U.S. Army)

14 flights away, and on May 27 only 11 landings were carried out. The rains also limited use of airfields outside Imphal Main and Palel after mid-May, resulting in congestion. Palel was further restricted by the threats of both Japanese infiltration and long-range shelling from the Shenam Saddle area.[55]

RAF 221 Group, which was based in Imphal, managed to maintain air supremacy over the area, with its Spitfires, Vengeances, and Hurricanes, but they could not prevent all Japanese air incursions. Nonetheless, the British, Indian, and Burmese fliers took to the air as often as possible to support the ground troops and the airlift. RAF planes helped 20th Indian Division hold Scraggy, while other interceptors guarded the eastern air approaches to Imphal Plain. By the end of the battle, the RAF had flown over 25,000 sorties and shot down 33 Japanese fighters with another 22 probable and 61 damaged, against a loss of 18 Spitfires.[56]

Despite the air efforts, Stamina's shortfalls limited IV Corps' fighting ability. Artillery firing was limited to six rounds per day, per gun, unless Corps headquarters authorized more firing. Fuel was at a premium, and trucks were often operated in tandem to save gasoline and oil. Rations were cut to a level unable to sustain active troops, and by mid-May hunger was prevalent in many formations. "Scaling hills became a problem and patrols were given extra food," remembered a lieutenant in Cowan's division. "We smoked a lot to stop thinking of hunger." Lack of rain gear and new clothing added to the hardships. "We had the means to ensure survival, but no more," recalled an officer on Roberts's staff. "Life during the siege of Imphal was strenuous for all and devoid of comfort and it imposed a strain on the nerves."[57]

Mutaguchi's army was little better off, but the general refused to accept defeat and ordered a new offensive. As the 33rd Division was the strongest single force left in his army, he decided this formation would lead the attack. He also reinforced the division with two battalions of infantry, the 14th Tank Regiment, and a battalion each of artillery and anti-tank weapons. Mutaguchi personally attended to the preparations and plans, which called for a three-pronged attack. The 213th Regiment, plus reinforcements, would attack northward through Potsangbam, while the 215th Regiment assailed Point 5846 from the west. Moving through the northern hills, the 214th Regiment would strike into Cowan's rear. The division was to be ready to move by May 15.[58]

Scoones also sought opportunities to attack on his northern and southern flanks. Briggs's 5th Indian Division received orders to probe northward along the Imphal–Kohima Road. This was not a breakout attempt (Slim had repeatedly made it clear that XXXIII Corps was to relieve Imphal), but rather an effort to try and meet Stopford's troops partway and ease their task. At Bishenpur, Cowan sought nothing less than to "destroy those elements of the Jap 33rd Division ... which are threatening Bishenpur from the north, south, and southwest." While 32nd Brigade held firm, 48th Brigade would march south and cut the Tiddim Road behind the Japanese. Then 63rd Brigade would attack south along the road and crush all forces "south of the Silchar Track." On May 15, Cowan ordered his troops to start the next day.[59]

Coincidentally, both sides also changed commanders at this point. Mutaguchi was still unsatisfied with the 33rd Division's performance, and viewed its current commander, General Yanagida, as defeatist. On May 15, Mutaguchi relieved Yanagida, effective May 24. Major General Tanaka Nobuo, coming from Rangoon, would assume command.[60]

The same day Mutaguchi fired Yanagida, Mountbatten indicated that he had lost confidence in his ground commander, General Giffard, and would request his relief. "Mountbatten feels that he cannot project his own energy and drive through so passive a man as Giffard," mused General Pownall in his diary. "With that I agree." General Sultan, Stilwell's deputy in New Delhi, added his concurrence in a message to Stilwell. "Determined aggressive leadership is needed," Sultan said, "if the Imphal situation is to be cleared up." For his part, Stilwell also endorsed the change. "Instead of the word desirability I would substitute the word necessary," he told Marshall the next day, "and my list would have more than one name on it."[61]

North of Imphal, Briggs's 5th Indian Division attacked toward Kanglatongbi and into the hills flanking the Imphal–Kohima Road. Despite its exhaustion, Yamauchi's division put up a stiff defense. "The ground was difficult, the jungle thick," declared one of Briggs's staff officers. Mud and rain also slowed operations. By May 21, Evans's troops had recaptured the former Lion Box; Colonel Clarence W. Bennett, Stilwell's liaison officer to IV Corps, found it "practically intact." Rain and stubborn resistance limited the division's advance to a point just north of Kanglatongbi, before heavy rain forced a pause in late May.[62]

At Shenam, Yamamoto tested the 23rd Indian Division. Roberts's defense centered on two major hill masses along the road. The eastern bastion was Scraggy and nearby Malta, while a mile to the west Gibraltar and Recce Hill formed the other. The Gibraltar/Recce Hill position also marked the last massifs before the road descended toward Palel.[63]

On the night of May 20, Yamamoto's infantry hurled themselves against Roberts's positions. Massed attacks hammered Scraggy through the night and into the next morning. Scraggy was defended by the 3/10 Gurkha Rifles. "Several times the battle was at very close range," reported an officer. "Shortly after dawn [on May 21] the Japs came yelling and screaming over the summit of Scraggy in three waves, many of them armed only with grenades and gelignite bombs. Our Brens spoke and slaughtered the incoming hordes." The Gurkhas counterattacked with kukri and bayonet and routed the attackers, saving the hill. Meanwhile, a flanking column of two understrength battalions tried to scale Gibraltar, which was being defended by 5/6 Rajputana Rifles. The defenders threw back the Japanese in a hail of rifle and machine gun fire, assisted by the divisional artillery.[64]

Yamamoto tried again on the night of May 23. Under cover of an artillery bombardment, Japanese infantry scaled Gibraltar and dislodged the Rajputs atop the hill. "Dawn came," noted an officer of Roberts's staff, "and revealed to the eyes of all a Japanese flag fluttering from the top of Gibraltar." It was essential to counterattack the Japanese before they had dug in, otherwise Gibraltar might be impregnable, which in turn would force the abandonment of all positions east of Recce Hill.[65]

The divisional artillery shelled Gibraltar at 9:01am, followed by an attack by the Rajputs from all sides. After two hours of close-quarters fighting, the Rajputs were nearing the crest, but lacked the strength to do more. A Company of 3/10 Gurkhas came from Scraggy and attacked at 11. "Over went the Gurkhas," recalled an officer, "past the trenches the Rajputs had regained, until grenades and shells halted the leading platoon on the crest. A second was ordered through to top the crest and come to grips with the last of the enemy on the reverse slope. The Japs made one final effort to hold on … in the ensuing hand-to-hand combat, where the bayonet went home and the kukri came out when there was not room for the bayonet … Fifty Japs fled from death by steel, only for many to fall before the weapons on Malta." That afternoon the flag came down, and Gibraltar was back in British hands. The Rajputs and Gurkhas lost 11 killed and 107 wounded, while killing 145 Japanese on Gibraltar and an unknown number around Malta. A stalemate settled over the Shenam Saddle.[66]

South and southwest of Imphal, Mutaguchi's and Cowan's offensives collided to produce the largest battles of the month. Cowan's movement started first, with Cameron's 48th Brigade moving rapidly south past Loktak Lake on May 16. By the afternoon of May 17, the brigade had cut the Tiddim Road at Milepost 33, just south of the village of Torbung and approximately 13 miles south of the front line. That evening, tanks and trucks, the latter with headlights blazing, unwittingly drove into the roadblock. Cameron's men shot them up.[67]

The 48th Brigade's appearance stunned the Japanese. Cameron's roadblock was north of the reinforcing units, and cut them off from the frontline troops. The 33rd Division's supplies were also south of the block, meaning the division soon faced severe shortages. General Tanaka Nobuo was unable to reach his new command when he arrived on May 18. In addition, 63rd Brigade's attacks were getting underway. "The 33d Division found itself under attack from all sides," noted a staff report.

The 33rd Division's supply chief, Lieutenant Colonel Matsuki, received orders to organize whatever he could and eliminate the roadblock. His first attempt with 100 men on the night of May 17 failed when the commanders misjudged the roadblock's location and inadvertently drove into Cameron's perimeter. Matsuki called up the reinforcements (1st Battalion, 67th Regiment; 2nd Battalion, 154th Regiment; and 14th Tank Regiment) intended for the major offensive, and send them to battle Cameron's brigade. A staff officer noted that their repeated attacks "were not only unsuccessful in dislodging the enemy, but [the units] also suffered extremely heavy losses."

Meanwhile, a frustrated General Mutaguchi ordered the division's frontline infantry to attack, and the 214th Regiment to proceed with its planned strike into Cowan's rear. The 215th Regiment battled with 32rd and 63rd Brigades to a stalemate. Colonel Bennett visited the 63rd Brigade on May 20, and "was immediately struck by the high morale of this outfit ... They are supremely self-confident and very pleased with their operations (which they have a right to be)."

These developments concerned Cameron, as it was clear 63rd Brigade would not be able to break through to his forces. In this event, Cowan had directed Cameron to "facilitate his [the enemy's] destruction ... by operating against him from the rear." Cameron decided to move north, pulling out on May 24. Two days later, his men occupied Moirang, then continued northward, cutting through Japanese units along the way, before reaching the 63rd Brigade's lines at Potsangbam on May 31. The Japanese were grateful for Cameron's withdrawal. "Had the roadblock been held only a few days longer," noted a staff report, "the 33rd would have been in serious straits regarding supply and in a most difficult tactical position."

While fighting raged along the front lines, Cowan also faced a threat to his rear. He had just moved divisional headquarters six miles north of Bishenpur, to a spot on the Tiddim Road overlooked by a hill marked on maps as Point 2926 and soon dubbed "Red Hill". At 2am on May 21, 2nd Battalion of the 214th Regiment (estimated by Cowan's headquarters as "two platoons plus") attacked the hill, but were kept off the crest by the Baluch platoon atop the feature. The Japanese took up a defense on Point 2926's the southeastern spur. The 214th's 1st Battalion occupied the nearby village of Maibam. Cowan sent the division's headquarters guard to attack the spur, under his operations officer, Captain J. A. Cumming; they attacked from two sides but were unsuccessful, and Cumming was killed.

On May 23, tanks and infantry cleared Maibam, routing the defending Japanese. Meanwhile, the Japanese on Red Hill held out through days of attacks. Cowan directed the battle in person, and by May 25 realized he needed help. Scoones sent 50th Parachute Brigade headquarters and a detachment of tanks from 3rd Dragoon Guards, and Cowan launched a major attack on the morning of May 27. His men made slow progress against the dug-in Japanese, but by the night of May 28, they had compressed the defenders into a small perimeter along the spur's southern face. Victory appeared imminent.

During this fighting, the Japanese battalions had been out of touch with headquarters. On May 27, they re-established radio contact and received orders to retreat. The Japanese pulled out on the night of May 28/29, retracing their steps westward. Of 380 men in the 214th's 1st Battalion who started the attack, only 17 remained; the regiment's 2nd Battalion counted 37 "fit for combat" out of 540. Cowan's troops occupied their deserted positions on May 29 and 30.

By May 31, a lull settled in on the Tiddim Road sector and in the hills around Imphal generally. Much fighting in the last two weeks of May had left the battle lines around Imphal essentially unchanged. But IV Corps' strength was ebbing away. "Chances of IV Corps sustained offensive appears remote," Colonel Bennett told Stilwell as May turned into June. "What IV Corps is doing can hardly be dignified by the word operations." Relief needed to come from the outside soon.[68]

* * *

Stopford's corps struggled to clear Kohima. Grover was now in command of his own division, plus elements of Messervy's 7th Indian Division, with the rest expected to arrive in about a week. Slim pressed Stopford to be aggressive.

On May 11, the British attacked all along the line after what one officer described as "the most terrific artillery concentration imaginable." The 1st Queen's charged up Jail Hill, now festooned with Japanese bunkers. "Fighting was now bitter and mostly hand-to-hand," noted a battalion officer. "Seen from tactical headquarters, what looked almost like a snowball fight was taking place on the west end of the crest. The snowballs, however, were not white; they there grey and burst, and when they burst men fell." The Queen's drove back the Japanese, and held their positions on Jail Hill despite heavy fire.[69]

Elsewhere, the tennis court and all of Kohima Ridge was cleared in three days of heavy fighting. Artillery and tank fire literally blasted Japanese from their dug-in positions, while those who fled were shot down by British rifles and machine guns. Brigadier Hawkins fell wounded as his brigade fought against dogged resistance to advance in Naga Village. 33rd Brigade Gurkhas cleared Treasury Hill on May 14, while the 2nd Royal Norfolks cleared the rest of GPT Ridge.[70]

The fighting had liberated Kohima, but also razed it. "Hillsides that had once been covered with forest were stripped bare by shellfire and were honeycombed with foxholes and bunkers. Parachutes still dangled from shattered trees," recalled Lieutenant Gilmore of the 4/8 Gurkhas. "It was exactly like the Somme in 1916," noted General Stopford. "One could tell how desperate the fighting had been." Brigadier Roberts, arriving with his 114th Brigade, recalled that Kohima was "a heap of ruins, shell holes, mud and shattered trees ... not even the fresh mountain air could entirely carry away the smell of death that crept with the mists up the mountain-sides and into the valleys."[71]

After a period of regrouping, Messervy's 7th Indian Division now took the lead, with its own 33rd and 114th Brigades and the 5th Indian Division's 161st Brigade under its command. The division attacked Naga Village on May 25, but failed to capture it against stiff opposition and fire from the commanding heights of Church Knoll and Gun Spur. On the night of the May 25, 4/1 Gurkhas infiltrated Gun Spur, and cleared it the next day with the assistance of artillery and mortars. The next few days were spent mopping up Japanese bunkers on the reverse slope of Gun Spur, while 4/15 Punjabs stormed Church Knoll. By May 31, virtually all of the Japanese positions in and around Kohima had been captured. Stopford could now look to turning his divisions southward to exploit the victory and open the road to Imphal.[72]

Sato understood what these developments meant. His division had suffered losses that made it a shadow of its former self. The monsoon was starting, and the wet weather combined with Perowne's Chindits to make his overland communications more fragile by the day. On May 25, Sato signaled Mutaguchi his intention to withdraw unless supplies arrived in the following days. None came, so on May 31, Sato ordered his men to leave Kohima. Most would go east, while a battalion-sized group under Miyazaki would fight a delaying action along the road to Imphal.

"Retreat and I will court-martial you," radioed Mutaguchi when informed of these orders. "Do as you please," Sato shot back. "I will bring you down with me."[73]

CHAPTER 9

The Balance Tips

Mutaguchi took stock after the battles of late May. "The balance of power had shifted very definitely to the enemy," noted a staff report, "and only the indomitable spirit of the 33rd Division enabled it to stave off defeat." Much the same could be said for Yamamoto Force and the 15th Division. Mutaguchi's forces had tried their hardest to break through to Imphal, and had scored some notable, if temporary, successes; but in the end, IV Corps still stood ready for another round.[1]

Fifteenth Army was not the only source of bad news for the Japanese. The balance of power on the entire Burma–India front was tilting toward the Allies. Wei's forces remained active, and a constant threat from the east. The loss of Myitkyina airfield eliminated a major Japanese airbase, and opened up a shorter, more southern route for Hump flights; after a period of fluctuations around 10,000 tons per month in the first five months of 1944, airlift tonnages to China would increase markedly in June and would never decrease until the war's end in 1945. The Chindits had moved north, but remained a potent force. Stilwell's NCAC advance had resumed, and it was clear that the withering strength of Tanaka's 18th Division would not hold it back for much longer.[2]

Nonetheless, Mutaguchi remained determined to capture Imphal. He ordered preparations for a new offensive. The 33rd Division would make the major attack, with supporting assaults coming from Yamamoto Force and the 15th Division. This would be an all-out effort, as General Tanaka Nobuo explained to his men in an Order of the Day on June 2. "Now is the time to capture Imphal," he said. "Our death-defying infantry group expects certain victory when it penetrates the main fortress of the enemy. The coming battle is a turning point. It will decide the success or failure of the Greater East Asia War ... Regarding death as something lighter than a feather you must tackle the job of definitely capturing Imphal. That's why it must be expected that the Division will be almost annihilated. I have confidence in your courage and devotion and believe that you will do your duty ... *On this one battle rests the fate of the Empire.* All officers and men, fight courageously."[3]

Three days after this order was issued, General Kawabe arrived from Rangoon to meet with Mutaguchi. Operation U-Go's lack of progress had become controversial in Tokyo. In late April, Imperial General Headquarters had sent observers to see the situation for themselves, and Mutaguchi had privately expressed to them pessimism about his chances for victory. When this information reached Tojo, he declared in a contentious meeting: "The battle must be fought to the end." Tojo had staked much political capital on the invasion of India, and may have felt the foundation of his government creaking at the prospect of failure. "The Imphal operation is now a problem not just for Burma but on the world stage," came a message from Tokyo to Kawabe's headquarters in Rangoon. "Whatever sacrifice is required, Burma Area Army must make it to take Imphal."[4]

Kawabe and Mutaguchi conferred on June 5. Mutaguchi greeted him emotionally. "We are at the crossroads," Mutaguchi said with tears in his eyes, "but have no fears." Kawabe, exhausted and ill from the six-day journey from Rangoon, took a break to review the grim situation—33rd Division, Yamamoto Force, and 15th Division all stymied around Imphal, 31st Division falling back from Kohima, and the entire Fifteenth Army seriously weakened due to sickness and battle casualties. Mutaguchi planned to renew the attack, and was in the process of ordering Sato to concentrate and move south to assist the 15th Division. General Yamauchi had just been relieved from command of the 15th Division due to ill health—the second of Mutaguchi's division commanders to lose his job in three weeks.[5]

The next day, June 6, Kawabe again met with Mutaguchi. The two men discussed the state of affairs in detail. Mutaguchi asked for reinforcements, and Kawabe promised to do his best to provide some. Both men fell silent. Kawabe could tell that Mutaguchi had something more on his mind, but did not ask for fear of raising an unpleasant topic. For his part, Mutaguchi desperately wanted to say "The time has come to give up the operation as soon as possible," but could not bring himself to do so, for fear of looking defeatist. The sentence "got as far as my throat; but I could not force it out in words," Mutaguchi later recorded in his diary. "But I wanted him to get it from my expression." The moment passed, and the meeting ended.[6]

If Kawabe understood Mutaguchi's silent meaning, he gave no sign of it. That evening Kawabe departed, telling Mutaguchi "I'm going back to Rangoon with confidence in you, and with peace of mind." He reported to Tokyo about Fifteenth Army's situation, without indicating that the operation needed to be cancelled. The fighting went on.[7]

* * *

On June 2, Sato's headquarters and infantry abandoned Naga Village. After a sharp fight in the Aradura area, Miyazaki's men retired southward toward Imphal on June 5. The British detected the slackening of Japanese resistance, and Stopford urged

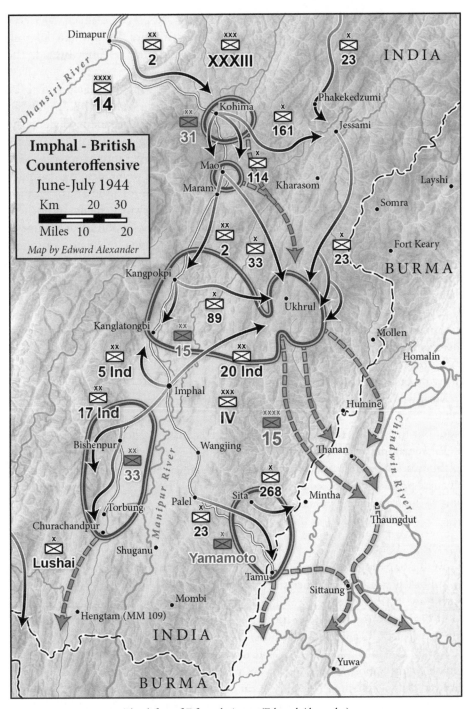

Dimapur

XX
2

XXX
XXXIII

x
23

INDIA

XXXX
14

Dhansiri River

Kohima

Phakekedzumi

XX
31

x
161

Jessami

Mao

x
114

Kharasom

Layshi

Maram

Somra

Imphal - British Counteroffensive
June-July 1944

Km   20   30

Miles 10   20

Map by Edward Alexander

XX
2

x
33

x
23

Fort Keary

BURMA

Kangpokpi

Ukhrul

Mollen

x
89

Homalin

Kanglatongbi

XX
15

XX
20 Ind

XX
5 Ind

Imphal

Humine

XX
17 Ind

XXX
IV

Chindwin River

Bishenpur

XX
33

XXXX
15

Thanan

Wangjing

Torbung

Palel

Sita

x
268

Mintha

Thaungdut

Churachandpur

Shuganu

x
23

x
Yamamoto

Tamu

Sittaung

Lushai

Manipur River

Mombi

INDIA

Hengtam (MM 109)

Yuwa

BURMA

The defeat of Fifteenth Army. (Edward Alexander)

his two division commanders, Grover and Messervy, to press the attack. Messervy moved his 7th Indian Division east and southeast toward Jessami and Ukhrul, while Grover directed his 2nd British Division south along the Imphal Road. The IV Corps' perimeter was 75 miles away.[8]

"As the advance progressed the magnitude of the Japanese defeat began to be realized," recalled Brigadier Roberts, whose 114th Brigade led the 7th Indian Division's advance. "Arms, equipment, and guns were found abandoned along the track in increasing quantities." Sato's retreat was becoming a rout.[9]

Messervy's men found worse when they penetrated deeper into Sato's rear areas. "In their cautious progress the brigade passed through and round deserted camps of leafy huts, concealed strongpoints, living accommodation for thousands," recalled an officer of the division artillery. "Unburied dead lay everywhere, many untouched, some fat and well-looking, others emaciated, filthy skeletons. Typhus, that scourge of armies, had done its work ... Naga tribesmen started bringing in Japanese prisoners too sick to move, filthy skeletons, raving, weeping and gibbering in their madness, the ultimate resistance of their minds broken by the unspeakable hardships to which their bodies had been subjected."[10]

Sato received orders to concentrate and move to attack Imphal. Knowing that the condition of his men made these instructions impossible to execute, he instead directed his troops toward Ukhrul, where there were some supplies. Mutaguchi sent a staff officer to meet with Sato. "First we must eat," Sato told him. "Carrying out Army orders comes after that." The withdrawal continued.[11]

Meanwhile, Grover's division pressed southward toward Imphal. Miyazaki's soldiers took up bridges, laid mines, and set up roadblocks on the narrow and twisty road, but the British kept a close pursuit. The Japanese made stands at the villages of Viswema and Mao Songsang, where the road narrowed between steep heights to the west and a deep valley to the east. Both times, British infantry flanked the Japanese position and forced a retreat. Grover rotated brigades to always keep a fresh unit at the front of the pursuit.[12]

* * *

Grover's troops could not arrive soon enough for the hungry and beleaguered men at Imphal. Despite the weather, an average of 259 tons of supplies per day arrived during the period June 4–15. Still, it was not enough, and rations were again cut. Most ominously, by mid-June, fuel and oil stocks for IV Corps were estimated to run dry in just over a week. The weather was extreme in Imphal and prevented many deliveries. On June 20, IV Corps had to report that "stocks in the RIASC [Royal Indian Army Supply Corps] depot are practically exhausted and unless petrol is received daily ... it will be necessary to eat down the very small ... reserves." In short, IV Corps was running out of food and gasoline. Help was needed, and quickly.[13]

During this time, Mutaguchi embarked on his last attempt to take Imphal. Yamamoto's depleted forces attacked Scraggy on the evening of June 9. They succeeded in wresting the hilltop from the Gurkha defenders, but could advance no further after heavy fighting lasting until June 10. Yamamoto's weakened force did not have the strength for another attempt. "We still barred the way," noted one of Roberts's staff officers, "and, grievous as our losses had been, the Japs had lost as heavily … [Yamamoto] had broken his head on a brick wall."[14]

Further south, Tanaka Nobuo sent his 33rd Division against Cowan's defenses. First on June 7 and then again on June 12, combined attacks by infantry and tanks struck the area of Potsangbam and nearby Ningthoukhong. Heavy fighting erupted in the villages, and British Grant tanks and PIAT anti-tank weapons took a heavy toll on Japanese armor, stalling both attacks. Exhausted and starving, the Japanese pulled back. Slim later paid tribute to "the supreme courage and hardihood of the Japanese soldiers" in the 33rd Division. Both sides settled into a bloody stalemate.[15]

On Imphal's northern front, Scoones put all his resources behind Briggs's effort to fight northward toward XXXIII Corps. While the 89th Brigade held the division's eastern flank, Briggs sent Evans's 123rd Brigade attacking northward up the road and through the hills overlooking it to the east. Meanwhile Salomons's 9th Brigade swung westward through flatter terrain to flank the Japanese. Despite heavy rains, the advance made two miles in five days. Briggs regrouped, and Salomons's brigade, with tanks, attacked into the hills while Evans's men swung west of the road and pressed northward. The Japanese pulled back to a hill called Liver, which covered the road and the surrounding area. Salomons's infantry, supported by airstrikes, repeatedly attacked Liver in heavy rain, but made no progress. On the night of June 21, the Japanese stole away to the east. Salomons's men occupied Liver without opposition on the 22nd, cleared a roadblock, and headed northward.[16]

* * *

By June 18, the 2nd Division stood at Mile Marker 80 on the road just north of Maram, 40 miles from Imphal. There, Miyazaki had organized a roadblock he thought could hold for 10 days. The 5th Brigade attacked down the road under cover of smoke and airstrikes, while a bulldozer followed behind to clear the block. The position fell within hours, the Japanese fleeing eastward. The 4th Brigade passed through and advanced another eight miles before overrunning Miyazaki's headquarters. The 6th Brigade next took up the southward advance.[17]

On the morning of June 22, the 2nd Durham Light Infantry, leading 6th Brigade of Grover's division, moved to the area of Mile Marker 109 in Kangpokpi. At 10:30am the Durhams opened fire on a group of infantry pushing northward, causing them to quickly take cover. After an urgent exchange of radio messages, it became clear that the targets were actually 1/17 Dogra, the advance elements of 5th

Indian Division. All firing ceased, and the men came forward to shake hands. That afternoon, Stopford, Grover, and Salomons met at Mile Marker 109 for a conference. After 85 days of isolation, IV Corps at Imphal again had land communication with the outside world. That night, a truck convoy drove from Kohima to Imphal with headlights blazing.[18]

* * *

In Burma, General Stilwell continued his offensive toward Kamaing and Mogaung. Sensing the kill, Chinese troops closed in on Tanaka's 18th Division from all sides. The Japanese fought stubbornly to hold back NCAC's advances despite heavy rain.

Nonetheless, Tanaka's position was desperate. All of his units were understrength by over 50 percent, and many had lost the majority of their officers. "The forces were suffering from the lack of capable leaders, ammunition, provisions, and other necessary supplies," recalled Tanaka. His artillery was limited to four shells per gun, and by June 9 had almost completely been overrun and captured.[19]

For the first time, signs of panic showed from the men of the Chrysanthemum Division. "The advance attack of the enemy from the north is unexpectedly swift; the enemy is advancing southward, threading through the gaps in our lines by wading chest-high through marshy zones," reported the 56th Regiment's commander on June 7. "I am unable to contact the 1 and 3 Battalions, which are under my command, and their situation is unknown … The regiment will cover the withdrawal of the main body of the division at the sacrifice of our lives. I believe this will be our final parting. Please give my best regards to the division commander."[20]

To avoid annihilation, Tanaka decided to evacuate the area around Kamaing. Using jungle trails, 5,000 men retreated southwest past the Chinese. A regiment of the Chinese 30th Division entered Kamaing on June 16 and sealed the victory. Six days later, Honda ordered Tanaka's division to withdraw southwest of Mogaung. The Mogaung Valley was now firmly in Allied hands.[21]

At the same time, Calvert's 77th Brigade approached Mogaung, which Calvert quickly realized "was a difficult place to attack." The city sits in a valley surrounded on three sides, except the south, by watercourses, with a range of hills to the southeast and east. The monsoons had flooded the low ground, and the terrain was waist-deep in water in places. Swinging east of the city, Calvert's troops set up a base, captured the part of the high ground, and secured the Tapaw Ferry. Motorboats and crews were airdropped, and the Chindits established a ferry of their own.[22]

The brigade now turned to attack Mogaung from the east. The Japanese 53rd Division was moving into the area with a view toward relieving Myitkyina; instead, it turned around to Mogaung and the area north and northwest of it to assist the 18th Division's withdrawal. Calvert attacked repeatedly from June 3–13, capturing several outlying villages, a massive field hospital, supply dumps, and campsites.

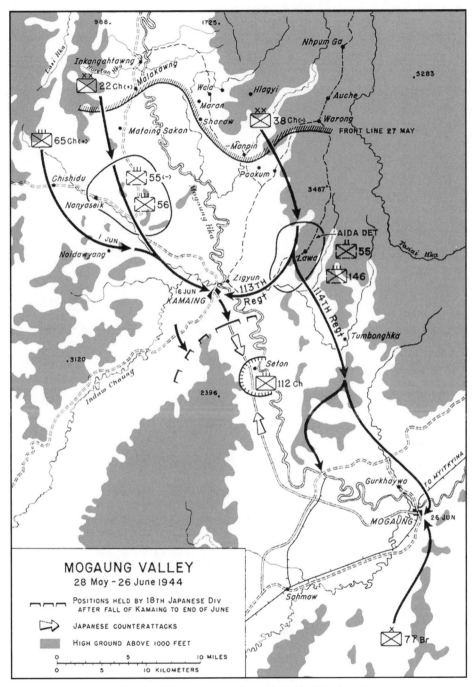

The NCAC front, May 28–June 26, 1944. (U.S. Army)

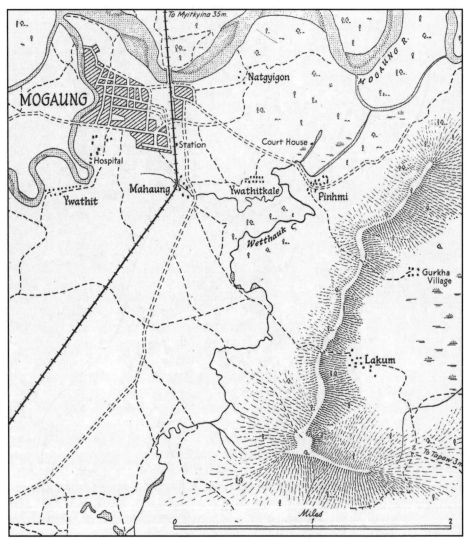

The Mogaung area. (U.K. Ministry of Defence)

Bladet Force arrived by parachute with flamethrowers, which sped up the advance. The Japanese fell back into Mogaung itself, leaving some 600 yards of open space between the Chindits and the town. Calvert called a pause after all of his battalion commanders[23] visited his headquarters and "said that however much they were willing to go on, these last series of attacks in rain and mud had exhausted their men and their casualties had reduced their numbers of fit men per battalion to a little more than a company strength each." Meanwhile, a reinforced battalion of the 53rd Division's 128th Regiment had arrived to defend Mogaung. "We had lost the race to Mogaung by 600 yards," lamented Calvert.[24]

On the evening of June 18, one of Calvert's staff officers reported "that he had a Chinese regiment waiting on the other bank of the Mogaung [River]." The unit turned out to be Colonel Li's 114th Regiment of Sun's 38th Division, sent specifically to assist with the capture of Mogaung. The Chindits and NCAC had at last made ground contact.[25]

Li's Chinese crossed between the June 18 and 22, taking up position on Calvert's left and enveloping Mogaung from the south. After several probing attacks, they occupied Mogaung's southern outskirts. Calvert then sent his brigade into town, assisted by heavy airstrikes from U.S. planes. The Chindits and Chinese cleared the town in three days of house-to-house fighting. On June 26, Mogaung was declared secure. The Japanese defenders died to a man, while 77th Brigade sustained 776 killed and wounded—over one-third of its strength. Calvert's men were exhausted and could do no more. The same was true of their commander. "I had no elation, no satisfaction, no positive emotion," recalled Calvert later. "Just to lie down for a while and rest."[26]

NCAC's press officers credited only Li's regiment for the victory. "Mogaung haven been taken by Chinese," radioed an exasperated Calvert to Lentaigne, "77th Brigade is proceeding to take Umbrage."[27]

* * *

The news from Myitkyina was not as promising. In the first days of June, General Boatner ordered an all-out offensive. The engineers attacked the defenses north of town with little success. The Chinese 42nd and 150th Regiments punched into Myitkyina from the south, making some progress before being held up by a nest of bunkers along the river. The 42nd pressed into the train station, and by day's end held "all the station but the ticket office," reported Boatner to Stilwell. "I really thought we'd get the town."[28]

In contrast to the battles waged in May, the early June attack included support from Morrisforce across the Irrawaddy. Morris reported on June 1 that he had three columns, each numbering 430 men each, less about 100 casualties. Boatner ordered him to attack Waingmaw, held by 100 Japanese, which Morris did albeit without success. Colonel Herring, also present with his Kachin Levies, reported "Waingmaw was full of pillboxes." Morris tried again on June 2, with little better result. Boatner ordered another offensive, which prompted Morris to ask if it was "a death or glory show." Boatner answered "definitely yes," citing previous orders from Mountbatten and Stilwell. "God knows I want to attack vigorously," Boatner told Stilwell.[29]

Despite Boatner's impatience, the lines fell into a stasis in early June. The Chinese commenced using siege tactics, including systematic digging toward the enemy positions. On the northern sector, the American units reorganized, trained, and patrolled. Colonel Hunter was assigned to command all U.S. units—both the 5307th and the two engineer battalions, grouped into a provisional regiment on June 8. Over the first week of June, more replacements arrived for the 5307th, and Hunter reorganized the unit into a regular regiment. Three battalions were organized: 1st Battalion "Old Galahad" made up of the remainder of the original 5307th, and the 2nd and 3rd "New Galahad" Battalions, comprising mostly replacements except for some key officers and NCOs transferred from Old Galahad. The combat teams were abolished, and the three battalions divided into companies as standard infantry units. The Old Galahad battalion numbered 300 men, while the New Galahad battalions contained 950 men each.[30]

Some of the replacements sent to these battalions were Marauders taken from their hospital beds; NCAC staff officers visited the 20th General Hospital and dispatched sick and wounded men to the nearby airfield for transport to Myitkyina. Doctors managed to stop most of the worst cases from boarding, but many men made the trip only to be re-evacuated almost immediately as unfit for combat. Many men had to be pressured to go back into battle, while some went willingly. One of the willing, Gilbert Howland, rejoined the units at the front despite still recovering from a wound sustained at Nhpum Ga. "Those were my buddies," he later said. "I couldn't let them down."[31]

Hunter wanted the Old Galahad 1st Battalion with him at the front, but for most of the siege they stayed behind at the airfield to protect the Myitkyina Task Force's flanks and rear. "The situation was one that must be unusual in war," observed Ogburn. "The besieging force was itself surrounded by enemy-held territory." Until Mogaung was taken, the Myitkyina Task Force needed to protect itself in all directions. The airfield was the only way in and out, and its security was critical to both the Task Force's success and its very survival.[32]

All of this made the Myitkyina Airfield a focal point of the battle, second only to the town itself. Except for six pack 75s in the U.S. sector and eight of the same in the Chinese sector, all support came from the P-40s of the 88th Fighter Squadron, based at the field. Japanese shelling and occasional air raids had left the field littered with wrecked C-47s, while off to the side stood tents made of old parachutes containing hospitals, offices, and quarters. Mud and rain added a bedraggled look to the scene.

"The effect," Ogburn wrote, "was an odd one, giving the scene an appearance of fair grounds—one in hell, attended by an army of the condemned."[33]

In mid-June, Brigadier General William H. Tunner, on an inspection of the Hump airlift operation, flew in to see the battle. As he landed, he saw Chinese soldiers firing into Myitkyina. Tunner visited Gordon Seagrave's hospital, in the open air on the airfield's eastern end. While they talked, Tunner recalled how "fighter planes were coming in and taking off right over our heads; our shells and bombs were bursting in and over the town. In all the confusion, Dr Seagrave was perfectly calm."[34]

General Boatner remained in his headquarters, preferring to deal directly with the Chinese and liaising with Hunter via his deputy, Colonel George W. Sliney. Boatner sent daily reports to Stilwell, in which he tried to put the best face on the situation. "Am pushing these troops just as hard as I can within what I believe are reasonable limits," he told Stilwell on June 12. To Cannon, NCAC's Chief of Staff, he was blunter. "This place is a real mess," Boatner told him. "With the help of God we will pull through OK but it's tough sledding … God knows what I ever did to pull a job like this." To another officer he said "I would be one helluva liar if I said all was OK. Sure wish I was in the AGD [Adjutant General's Department] or SOS [Service of Supply]." Stilwell picked up on this attitude, which he termed "up and down."[35]

In Myitkyina itself, the Japanese remained confident. A Burmese spy reported 30–50% losses among the Allies, while the defenders numbered approximately 3,500 with ample supplies on hand for three months' consumption. General Mizukami assumed command on May 31, with orders to hold to the last. Between fighting, Mizukami kept his men busy by improving their defenses. Boatner dropped leaflets demanding surrender and calling the garrison "doomed," but these were greeted with laughter and scorn by the Japanese.[36]

On June 14, Boatner launched a new offensive against Myitkyina, which made little gain. "There can be no withdrawal or slackening of our efforts," Boatner messaged Hunter. The offensive resumed on June 15 and 16, gaining some ground. Across the river, Morrisforce failed to make significant progress. On June 17, in one final push, Hunter's men reached the Irrawaddy north of Myitkyina and formed a firm ring around the town. This effort cost the Allies 200 casualties, against an estimated 100 Japanese killed.[37]

During the battle, Boatner reported to Stilwell about "complete disorganization and fear in U.S. units. They are in many cases simply terrified of the Jap." Stilwell exploded at this news. "That last report was very disturbing," he wrote Boatner. "If we can't depend on U.S. units, where the hell are we? I assume you verified those reports of bad conduct; that's something I never thought would enter our picture." Stilwell hoped that more battlefield experience would help. In the meantime, all attacks would stop and siege operations would resume. "I don't like the idea of a siege," he told Boatner, "but it may be the proper solution." Boatner said he would stop attacks "until our troops are steadied and a favorable opportunity presents itself."[38]

Stilwell flew to Myitkyina on the afternoon of June 17 to see the situation for himself. Brigadier General Theodore F. Wessels, a former Infantry School instructor who had arrived in SEAC hoping to help train the Chinese Army, went along. To Stilwell's displeasure, he found that Boatner had never visited the front. Over the next two days, Stilwell and Wessels traveled all along the lines. "Saw Hunter and talked it over," Stilwell recorded in his diary. "Not so bad as painted." Stilwell departed on June 20, leaving Wessels behind to observe and help plan new operations.[39]

Three days later, Stilwell returned. "I don't know what to do," said Boatner, "and neither does anyone else." Boatner had lost his energy, and remained tied to his headquarters. "He is not a Commander," Stilwell fumed. Two days later, Boatner reported sick with malaria, and on June 26 Stilwell used this to put Wessels in command. Boatner "cried and protested," noted Stilwell in his diary. "Told him no argument. He was a staff officer and not a Commander."[40]

* * *

Imphal's relief signaled the final failure of Mutaguchi's invasion. He accepted defeat in early July and ordered his shattered forces back to Burma. "All hope of capturing Imphal or Palel was now gone," stated a staff report, "and the Fifteenth Army realized it would be fortunate if it could extricate itself from its extremely hazardous position without greater losses." The dream of a March on Delhi had gone glimmering.[41]

Subhas Chandra Bose digested the reports from the front. His INA units had lost heart, and were caught up in the Japanese retreat. Many INA soldiers had been surprised that the Indian soldiers in Slim's army had not defected to their side; instead, significant numbers of INA troops were deserting to the British. Bose's dreams of a second "Quit India" uprising were also dying. In desperation he broadcast directly to Gandhi and the Congress Party leaders on July 6. "Nobody would be more happy than ourselves if by any chance our countrymen at home should succeed in liberating themselves through their own efforts or by any chance, the British Government accepts your 'Quit India' resolution and gives effect to it," he read to his old prewar political comrades. "We are, however proceeding on the assumption that neither of the above is possible and that a struggle is inevitable." Bose then bestowed a title on Gandhi that has endured ever after. "Father of our Nation in this holy war for India's liberation, we ask for your blessings and good wishes." No reply came.[42]

Slim was not about to let up on the pursuit. Stopford received command of all troops north and east of Imphal, with orders to drive the Japanese back across the frontier and to the Chindwin. As Messervy's 7th Indian Division and Gracey's 20th Indian Division closed in on Ukhrul, Perowne's 23rd Brigade continued to slash into the Japanese rear. Meanwhile Roberts's 23rd Indian Division stormed Shenam against weakening Japanese resistance, compelling Yamamoto Force to retreat. On the Tiddim Road, 5th Indian Division relieved Cowan's 17th Indian Division and attacked southward.[43]

As these movements got underway, Stopford, increasingly dissatisfied with Grover's cautious methods, relieved Grover on July 4 and sent him home to Britain. "The shock to the 2nd Division was considerable," recalled Arthur Swinson of the Division's staff. "Not only the officers, but the troops, were quite bewildered." Major General Cameron Nicholson took command.[44]

The next day, Sato was removed from command of 31st Division. Mutaguchi had now relieved all three of the division commanders with which he had started the March on Delhi. "I do not intend to be censured by anyone," Sato announced to his staff before he departed. "Our 31st Division has done its duty."[45]

On the Tiddim Road, the 33rd Division fell back in the face of British attacks. As the 5th Indian Division pressed south in pursuit of the Japanese, they found signs of collapse. "Mud-clogged rifles and splintered packing cases kept company with dirty webbing equipment, hand grenades and blood-stained, muddy, rain-soaked corpses," recalled an officer of the division staff. "From beneath mounds of loose earth appeared legs and arms, even a solitary hand. Over all, and on almost every stretch of the road, hung the sickly smell [of death]." Retreating men had collapsed on the roadside and died where they lay. Patrols overran a deserted hospital where patients had been killed or committed suicide, while the 33rd Division's former headquarters site showed signs of hasty flight and yielded many souvenirs. Similar scenes played out elsewhere as the Japanese retreated. The Japanese later dubbed the path from Ukhrul the "Road of Bones."[46]

By July 31, after five weeks of marching and fighting in mud and rain, the Fourteenth Army had evicted virtually all Japanese from India. Slim called back his units for rest and rehabilitation. After the monsoon, Fourteenth Army would resume campaigning.[47]

Operation U-Go, the March on Delhi, had been soundly defeated. In four months of combat around Imphal, IV Corps lost 12,600 casualties killed, wounded, and missing. The British lost 4,064 casualties in the two months of combat at Kohima. Richards's garrison contributed 401 to this total, while 161st Brigade lost 462—a combined approximate total of one in three. Grover's 15,000-man 2nd Division lost 2,125 men around Kohima, while Messervy's division lost 623 of 12,000 in three weeks of battle and one month of pursuit. When the losses for Imphal and Kohima are added together, stopping the March on Delhi cost the British 17,500 personnel.

As for the Japanese, Fifteenth Army was shattered. Of 84,000 Japanese assigned to Mutaguchi's army at U-Go's opening on March 15, only 30,000 were "available for duty" five months later, and the majority of those were so weak they could perform only the lightest tasks. Of the 53,000 men who returned to Burma, 23,000 required immediate hospitalization. The three divisions were each shattered: 31st Division took 15,000 men into India; 6,264 were killed, mortally wounded, or died of disease. The 15th Division lost 8,268 dead of 15,280, while 33rd Division lost 7,970 of its 18,000 men. Eight thousand more deaths came from attached units like the 14th Tank Regiment, the artillery, and army support units. In total, 30,000 Japanese died in the hills around Imphal and Kohima.[48]

These losses were not recoverable—indeed, Mutaguchi had presided over the greatest defeat in the history of the Imperial Japanese Army. Although much hard fighting remained, from July 1944 to war's end Slim's army would have the advantage.

* * *

Fighting in Burma also continued through July. The Chindits were approaching their physical limits. In the weeks after Blackpool, Masters noticed that his men had an "absolute lack of reserve strength" in their bodies. "Men died from a cold, from a chill, from the exertion of a patrol to the nearest village four miles away," he recalled. "A high proportion of the British troops, officers and men, were in fact on the threshold of death from exhaustion, undernourishment, exposure, and strain." Similar conditions were reported in other brigades.[49]

Despite the difficulties, the Chindits fought on to the best of their ability. Led by 111th Brigade, the forces near Indawgyi Lake moved east to harass the railroad south of Mogaung. In a 10-day battle for Point 2171, a commanding hill, 14th and 111th Brigades captured it in bitter fighting during heavy rains.[50]

Stilwell appeared not to understand the Chindits' condition. He blamed them for failing to hold Blackpool, and could not understand the men's subsequent slow movement and apparent reluctance to act. Several times he raged in his diary about Lentaigne "crying" about his troops. Communication between Stilwell and Lentaigne broke down at points. Slim and Mountbatten both came out to referee, with varying degrees of success. "Stilwell's orders on the face of it were sound enough," recalled Slim, but the Chindits were "physically incapable" of executing them. Nonetheless, all British, American, and Chinese units had to stay in the battle to the end, lest withdrawals start accusations about favoring one nation over another. Special Force would not be fully extracted until Myitkyina's fall, when the fresh 36th Division, on its way to NCAC from India, would relieve them.[51]

In the midst of all this, Stilwell ordered Calvert to march his brigade to Myitkyina, where it would be flown to India. Fearing that his men would be sucked into the battle at Myitkyina, Calvert instead shut down his radio and marched up to Kamaing over flooded roads. "This was totally wrong of me," he later admitted, "and my disobedience of an order was not even justified by success. The route to Myitkyina would have been far easier and our evacuation far quicker and simpler."[52]

Stilwell summoned Calvert to meet him at Shaduzup, along with Lentaigne and Henry Alexander, now a Brigadier and Special Force's chief of staff. Calvert arrived on July 10 "spitting blood" and ready to lay in to Stilwell, but after a night's rest decided to take a different approach with the American general when they met the next day.

Stilwell greeted Calvert and motioned him to sit. "Well, Calvert," said Stilwell, "I've been wanting to meet you for some time."

"I've been wanting to meet you too, sir," replied Calvert.

"You send some very strong signals, Calvert," said Stilwell.

"You should see the ones my brigade major won't let me send," countered Calvert.

At this, Stilwell burst out laughing. "I have just the same trouble with my own staff officers when I draft signals to Washington," he replied. Stilwell then asked Calvert to explain what his brigade had done, and listened intently to 77th Brigade's story from the Broadway fly-in through the capture of Mogaung. Several times Stilwell expressed surprise at what Calvert was saying, and repeatedly asked his staff "why wasn't I told?" Stilwell "explained that he appreciated the fighting that the brigade had done." The men discussed tactics and lessons learned, and Stilwell offered to decorate five men from 77th Brigade with the Silver Star. The British soldiers then departed, leaving Stilwell with the impression that "they were in a hurry to get out before there was any question of 'failing to obey orders' brought out into the open." Several days later, 77th Brigade was flown to India.[53]

After the capture of Point 2171, medical personnel evaluated the remaining Chindits. The 14th and 3rd West African Brigades were tired, but still generally fit for duty. Of 111th Brigade's 2,200 men, Masters reported that "we had a dietary deficiency of 800 calories per day for 110 days. The average weight loss per man was between 30 and 40 pounds." Only 118 men, plus Masters, were still fit for any duty; Masters ordered the unfit men to evacuate to India, formed a unit he sarcastically called "111 Company," and asked Stilwell for orders. Stilwell sent them to guard a Chinese artillery battery near Mogaung, an assignment that lasted until the end of July when the company was flown to India. The 36th Division arrived in mid-August, and the remainder of Special Force left for India.[54]

Developments elsewhere also reverberated in the theater. In early July, the deteriorating situation in eastern China caused the War Department and President Roosevelt to push for Stilwell's appointment to command all Chinese armies and all Allied forces in China Theater. On July 8, Stilwell was nominated for a fourth star, and his promotion took effect August 1. Joseph Stilwell was now one of the highest-ranking officers in the U.S. Army, behind only George C. Marshall, Hap Arnold, Douglas MacArthur, and Dwight Eisenhower. Ten days after Stilwell's promotion was announced, Tojo's government in Tokyo fell—a victim of bad news from the battlefield. The March on Delhi's defeat had weakened the government to the point of collapse, and the U.S. victory at Saipan in the Mariana Islands finished it off.[55]

All eyes were on Myitkyina, where Wessels had taken charge with a firm hand. Stilwell had sketched plans for penetrating the line with massed attacks against various Japanese strongpoints. The first one, an attack by the Chinese 42nd Regiment from the north, failed, but later plans showed more promise.[56]

General Wessels assumed command the same day that Mogaung was captured, and quickly reaped the benefits. With a secure land communication, he received supplies in comparative abundance to his predecessors, who had often had to live with only one or two days' worth of food and ammunition reserves on hand. Reinforcements also arrived. Most importantly, Wessels could now concentrate his strength on Myitkyina, without worry about his flanks or rear.[57]

Across the river, Morrisforce was wasting away. Of 1,300 men on hand, Morris reported that only four platoons' worth, or approximately 10%, were effective. The others were incapacitated due to fatigue and disease. "It is apparent that the Force is no longer capable of anything beyond purely static duties and even then will continue to waste away," Lentaigne advised Stilwell on July 14. "I very much regret that the Force has not been able to last out the Myitkyina Operation, which has lasted for longer than expected." Stilwell ordered Morrisforce to India, with Herring's Kachin Levies replacing it on July 27. Morris's men crossed the river and marched to Myitkyina airfield, joining Masters's 111 Company for the flight out.[58]

The Myitkyina Task Force renewed the offensive on July 12, but the attack proved ineffective when American planes dropped their bombs short, causing casualties among the attacking units and disrupting them. Wessels reverted to siege tactics, building gradual pressure on the Japanese. The U.S. Office of War Information sent a detachment which broadcast news, music, and propaganda to the defenders. This effort persuaded 244 Myitkyina residents to cross into Wessels's lines, where they reported that the messages were having an effect. The music in particular eroded morale, "invariably [making] the listener lonely, homesick and discouraged," wrote an officer. "Native witnesses saw Japanese crying openly." During the latter part of July, 24 Japanese personnel tried to surrender, with over a third being shot in the attempt.[59]

In Myitkyina, General Mizukami and Colonel Maruyama sensed the end was near. On July 30, Mizukami ordered Maruyama to evacuate his regiment. Mizukami would remain behind and fight to the last man with the wounded and the garrison's remnants. Other escapees joined Maruyama's regiment, and an estimated 800 people escaped downriver by boats over the next several nights. Mizukami died by suicide on August 1.[60]

On the morning of August 3, led by a Chinese penetration force, the Allies entered Myitkyina and cleared the last resistance. They captured 187 Japanese personnel, plus 21 Korean comfort women. At 3:45pm that day, the town was declared secure after 79 days of battle. The Siege of Myitkyina ended in a major Allied victory.[61]

The fighting had been neither cheap nor easy. The siege cost 5,383 Allied casualties and a further 1,168 sick. Of approximately 4,200 Japanese defenders, 800 escaped, 187 were captured, and remaining 3,213 killed. Most importantly, a key Japanese base had been eliminated, north Burma was firmly secured in Allied hands, and a jump-off point had been set for future advances into Burma and toward China.

Epilogue

General Stilwell was not present for the capture of Myitkyina. He was in Kandy, serving as acting Supreme Commander while Mountbatten was in London for consultations. Stilwell would spend most of August in the Ceylon city, where his hands-off management style endeared him to many of SEAC's staff.

The news of Wessels's victory made a great impression. "Radio about Myitkyina," Stilwell recorded in his diary. "Over at last ... Thank God."

Myitkyina's fall marked the end of the decisive period of World War II in Burma and India. Both sides stopped major operations to take stock of recent events and prepare for new campaigns after the monsoon ended. A year earlier, the front had stood in precarious balance between Axis and Allied forces, with either side capable of seizing an advantage. Now, the balance had tipped irrevocably toward the Allies following the series of battles that occurred over the first eight months of 1944.

These victories were won by the tenacity and skill of the common soldiers on the Allied side. American, British, Canadian, Chinese, Gurkha, Indian, Kachin, Kenyan, Nigerian, Nepalese, and many other soldiers combined to prevail despite significant challenges of weather and terrain. Their officers, up to and including corps and division command, with few exceptions led them with considerable skill. The names Stopford, Scoones, Merrill, Boatner, Wessels, Messervy, Briggs, Evans, Gracey, Roberts, Grover, Cowan, Sun, Liao, Fergusson, Calvert, Brodie, Perowne, Lentaigne, Hunter, Richards, Masters, and many others occupy important places in the history of World War II on the Asian mainland and in the story of the war against Japan as a whole.

Among the Allied leaders, the titan of the period just concluded was William Slim. He trained and organized Fourteenth Army, and led it to victory. He did this across a wide front and over some of the toughest terrain in the world, while leading an unprecedentedly diverse force of many nations and religions. Slim's handling of the many crises between February and May 1944 showed his steadiness and grasp of operations. The informal command agreement with Stilwell worked superbly due to the two men's mutual regard, and Slim showed a deftness in handling Stilwell that resounds to his credit. An outstanding leader, General Slim's performance in 1944 ranks him among the foremost commanders of World War II, if not the 20th century.

Aside from Slim, the most important Allied player in the campaigns was Joseph Stilwell. His conduct of operations in the Hukawng and Mogaung Valleys demonstrated his excellence at managing a campaign. He succeeded despite Japanese resistance, Chiang's interference, and SEAC's belief that the task was impossible. The Marauders' flanking operations and the movement to Myitkyina were brilliant feats of American arms. However, some of this success was offset by his difficult personality and stubbornness regarding SEAC's wishes and demands. Stilwell's conduct of Myitkyina's siege, and his relations with the Chindits, mar an otherwise great victory. General Stilwell is the dominant figure in America's involvement in Asia during World War II.[1]

In his memoirs, Slim paid Stilwell a high compliment. "The capture of Myitkyina, so long delayed, marked the complete success of the first stage of Stilwell's campaign," he wrote. "When all was said and done, the success of the northern offensive was in the main owing to the Ledo Chinese divisions—and that was Stilwell."

Both Slim and Stilwell received vital assistance from the Chindits in Operation Thursday. The March fly-in was one of high drama and adventure. Wingate's death took something out of the force, but it fought on with tenacity and skill for another four months. After the war, Japanese commanders clearly and repeatedly stated that the Chindits made them divert units from northern Burma and U-Go. Mutaguchi claimed they were a reason for his defeat, by sucking away two battalions from the 15th Division, the entire 53rd Division, and other units that had been in reserve for U-Go. When one considers that the presence of one or two more battalions with the 15th Division might have made the difference between victory and defeat at the Lion Box in April 1944, one must concede Mutaguchi's point.

Operation Thursday had been the brainchild of Orde Wingate. A fierce debate about the man and his methods has raged since the war's end, with little sign of abating. Wingate inspired many people to support and follow him, but his manners and methods also alienated many potential supporters. Wingate's performance in the last weeks of his life leaves one wondering if he was out of his depth commanding a force in battle larger than a brigade. The judgment of S.W. Kirby, the British official historian and a former staff officer in Delhi, seems just: "Wingate had many original and sound ideas. He had the fanaticism and drive to persuade others that they should be carried out, but he had neither the knowledge, stability, nor balance to make a great commander."

None of the victories in 1944 would have been possible without Southeast Asia Command and India Command. India Command provided essential support and transport, and was key to getting XXXIII Corps headquarters and 2nd British Division by rail to Dimapur. Much of this credit goes to General Auchinleck and the American railroad units. SEAC's creation brought essential clarification to the command structure on the Burma–India front, just in time for the demands of the 1944 operations. While Mountbatten may be criticized for his vanity, the size and operation of his headquarters, clinging too long to impracticable plans like Culverin, and the timing of his move to Kandy, he must be credited for firmness and decision on the matter of transport planes for the Admin Box and Imphal. His backing also enabled Slim and Wingate to prosecute their campaigns.

On the Japanese side, the commanders for the offensives in both the Arakan and in Assam pressed home their attacks with great ferocity. Where the wisdom of their plans may be open to question, the aggressive execution is not. Fifteenth Army's division commanders generally performed well, and managed to extract the utmost from their formations. Mutaguchi's strategy, however, left much to be desired, especially with its reliance on questionable logistical plans. He recognized the failure of his operation, but had so much personally staked on U-Go's success that he could not recast his plans or admit defeat to his superiors. The result was disaster unlike any in the history of the Imperial Japanese Army.

In one aspect, Mutaguchi's strategy was sound: the 31st Division should have struck for Dimapur in force. Capturing that town and thereby cutting the Bengal–Assam Railway which fed Fourteenth Army, NCAC, the Ledo Road construction, and the Hump airlift to China, would have short-circuited Allied operations from Calcutta to Manchuria. Allied commanders were aware of this, and reacted strongly to even the possibility of an advance on Dimapur. Kawabe's overruling of that movement was a serious error, one that threw away what might have been the best opportunity of success for the March on Delhi.

Arguably the best Japanese commander in these campaigns was General Tanaka of the 18th "Chrysanthemum" Division. He commanded a first-class unit, which held back superior numbers of Chinese and Americans for six months despite little support, mounting casualties, and disrupted supply lines. Tanaka handled his division with considerable ability, and the division fulfilled its mission of defense and delay the best it could. Any analysis of NCAC's performance in 1944 should take the skill of its opponent into account.

* * *

The war went on. When Mountbatten returned to Kandy, Stilwell moved to Chungking. Chiang had agreed to give Stilwell field command of the Chinese armies, but dragged out negotiations about Stilwell's exact powers and relationship to Chiang as Supreme Commander of China Theater. Matters came to a head on September 19, when Stilwell delivered to Chiang a sharp note from Roosevelt demanding action. Stung by this rebuke and the loss of face, Chiang instead maneuvered to get Stilwell recalled, which occurred on October 19. Albert Wedemeyer took Stilwell's place in China. Daniel Sultan assumed command of a reorganized India–Burma Theater.

After the monsoon passed, Fourteenth Army started a new offensive, codenamed Operation Capital. Scoones had been promoted to a command in India, and Messervy took command of IV Corps; Stopford retained command of XXXIII Corps. Slim's forces crossed the Chindwin and secured jump-off points into central Burma. The Japanese fell back to the Irrawaddy River, where they planned to make their major stand in defense of Burma.

In northern and eastern Burma, NCAC pursued its mission of opening a land route to China. The Marauders had been disbanded on August 10, 1944, and the survivors became the cadre for the new 475th Infantry Regiment. Joined by the dismounted 124th Cavalry Regiment and assisted by U.S. and Chinese artillery, this division-sized unit, known officially as the 5332nd Infantry Brigade (Provisional) but more commonly as Mars Task Force, helped spearhead the opening of the Burma Road. As NCAC pushed south and east in the last months of 1944, Wei's Y Force advanced west, meeting NCAC near Bhamo in January 1945.

On January 28, 1945, 362 days after Wedemeyer predicted that its completion before 1946 was impossible, the first truck convoy entered China over the new Ledo Road. Chiang christened the route the Stilwell Road, "in memory of his distinctive contribution and of the signal part in which the Allied and Chinese forces under his direction played in the Burma campaign and in the building of the road." Soon, NCAC's forces were being flown and driven to China, leaving SEAC to continue the war in Burma largely alone.

By this point, SEAC's war was running well, thanks to the skill of Slim, Stopford, Messervy, and the Fourteenth Army as a whole. Indeed, the weapon forged in the victories of 1944 proved to be quite powerful in 1945. After feinting north of Mandalay in February, Slim crossed Messervy's corps south of the city and seized the key Japanese base of Meiktila. Messervy's troops withstood a major siege for a month, while Stopford's forces secured Mandalay. The Japanese retreated southward, closely pursued by Slim's army with Cowan's 17th Indian Division leading the way. Christison's XV Corps took Rangoon by sea and air, and met Cowan's troops north of the city in early May, just as the monsoon broke. After several battles with Japanese stragglers and die-hard resisters, the war in Burma ended with Japan's surrender on August 15, 1945. The India–Burma battles of 1944 and 1945 thus became the last great victories of the British Empire.

For Bose and the INA, these events were nothing short of a disaster. Bose himself tried to reach the Soviet Union, but died after his plane crashed in northern Formosa (modern Taipei, Taiwan) on August 18, 1945. His ashes are buried in Japan, although theories of his survival persist. The remaining INA personnel either fell into British captivity or escaped into the disorder of the war's end.

The INA would likely have passed into obscurity but for the British desire to make an example of its leaders. In 1943 and 1944, captured INA personnel had been quietly court-martialed on the charge of "making war against the King-Emperor." The INA's senior leaders would be handled differently. In November 1945, British authorities started proceedings against three of the most senior leaders in a public trial in Delhi's Red Fort. Among the defendants was Major General Shah Nawaz Khan, the commander of the INA division that accompanied Mutaguchi's invasion of India. Nehru, newly released from prison, served as a defense counsel.

The three defendants were convicted and sentenced to deportation for life, but the trial had galvanized Indians, most of whom knew nothing of the INA but remembered Bose from his prewar activities. The proceedings brought to light the INA's mission and activities; as fighters for a Free India, the INA men came to be popularly regarded as Indian patriots. The verdicts resulted in shock, which soon turned to anger and protests. The Royal Indian Navy mutinied, and the Indian Army saw signs of unrest and disobedience in its ranks toward British officers. Auchinleck commuted the sentences, and the defenders went free after a dishonorable discharge from the Indian Army.

The Red Fort trials had lit a fuse that could not be extinguished, and pro-independence demonstrations broke out across India. Sectarian violence also erupted. Pressure built on the British administration to find a solution. In February 1947, Mountbatten arrived in New Delhi as Viceroy, with orders to oversee India's transition to independence in 1948. As power-sharing negotiations failed and sectarian divisions deepened, Mountbatten pushed up the time of India's independence to midnight, August 14/15, 1947. India would be partitioned into two countries, majority-Hindu India and majority-Muslim Pakistan. The contentious split resulted in violence and mass migrations on both sides, with much death and misery. Tensions between India and Pakistan remain, with no signs of abatement. Both nations have repeatedly fought wars since 1947, and are now both nuclear powers.

This connection of the events of 1944 to the Partition of India demonstrates that the India–Burma battles of 1944 not only determined the winners and losers of World War II in Southeast Asia, but also influenced the postwar future of that region. As World War II progressed, the United States had assumed a key position regarding the conduct of the war in the China–Burma–India Theater. After Japan's surrender, the United States remained engaged in Southeast Asia. The fall of Saigon in 1975 ended 33 years of continuous American involvement in the region, stretching back to General Stilwell's arrival in 1942.

Burma followed India out of the British Empire in 1948, as did Ceylon, which became the independent nation of Sri Lanka. These developments unleashed sectarian violence in both nations and in eastern India. For much of the past 75 years, the battlegrounds of 1944 have echoed with gunshots as national armies battled insurgents. Part of northern Burma is still effectively closed to tourists, along with the Arakan battlefields, while Imphal and Kohima opened to tourists in 2013 and 2014, respectively. Today, people from formerly Axis and Allied nations visit these places, often motivated to stand where a relative served or died.

In 1946, China plunged into civil war between the forces of Chiang's Nationalists and Mao's Communists. Mao declared victory in October 1949, although the last

Nationalist forces were not evicted from mainland China until the spring of 1950. Chiang retreated to the island of Taiwan, a former Japanese possession which had been returned to China in 1945, where the Republic of China still rules.

Here, too, the 1944 India–Burma campaigns had an influence. "By keeping intact the blockade of China for another year," noted the U.S. Army historians of the CBI Theater, "the 18th Division and Tanaka may have profoundly affected the history of Asia. If Stilwell had won a speedy victory in North Burma, the position of [Chiang's] government in China could have been greatly strengthened by the return of good Chinese troops and the delivery of trucks and artillery in 1944." A stronger and better-equipped Nationalist Chinese Army would have been a great asset in the 1945 China campaigns and the subsequent Chinese Civil War, perhaps altering the outcome of the latter.

Today, Britain remembers Imphal and Kohima jointly as its greatest land battle of all time. The Kohima Museum in York, England recalls the battle and 2nd Division, while local museums in Imphal and Kohima also tell the story. Japan recognizes Imphal-Kohima as one of its worst defeats but also one of its largest battles. The U.S. military carries the lineage of Merrill's Marauders, the 1st Air Commando, and other U.S. units from CBI forward to the present. The militaries of India and Pakistan also recall the victories of 1944, while Bose and the INA are celebrated in India. Bose's home in Calcutta is a museum, and Moirang hosts a museum and library decided to the INA. Calcutta's airport and an island in the Andaman Islands are both named for Bose, as are streets and squares in many Indian cities. Films have been made featuring him and the INA story. In China, the memory of World War II is used to link the People's Republic with the United States. General Stilwell's former headquarters in Chungking is now a museum, which recalls him as a friend to China, while a Flying Tigers museum stands near the former Kweilin airfield complex.

Many decades later, the India–Burma battles of 1944 continue to be a part of the fabric of the modern world—echoes of a time of high drama, when nations stood in the balance.

Major Characters and their Fates

What follows are brief statements about the fate of many of the major characters in this book after August 1944. The list is organized alphabetically by family name.

John Alison commanded the 3rd Air Commando Group in the Liberation of the Philippines and the battle of Okinawa. He stayed in the newly-independent U.S. Air Force after the war, retiring at the reserve rank of Major General. A respected figure dubbed the "Father of Air Force Special Operations," Alison died in 2011.

Claude Auchinleck led the Indian Army until late 1947, when he became Supreme Commander of India and Pakistan. He left active service on December 1, 1948, embittered about the Partition of India and the Indian Army. He retired to England and later North Africa, where he died in 1981.

Haydon Boatner continued with NCAC until 1945. After the war, he served as Commandant of Cadets at Texas A&M University. In 1951, he went to Korea, where a year later he was a key figure in putting down the Koje-do POW uprising. He was Provost Marshal General of the U.S. Army from 1957 until his retirement in 1960. He died in 1977.

Harold Briggs commanded the postwar occupation force in Burma until 1948. He later helped develop a strategy to end the Malayan Emergency. He died in 1952.

Rothwell Brown held advisory positions in Korea and Indochina. He also commanded the 6th Cavalry Regiment in Germany during the Korean War period.

Tom Brodie returned to his regiment after the war, serving in Palestine. In 1950 and 1951, he commanded the British 29th Infantry Brigade in Korea, fighting in the second battle of Seoul and battle of the Imjin River. He later commanded the British 1st Infantry Division before retiring. He died in 1993.

Mike Calvert ended the war in command of the Special Air Service Brigade in Germany. He later fought in the Malayan Emergency, albeit with less success than in Burma. In 1952, he was dismissed from the British Army after being convicted at a court-martial of indecency with underage German boys. That year, Calvert published his first book on the war in Burma, and later became a commentator on World War II. He battled alcoholism and held various jobs in Britain and Australia before his death in 1998.

Claire Chennault commanded the Fourteenth Air Force until being relieved in the summer of 1945. After the war, he founded Civil Air Transport (later Air America), and assisted in covert operations throughout Asia. He died in 1958.

Chiang Kai-Shek remained in charge of the Republic of China until his death in 1975. He is buried in Taiwan in a temporary mausoleum. Once Communist rule ends on mainland China, his body will be buried in the family cemetery outside Ningbo.

Chiang Soong May-ling (Madame Chiang) accompanied her husband to Taiwan, where she became an international figure of considerable note until Chiang Kai-Shek's death in 1975. She emigrated to New York, where she died in 2003 at the age of 105. She is buried in Hartsdale, New York, with arrangements to be moved to Ningbo with Chiang's body at the appropriate time.

Philip Christison was knighted in Imphal in December 1944 for his role in the victories of that year. He commanded his corps with distinction in 1945, and took the surrender of Japanese forces in Singapore. He later led the occupation of the Dutch East Indies and tried to prevent an uprising. He returned to Britain and held several senior army posts before retiring to Scotland in 1949. Christison died in 1993, just after his 100th birthday.

Phil Cochran left the U.S. Army Air Forces in 1945 and went into business in Pennsylvania. He later worked in Hollywood. He died of a heart attack in 1979.

David T. "Punch" Cowan commanded 17th Indian Division with great distinction until the end of the war. After the Japanese surrender, he led the British Commonwealth Occupation Force in Japan until his retirement in 1947. He died in 1983.

John Paton Davies left China in 1945 after disagreements about policy. He held several senior State Department posts before being fired in 1954 at the height of the McCarthy anti-Communist crusade. His firing was overturned in 1969. Davies moved to South America and later Spain before returning to the United States for good. He died in 1999.

Frank Dorn was sent home by Wedemeyer in January 1945. He served on Stilwell's staff until the end of the war, then held several posts in the U.S. Army's public affairs section. He retired in 1953 and died in 1981. His memoirs were published in 1972.

Geoffrey Evans led 5th Indian Division until he was disabled by typhoid. Upon recovery, he succeeded Messervy in command of 7th Indian Division, which he led with distinction in the 1945 Burma campaign. After the war, he held senior commands in Thailand, Hong Kong, and the United Kingdom. He later became a noted writer of military history, especially World War II in North Africa and Southeast Asia.

Bernard Fergusson published two memoirs in 1945 and 1946 about his time in the Chindits. He saw service in Palestine and during in the Suez Crisis before retiring in 1958. From 1962 to 1967, Fergusson was Governor-General of New Zealand, a post previously held by his father and grandfather. He became Baron Ballantrae in 1972, and died in 1980.

George Giffard held several honorary positions before his retirement in 1946. He died in 1964.

Douglas Gracey commanded 20th Indian Division with distinction in the 1945 Burma campaign. After the war, he led the initial occupation of southern Indochina. He commanded in India and after Partition became Messervy's deputy in command of the Pakistani Army. Gracey succeeded Messervy in 1948 and retired in 1951. He died in 1964.

John Grover held administrative posts in England until 1945. He greeted the 2nd British Division upon its return from India, and was loudly cheered. He retired in 1948 and died in 1979.

Charles Hunter returned to the United States and held a variety of staff positions. He published a memoir in 1963 and died in 1970.

Mohammad Ali Jinnah served as first president of independent Pakistan. He died in office in 1948, 13 months after Partition.

Kawabe Masakazu was relieved at the end of August 1944, and returned to Tokyo. He was convicted of war crimes and was hanged in 1948.

Joe Lentaigne held a variety of senior posts in the India Command, and turned down a senior appointment in the post-Partition Indian Army. He commanded the

Staff College in Wellington, New Zealand, from 1948 to his retirement in 1955. He died two months later.

Liao Yu-Sheng was promoted to command New Sixth Army in 1945. In the Chinese Civil War, he commanded all Nationalist forces in Manchuria before being defeated and taken captive in late 1948. He was a prisoner of the Communists until 1961, and died in 1968 during the Cultural Revolution.

John Masters became a senior staff officer in the 19th Indian Division during the 1945 Burma campaign. He later embarked on a noted career as a writer of fiction and non-fiction, with special emphasis on Britain's experience in India, before dying in 1983 in New Mexico. His stepson is British General Michael Rose.

Frank Merrill held senior staff positions in SEAC and under Stilwell until 1946. He later served as highway commissioner of New Hampshire. He died of a heart attack in 1955.

Frank Messervy commanded IV Corps in 1945 with great distinction. After Partition he became the first commander of the Pakistan Army, a post he held until his retirement in 1948. He died in 1974.

Louis Mountbatten took the title Earl Mountbatten of Burma. After serving as Viceroy and Governor-General of India, he resumed his Royal Navy career. In 1954, he fulfilled his ambition to avenge his father's disgrace by becoming First Sea Lord. He later served as Chief of Defense Staff until 1965. An international figure of note, Mountbatten became involved with many political and cultural pursuits while mentoring a young Charles, Prince of Wales. On August 27, 1979, the Irish Republican Army assassinated him by blowing up his yacht.

Mutaguchi Renya was relieved of command and forced into retirement. He remained publicly reticent about U-Go, but privately maintained that his offensive came very close to victory. He died in 1966.

Jawalharlal Nehru became the first Prime Minister of independent India. He died in office in 1964.

Charlton Ogburn served in the U.S. State Department into the 1950s. He later became a writer known for his semi-autobiographical history of Merrill's Marauders, works on Shakespeare, and several novels. He died in 1998.

Richard Peirse was recalled from India in late 1944 after an affair with Lady Auchinleck. She divorced General Auchinleck a year later and married Peirse. The scandal, and the fact that Peirse had neglected his duties to court her, effectively ended his career. He died in 1970.

William Peers joined the CIA after World War II, running Nationalist agents in Communist China. He helped set up the U.S. Army's Special Operations Command, and later commanded 4th Infantry Division and I Field Force in Vietnam. In 1969, he headed the investigation into the My Lai Massacre. He retired in 1973 and died in 1984.

Lewis Pick led the first convoy on the Ledo Road from Ledo to Kunming. In 1949, he became Chief of Engineers of the U.S. Army. He retired in 1953 and died three years later.

M. A. Rahman served with his regiment in the 1945 Burma campaign. He joined the Pakistan Army upon Partition, becoming the chief instructor of its military academy. He moved on to a variety of senior military and civil posts, including Vice Chief of the General Staff and Governor of the Punjab. He died in 1996.

I. S. Ravdin returned to the University of Pennsylvania and remained on faculty until shortly before his death in 1970. The medical school's main building is named for him.

Hugh Richards received a promotion to Brigadier for his defense of Kohima. Upon his return to Delhi, he thanked his superiors "for sending me to Kohima."

Dean Rusk held several senior staff positions in the U.S. State Department after the war. He was Secretary of State for John F. Kennedy and Lyndon Johnson, serving the second-longest tenure of anyone in that post. He died in 1994.

Charles Russhon was one of the first Westerners into Hiroshima after the war. He later served as technical advisor to the first James Bond films, and appeared in cameos in *Thunderball* and *Goldfinger*. He died in 1981.

Sato Kotoku requested a court-martial to clear his name, but doctors declared him unfit because of a mental breakdown. He returned to staff duty in the Dutch East Indies and Japan, where he ended the war. He devoted his time to helping veterans of Kohima and memorializing the campaign. He died in 1959.

Harold Scheie returned to the University of Pennsylvania and rejoined the faculty. He and Mountbatten kept up a connection and warm correspondence until the latter's death in 1979. Scheie died in 1990. The medical school's eye center is named for him.

Geoffrey Scoones was knighted at Imphal in December 1944 for his role in the victories of that year. He held administrative posts in India from 1944 to 1947. From 1953 to 1957, he was High Commissioner to New Zealand. Scoones died in 1975.

William Slim was knighted at Imphal in December 1944 for his role in the victories of that year. After commanding Fourteenth Army in the 1945 campaign, he returned home. He became Chief of the Imperial General Staff from 1948 to 1951, and later Governor-General of Australia. In 1964, he represented Queen Elizabeth II at General Douglas MacArthur's funeral. He died in 1970. Mountbatten visited Slim shortly before his death and told him, "We did it together, old boy."

James Somerville left Ceylon to head the British naval delegation to Washington, a post he held for the rest of the war. He retired from the Royal Navy in 1946 and died in 1949.

Joseph Stilwell returned to the United States in November 1944. He commanded Army Ground Forces and later Tenth Army on Okinawa after the death of Lieutenant General Simon B. Buckner, Jr. Stilwell was the senior U.S. Army observer at Japan's surrender on September 2, 1945. He commanded Sixth Army in San Francisco and attended the Bikini Atoll nuclear tests. General Stilwell died of stomach cancer on October 12, 1946, still on active duty.

Montagu Stopford was knighted at Imphal in December 1944 for his role in the victories of that year. He commanded XXXIII Corps and Twelfth Army with distinction in 1945, taking the surrender of all remaining Japanese forces in Burma. After the war, he held a succession of senior posts in Southeast Asia and the United Kingdom. He died in 1971.

George Stratemeyer commanded strategic air forces in Asia until 1946. After command tours in the United States, he returned to Asia and led strategic air forces during the opening year of the Korean War. After a heart attack in 1951, he retired in 1952 and died in 1969.

Daniel Sultan commanded the India–Burma Theater until July 1945, when he returned home to become Inspector General of the U.S. Army. He died in 1947 while on active duty.

Sun Li-jen toured Europe in 1945 and led New First Army in the closing stages of World War II. He held senior commands under Chiang in the Chinese Civil War, fleeing to Taiwan with the Nationalists. Sun commanded the Chinese Army from 1950 to 1954, when Chiang removed him to prevent Sun from becoming a rival for power. Sun was placed under house arrest a year later, and remained confined until 1988, two years before his death. His name was cleared in 2001.

Tanaka Shinichi was promoted in September 1944 to be the Burma Area Army's chief of staff. In May 1945, he transferred to Japan, where he took ill and ended the war in a hospital. After the war, he consulted with U.S. Army historians Charles Romanus and Riley Sunderland on their history of the 1944 northern Burma campaign.

William Tunner systematized and led the Hump airlift to great success until the war's end. In 1948 and 1949, he commanded the Berlin Airlift. During the Korean War he led the Combat Cargo Command in support of U.N. forces; his planes airdropped a key bridge to help forces escape from the Chosin Reservoir to Hungnam. He retired from the Air Force in 1960 and died in 1983.

Dermot F. W. Warren succeeded Evans in command of 5th Indian Division. He died in a plane crash on February 9, 1945.

Albert Wedemeyer commanded in China Theater until the end of the war. A staunch supporter of Chiang, he became heavily involved in anti-Communist movements in the United States. He retired from the U.S. Army in 1951 and died in 1989.

Wei Li-huang commanded Y Force throughout 1945. He held several senior commands under Chiang in the Chinese Civil War, but his campaigns showed disappointing results. Recently-released documents suggest he was bribed by the Communists during this time. In 1949, he fled to Hong Kong, before moving to the People's Republic of China in 1955. He died in 1960.

Samuel Wilson stayed in the U.S. Army after 1945. He fulfilled his plan to study the Russians, and spent the next three decades involved in the Cold War and Vietnam with the Army, the CIA, USAID, and other government agencies. He also helped develop special warfare doctrine and coined the term "counterinsurgency." His last post before his retirement in 1977 was Director of the Defense Intelligence Agency. He later led Hampden-Sydney College and remained an influential advisor to the U.S. government. He died in 2017.

Yamauchi Masabumi died of tuberculosis on the retreat out of India.

Yanagida Motoso was sent home to Japan in disgrace, and saw no further active service.

Outline Orders of Battle

The Admin Box

British

XV Corps— Lieutenant General Philip Christison
5th Indian Division—Major General Harold R. Briggs
9th, 123rd, 161st Brigades
7th Indian Division— Major General Frank Messervy
33rd, 89th, 114th Brigades
81st West African Division— Major General Christopher G. Woolner
5th, 6th West African Brigades

Japanese

55th Division—Lieutenant General Hanaya Tadashi

The Chindits

Special Force or 3rd Indian Infantry Division

Major-General Orde C. Wingate (killed March 24, 1944)
Major-General W. D. A. "Joe" Lentaigne

3rd West African Brigade

Brigadier A. H. Gillmore (to April 29, 1944)
Brigadier A. H. G. Ricketts
10 HQ column
6th Battalion, Nigeria Regiment: 66 and 39 Columns
7th Battalion, Nigeria Regiment: 29 and 35 Columns
12th Battalion, Nigeria Regiment: 12 and 43 Columns
3rd West African Field Ambulance

British 14th Infantry Brigade

Brigadier Thomas Brodie
59 HQ column

2nd Battalion, Black Watch: 42 and 73 Columns
1st Battalion, Bedfordshire and Hertfordshire Regiment: 16 and 61 Columns
2nd Battalion, York and Lancaster Regiment: 65 and 84 Columns
7th Battalion, Leicestershire Regiment: 47 and 74 Columns
54th Field Company Royal Engineers & Medical Detachment

British 16th Infantry Brigade

Brigadier Bernard E. Fergusson
99 HQ column
2nd Battalion, The Queen's Royal Regiment (West Surrey): 21 and 22 Columns
2nd Battalion, Leicestershire Regiment: 17 and 71 Columns
51/69 Field Regiment Royal Artillery: 51 and 69 Columns
45th Reconnaissance Regiment: 45 and 54 Columns
2nd Field Company Royal Engineers & Medical Detachment: support

77th Indian Infantry Brigade

Brigadier Mike Calvert
25 HQ column
1st Battalion, The King's Regiment (Liverpool): 81 and 82 Columns
1st Battalion, The Lancashire Fusiliers: 20 and 50 Columns
1st Battalion, South Staffordshire Regiment: 38 and 80 Columns
3rd Battalion, 6th Gurkha Rifles: 36 and 63 Columns
3rd Battalion, 9th Gurkha Rifles: 57 and 93 Columns
142 Company, Hong Kong Volunteers & Medical and veterinary detachments

111th Indian Infantry Brigade

Brigadier W. D. A. Lentaigne, (to March 27, 1944)
Major John Masters (to August 1944)
Brigadier J. R. Morris (see below)
48 HQ Column
1st Battalion, The Cameronians: 26 and 90 Columns
2nd Battalion, The King's Own Royal Regiment (Lancaster): 41 and 46 Columns
3rd Battalion (part), 4th Gurkha Rifles: 30 Column
Mixed Field Company Royal Engineers/Royal Indian Engineers & Medical and veterinary detachments

Morrisforce

Lieutenant Colonel (later Brigadier) J. R. Morris
4th Battalion, 9th Gurkha Rifles: 49 and 94 Columns
3rd Battalion (part), 4th Gurkha Rifles: 40 Column

Dahforce

Lieutenant Colonel D. C. Herring
Kachin Levies

Bladet (Blain's Detachment)

Major Blain
Commando Engineers Detachment

Divisional Troops

R, S and U Troops 160th Field Regiment Royal Artillery (all 25 pounders)
W, X, Y, and Z Troops 69th Light Anti Aircraft Regiment (40mm Bofors)

Support Units

2nd Battalion Burma Rifles—one section assigned per column except for columns
in the 3rd
145th Brigade Company RASC
219th Field Park Company, Royal Engineers
61st Air Supply Company RASC
2nd Indian Air Supply Company, RIASC

Attached Units

1st Air Commando U.S. Army Air Forces—Colonel Philip Cochran
900th Field Unit, U.S. Army

U-Go

British

Fourteenth Army—General William Slim
IV Corps—Lieutenant General Geoffrey A. P. Scoones
Kohima Garrison—Colonel Hugh Richards (brigade-sized composite unit created
March 22, 1944; detached to XXXIII Corps April 3, 1944)
5th Indian Division—Major General H.R. Briggs (two brigades flown in to Imphal
March 19–26, 1944; third brigade flown to Dimapur 26–28 March)
17th Indian Division—Major General David T. Cowan
20th Indian Division—Major General Douglas Gracey
23rd Indian Division—Major General Ouvrey Roberts
254th Tank Brigade—Brigadier C. Scoones
50th Indian Parachute Brigade—Brigadier M. Hope-Thomson

XXXIII Corps—Lieutenant General M. G. N. Stopford (arrived Dimapur April 3, 1944)
Kohima Garrison—Colonel Hugh Richards (April 3–20, 1944; unit dissolved after relief)
2nd British Division—Major General J. M. L. Grover
7th Indian Division—Major General Frank Messervy (attached May 1, 1944)
268th Lorried Infantry Brigade (attached May 1, 1944)
23rd Brigade—Brigadier L. Perowne (attached May 1, 1944)

Japanese
Fifteenth Army—Lt. Gen. Mutaguchi Renya
15th Division (Lt. Gen. Yamauchi Masabumi)
31st Division (Lt. Gen. Sato Kotoku)
33rd Division (Lt. Gen. Yanagida Motoso)
Yamamoto Force (Maj. Gen Yamamoto Tsunoru) (brigade-sized unit created March 16, 1944 out of Right Column, 33rd Division, and Left Column, 15th Division)
14th Tank Regiment

Kohima Garrison

1st Battalion Assam Regiment
One company, 3rd/2nd Battalion Punjab Regiment
One company, 1st Garrison Battalion Burma Regiment
One company, 5th Battalion Burma Regiment
Two platoons, 27th Garrison Battalion, 5th Mahratta Light Infantry Regiment
3rd Battalion Assam Rifles (Naga Hills Battalion)
Detachments "V" Force
The Shere Regiment
221st Line Construction Section
Detachment Burma P&T Signals
Detachment IV Corps "R" Signals
Detachment "T" Line of Communication Signals
80th Light Field Ambulance
Detachment 53rd Indian General Hospital
19th Field Hygiene Section
49th General Purposes Transport Company, RIASC
39th Cattle Conducting Section, RIASC
87th Indian Field Bakery Section, RIASC
622nd Indian Supply Section, RIASC
1432nd Company, Indian Pioneer Corps
24th Reinforcement Camp
Administration Kohima Garrison

Reinforcements from 5th Indian Division, April 5, 1944
2nd Field Company, Bengal Sappers and Miners, IE
20th Mountain Battery, Indian Artillery
4th Battalion Royal West Kent Regiment
75th Field Ambulance

North Burma

Chinese Army in India/Northern Combat Area Command
Lieutenant General Joseph W. Stilwell

Chinese

22nd Division—Lieutenant General Liao Yao-sheng
38th Division—Lieutenant General Sun Li-jen
1st Tank Group (Provisional)—Colonel Rothwell Brown (U.S.A.)

U.S.

U.S. Liaison Teams
OSS Detachment 101
5307th Composite Unit (Provisional) (added February 1944)
209th Engineer Battalion (added May 1944)
236th Engineer Battalion (added May 1944)

Chinese Units Added April 1944

14th Division—Major General Long Tian-wu
30th Division—Major General Tang Shu-chi
50th Division—Major General Pan Yu-kun

British

Special Force/3rd Indian Division (attached 17 May 1944)

Japanese

18th Division—Major General Tanaka Shinichi
55th Regiment
56th Regiment
114th Regiment
Divisional Artillery
4th Regiment, 2nd Division (attached May 1944)
146th Regiment, 56th Division (attached May 1944)

Bibliography

Primary Sources

Unpublished Primary Sources

Author's Collection
    Denis Short Memoir
    Bob Passanisi Correspondence
    Jay Vinyard Correspondence
George C. Marshall Library
    Louis Mountbatten Oral History
Hoover Institution at Stanford University
    Haydon L. Boatner Papers
    Robert M. Cannon Papers
    Frank Dorn Papers
    Carl Eifler Papers
    Donald McBride Diary
    Joseph W. Stilwell Papers
    Alfred H. Suehsdorf Papers
John Easterbrook Personal Collections
MacArthur Memorial Archives Collections
    Record Group 3 SWPA/ATIS Records
    Record Group 15 Contributions From the Public
U.K. National Archives
    Special Force Summary of Operations
    War Diaries Collection
University of Pennsylvania Special Collections
    20th General Hospital Papers
    Harold G. Scheie Papers
    I. S. Ravdin Papers
U.S. Air Force 1st Special Operations Wing Collections
    Philip Cochran Oral History
U.S. Army War College Collections
    Stephen K. Fitzgerald Monograph
U.S. National Archives
    Record Group 493 Papers of the China–Burma–India Theater

Books

Belden, Jack. *Retreat With Stilwell*. New York: Da Capo 1975.

Brett-James, Antony. *Ball of Fire: The Fifth Indian Division In the Second World War*. Aldershot: Gale & Polden 1951.

Calvert, Michael. *Prisoners of Hope*. London: Leo Cooper 1971.

Chennault, Claire. *Way of A Fighter*. New York: Putnam 1949.

Davies, John Paton. *China Hand: An Autobiography*. Philadelphia: University of Pennsylvania Press 2012.

Doulton, A. J. F. *The Fighting Cock: Being The History of 23d Indian Division, 1942–1947*. Sussex: Naval & Military Press 2002.

Dunlop, Richard. *Behind Japanese Lines: With The OSS In Burma*. New York: Rand McNally 1979.

Eldridge, Fred. *Wrath in Burma*. New York: Doubleday 1946.

Esherick, Joseph W., ed. *Lost Chance in China: The World War II Despatches of John S. Service*. New York: Vintage 1974.

Evans, Geoffrey C. *The Desert and the Jungle*. London: Kimber 1959.

Fergusson, Bernard. *Beyond the Chindwin*. London: Pen & Sword 2009.

—. *The Wild Green Earth*. London: Collins 1946.

Gause, Damon. *The War Journal of Major Damon "Rocky" Gause*. New York: Hyperion 1999.

Gilmore, Scott. *A Connecticut Yankee in the 8th Gurkha Rifles*. Washington, D.C.: Brasseys 1995.

Hayashi, Saburo. *Kogun: The Japanese Army in the Pacific War*. Quantico: Marine Corps Association 1959.

Hingorani, Ananad T., ed. *Gandhi on Nehru*. New Delhi: Thomson 1993.

Hopkins, James E.T. and John M. Jones, *Spearhead: A Complete History of Merrill's Marauder Rangers*. Baltimore: Galahad Press 1999.

Mountbatten of Burma, Earl. *Report to the Combined Chiefs of Staff by the Supreme Allied Commander Southeast Asia 1943–45*. London: His Majesty's Stationery Office 1951.

Ogburn, Charlton. *The Marauders*. New York: Harper 1959.

Pownall, Henry. *Chief of Staff: The Diaries of Lieutenant General Sir Henry Pownall Volume II*. London: Leo Cooper 1974.

Rahman, M. Attiqur. *Back to the Pavilion*. Oxford: Oxford University Press 2005.

Roberts, M. R. *Golden Arrow: The Story of the 7th Indian Division*. East Sussex: Naval & Military Press 1951.

Rusk, Dean. *As I Saw It*. New York: Norton 1990.

Slim, William. *Defeat Into Victory*. London: Cassell 1961.

Swinson, Arthur. *The Battle of Kohima*. New York: Stein and Day 1966.

Tulloch, Derek. *Wingate in Peace and War*. London 1972.

Tunner, William. *Over The Hump*. Washington D.C.: Office of Air Force History 1964.

Wedemeyer, Albert C. *Wedemeyer Reports!* New York: Henry Holt 1958.

White, Theodore, ed. *The Stilwell Papers*. New York: Da Capo 1991.

Ziegler, Philip, ed. *Personal Diary of Admiral The Lord Louis Mountbatten, 1943–46*. London: Collins 1988.

Periodicals and Newspapers

CBI Roundup

Ex-CBI Roundup

London Gazette

New York Times

Washington Post

Secondary Sources

Books

Allen, Louis. *Burma: The Longest War.* New York: St. Martin's 1984.

Barker, A. J. *The March on Delhi.* Dehra Dun: Natraj 1990.

Bayly, Christopher and Tim Harper. *Forgotten Armies: The Fall of British Asia, 1941–1945.* Cambridge: Harvard University Press 2004.

Blair, Clay. *Hitler's U-Boat War Volume II.* New York: Random House 1998.

Bond, Brian and Kyoichi Tachikawa, eds. *British and Japanese Military Leadership in the Far Eastern War 1941–1945.* New York: Routledge 2012.

Byrd, Martha. *Chennault: Giving Wings to the Tiger.* Tuscaloosa, AL: University of Alabama Press 1987.

Chaise, Charles and Harry Fecitt, *The Road to Kohima: The Naga Experience in the 2d World War.* Norway: Barkweaver 2017.

Cray, Ed. *General of the Army: George C. Marshall Soldier and Statesman.* New York: W. W. Norton 1990.

Croke, Vicki. *Elephant Company: The Inspiring Story of an Unlikely Hero and the Animals Who Helped Him Save Lives in World War II.* New York: Random House, 2014.

Fuller, Richard. *Shokan: Hirohito's Samurai.* London: Arms and Armour 1992.

Glines, Carroll V. *Chennault's Forgotten Warriors: The Saga of the 308th Bomb Group in China.* Atglen, PA: Schiffer 1995.

Hantzis, Steven. *Rails of War: Supplying the Americans and Their Allies in China-Burma-India.* Lincoln, NE: Potomac 2017.

Hogan, David W. *U.S. Army Special Operations in World War II.* Washington D.C.: US Army 1992.

Holland, James. *Burma '44: The Battle That Turned Britain's War in the East.* London: Bantam 2016.

Hough, Richard. *Mountbatten: A Biography.* New York: Random House 1981.

Katoch, Hemat Singh. *Imphal 1944: The Japanese Invasion of India.* Oxford: Osprey 2018.

Keane, Fergal. *Road of Bones.* London: HarperCollins 2011.

Kirby, Major General S. Woodburn. *The War Against Japan Volumes I–V.* London: His Majesty's Stationary Office 1957–1969; Naval & Military Press reprint 2004.

Kurtz-Phelan, Daniel. *The China Mission: George Marshall's Unfinished War, 1945–47.* New York: W. W. Norton 2018.

Larrabee, Eric. *Commander in Chief.* New York: Harper & Row 1987.

Lee, Ulysses. *The Employment of Negro Troops.* Washington D.C.: U.S. Army 1965.

Lewin, Ronald. *Slim: The Standardbearer.* London: Leo Cooper 1976.

Li, Laura Tyson. *Madame Chiang Kai-Shek: China's Eternal First Lady.* New York: Atlantic Monthly Press 2006.

Lucas-Phillips, C. E. *Springboard To Victory.* London: Heinemann 1966.

Lyman, Robert. Slim, *Master of War: Burma and the Birth of Modern Warfare.* London: Constable 2004.

Madan, N.N. *The Arakan Operations, 1942-45.* New Delhi: Government of India 1954.

Matloff, Maurice. *Strategic Planning for Coalition Warfare, 1943–44.* Washington D.C.: US Army 1958.

McLynn, Frank. *The Burma Campaign: Disaster Into Triumph 1942–45.* London: Vintage 2011.

Moriera, Peter. *Hemingway on the China Front.* Washington D.C.: Potomac 2006.

Mukherjee, Rudrangshu. *Nehru & Bose: Parallel Lives.* Haryana: Penguin India 2014.

Parshall, Jonathan, and Anthony Tully. *Shattered Sword: The Untold Story of the Battle of Midway.* Washington D.C.: Potomac Books 2010.

Plating, John D. *The Hump: America's Strategy for Keeping China in World War II.* College Station: Texas A&M Press 2011.

Prasad, Bisheshwar. *The Reconquest of Burma Volumes I–II.* New Delhi: Government of India 1958, reprint 2014.

Probert, Henry. *Forgotten Air Force: The Royal Air Force in the War Against Japan, 1941–45*. Lincoln, NE: Potomac 1995.

Raghavan, Srinath. *India's War*. New York: Basic 2016.

Romanus, Charles F. and Riley Sunderland. *Stilwell's Mission to China*. Washington D.C.: U.S. Army 1953.

—. *Stilwell's Command Problems*. Washington D.C.: U.S. Army 1954.

—. *Time Runs Out in CBI*. Washington D.C.: U.S. Army 1958.

Rooney, David. *Stilwell The Patriot: Vinegar Joe, The Brits, and Chiang Kai-shek*. London: Greenhill 2005.

Short, Philip. *Mao: A Life*. New York: Henry Holt 1999.

Spector, Ronald. *Eagle Against The Sun*. New York: Vintage 1985.

Taylor, Jay. *The Generalissimo: Chiang Kai-shek and the Struggle for Modern China*. London: Belknap 2011.

Thomas, Lowell. *Back to Mandalay*. New York: Greystone 1951.

Todd, Ann. *OSS Operation Black Mail: One Woman's Covert War Against the Imperial Japanese Army*. Annapolis: U.S. Naval Institute Press 2017.

Tuchman, Barbara W. *Stilwell and the American Experience in China 1911–45*. New York: Macmillan 1971.

Willmott, H. P. *June 1944*. New York: Sterling 1984.

—. *The Second World War in the Far East*. London: Cassell 2000.

Yamaguchi, Jiso. *Burma Operations Record: 15th Army Operations in Imphal Area and Withdrawal to Northern Burma (Monograph No. 134)*. Washington: U.S. Army 1958.

Ziegler, Philip. *Mountbatten*. New York: Knopf 1985.

Articles

Robert F. Dorr, "The First Helicopter Rescue: Where the Special Operations Combat Rescue Mission Began," Defense Media Network, 15 January 2015.

Christopher L. Kolakowski, "'The Coming of Modern War': The Coalition War in North Burma," in *Army History* Spring 2018.

—, "'Is That the End Or Do We Go On': The Battle of Kohima, 1944," in *Army History*, Spring 2019.

—, "Gallantry, Courage, and Devotion to Duty: Merrill's Marauders in Burma," in *Army History*, Summer 2020.

—, "Stout Pilots and Aircraft: Air Transport in the 1944 Burma-India Campaigns," in *The Air Force Journal of Indo-Pacific Studies* Volume 3 Issue 4, Winter 2020.

—, "'Tonight You Are Going To Find Your Souls': The Fly-in of Wingate's Chindits, March 1944," in *Army History*, Fall 2021.

Joe G. Taylor, U.S. Air Force Historical Studies No. 75: *Air Supply in the Burma Campaigns*.

U.S. Army Engineer Office publication EP-870-1-42: Builders and Fighters—U.S. Army Engineers in World War II.

Sam Wilson, "You Volunteered For This," in *World War II*, August 2018.

Endnotes

Prologue

1 Bernard Fergusson, *Beyond the Chindwin* (London 2009), 20.
2 For background on the organization and training of 77th Brigade, see Derek Tulloch, *Wingate in Peace and War* (London 1972), 54–94; Bisheshwar Prasad, *The Reconquest of Burma Vol. I, June 1942–June 1944* (New Delhi 1958, reprint 2014), 85–97; and Fergusson, *Beyond the Chindwin*, 15–50.
3 Prasad, *Reconquest of Burma*, 89, 99.
4 Ibid, 100–2. See also Fergusson, *Beyond the Chindwin*.
5 Tulloch. *Wingate*, 76–7.
6 Unless otherwise cited, this section is based on Prasad, *Reconquest of Burma*, 98–137; Fergusson, *Beyond the Chindwin*, passim; and Tulloch, *Wingate*, 65–89.
7 Yamaguchi Jiso, *Burma Operations Record: 15th Army Operations in Imphal Area and Withdrawal to Northern Burma* (Monograph No. 134) (Washington: U.S. Army 1958), 7–10. This is an official Japanese account, prepared under the aegis of the U.S. Army and based on records from the operations and recollections of the officers involved. Hereafter cited as BOR.
8 Major Bromhead is a descendant of Lieutenant Gonville Bromhead, who won the Victoria Cross in 1879 for the defense of Rorke's Drift.
9 Lockett is quoted in Tulloch, *Wingate*, 79–80.
10 BOR, 7–10.
11 Fergusson, *Beyond the Chindwin*, 123.
12 Prasad, *Reconquest of Burma*, 126–37.
13 Ibid, 134.
14 Fergusson, *Beyond the Chindwin*, 241.
15 Full Chinese and Japanese names will be rendered with surname first.

Chapter 1

1 William Slim, *Defeat Into Victory* (London: Cassell 1961), 325.
2 A. J. Barker, *The March on Delhi* (Dehra Dun: Natraj 1990), 53–70.
3 Because of the International Date Line, the bombing of Pearl Harbor on the morning of December 7, 1941 occurred in the early hours of December 8 in the Far East.
4 Unless otherwise cited, the paragraphs in this section are based on several excellent popular histories of the Burma operations, specifically: Louis Allen, *Burma: The Longest War* (New York: St. Martin's 1984) and Frank McLynn, *The Burma Campaign: Disaster Into Triumph 1942–45* (London: Vintage 2011). For official accounts, see Major General S. Woodburn Kirby, *The War Against Japan Volumes I–V* (London: H.M. Stationery Office 1957–1969; Naval & Military Press

reprint 2004); Charles F. Romanus and Riley Sunderland, *Stilwell's Mission to China* (Washington DC: U.S. Army 1953); Charles F. Romanus and Riley Sunderland, *Stilwell's Command Problems* (Washington DC: U.S. Army 1954) and Charles F. Romanus and Riley Sunderland, *Time Runs Out in CBI* (Washington DC: U.S. Army 1958).

5   Srinath Raghavan, *India's War* (New York: Basic 2016), 256–75. Gandhi's full remarks are in Ananad T. Hingorani, ed. *Gandhi on Nehru* (New Delhi: Thomson 1993), 308–313. A week later Gandhi wrote Linlithgow that "No Imperial Power likes to be told that it is in peril."

6   Raghavan, *India's War* 256–75; see also Christopher Bayly and Tim Harper, *Forgotten Armies: the Fall of British Asia, 1941–1945* (London: Penguin 2004).

7   Allen, *Burma*, 95–112.

8   Bayly and Harper, *Forgotten Armies*, 281–95.

9   Ibid; Fergusson, *Beyond the Chindwin*, 54.

10 For background on Mutaguchi see Richard Fuller, *Shokan: Hirohito's Samurai* (London: Arms and Armour 1992), 159–60.

11 Quoted in Bayly and Harper, *Forgotten Armies*, 361.

12 Kirby, *The War Against Japan* Vol. III, 71–81. Unless otherwise noted, all citations to Kirby will be to this volume.

13 BOR, 1–31.

14 This and the preceding paragraph are based on Maurice Matloff, *Strategic Planning for Coalition Warfare, 1943–44* (Washington DC: US Army 1958) 211–43.

15 Quoted in Tulloch, 114. Nine months after this trip, the Wingates' son, Orde Jonathan, was born.

16 Tulloch, *Wingate*, 118–21; Arnold is quoted in Eric Larrabee, *Commander in Chief* (New York: Harper & Row 1987) 551.

17 Earl Mountbatten of Burma, *Report to the Combined Chiefs of Staff by the Supreme Allied Commander Southeast Asia 1943–45* (London: His Majesty's Stationery Office 1951) 6–9. Hereafter cited as Mountbatten Report.

18 Larrabee, *Commander in Chief*, 538–47; for a slightly different perspective see Jay Taylor, *The Generalissimo: Chiang Kai-shek and the Struggle for Modern China* (London: Belknap 2011), passim.

19 Hemingway's trip report is quoted in Peter Moriera, *Hemingway on the China Front*, (Washington DC: Potomac 2006), 201–8; the specific quote is from page 202. Emphasis is in the original.

20 David Rooney, *Stilwell The Patriot: Vinegar Joe, The Brits, and Chiang Kai-shek* (London: Greenhill 2005), 13. For other insights into Stilwell's background and personality, see Larrabee, 509, 516–21; Barbara W. Tuchman, *Stilwell and the American Experience in China 1911–45* (New York: Macmillan 1971), passim. General Stilwell's diaries and papers are in the Hoover Institute Archives at Stanford University, while select of his writings from 1941–1944 were edited by Theodore White and published as *The Stilwell Papers* in 1948. The latest version is Joseph Stilwell, *The Stilwell Papers* (New York: Da Capo 1991); hereafter cited as SP.

21 Romanus and Sunderland, *Stilwell's Mission to China*, 191–8; Romanus and Sunderland, *Stilwell's Command Problems*, 258–9.

22 Dean Rusk, *As I Saw It* (New York: Norton 1990), 105; CBI History Staff Narratives, Stilwell Papers, Hoover Institution; Slim, 178; Robert M. Cannon remarks, Robert M. Cannon Papers, Hoover Institution.

23 Joseph W. Esherick, ed. *Lost Chance in China: The World War II Despatches of John S. Service* (New York: Vintage 1974), 38–40.

24 See Stilwell's diary entries for February 8–16, 1918, also undated typescript titled "THE BRITISH." Both are in the Joseph W. Stilwell Papers, Hoover Institution. General Stilwell's diary will henceforth be cited as SD.

25 See Claire Lee Chennault, *Way of a Fighter* (New York: Putnam's 1949), passim; and Martha Byrd, *Chennault: Giving Wings to the Tiger* (Tuscaloosa, AL: University of Alabama Press 1987).
26 Chennault is quoted in *Way of a Fighter*, 204; Stilwell is quoted in Romanus and Sunderland, *Stilwell's Mission to China*, 176.
27 Chennault, *Way of a Fighter*, 212–6. Chennault later asserted that the number 105 was meant to read 150.
28 John D. Plating, *The Hump: America's Strategy for Keeping China in World War II* (College Station: Texas A&M Press 2011), passim. See also Jay Vinyard, correspondence with the author, August 24, 2018.
29 Vinyard correspondence; see also Donald McBride Diary, entry of February 27, 1944, in the collections of the Hoover Institution.
30 Plating, *The Hump*, 159.
31 Matloff, *Strategic Planning for Coalition Warfare 1943–44*, 234–40. Southeast Asia Command's designation is the first use of the term *Southeast Asia* to describe the region south of China and east of India.
32 McLynn, *Burma*, 188–94.
33 Philip Ziegler, *Mountbatten* (New York: Knopf 1985), 1–36; see also Richard Hough, *Mountbatten: A Biography* (New York: Random House 1981), passim.
34 Hough, *Mountbatten*, 138–61.
35 Ziegler, *Mountbatten*, passim; Hough, *Mountbatten*, passim; McLynn, *Burma*, 188–194; Mountbatten, interview with Forrest Pogue, George C. Marshall Foundation archives.
36 The directive is quoted in Mountbatten Report, 221–2. See also Hough, *Mountbatten*, 184–188.

Chapter 2

1 Hough, *Mountbatten*, 166–168; McLynn, *Burma*, 194.
2 Lowell Thomas, *Back to Mandalay* (New York: Greystone 1951), 26–9.
3 Ibid, 29–56.
4 Ibid, 71–107.
5 Charlton Ogburn, *The Marauders* (New York: Harper 1959), 14–15; James E. T. Hopkins and John M. Jones, *Spearhead: A Complete History of Merrill's Marauder Rangers* (Baltimore: Galahad Press 1999), 31–41.
6 Henry Pownall, *Chief of Staff: The Diaries of Lieutenant General Sir Henry Pownall Volume II* (London: Leo Cooper 1974), 108–9. Hereafter cited as Pownall Diaries.
7 Mountbatten Report, 8–12.
8 Ibid.
9 Pownall Diaries, 126–8. This is his entry for Christmas Day, 1943.
10 Slim, *Defeat Into Victory*, 167.
11 Slim, *Defeat Into Victory*, 195.
12 Munro's report is in the Stilwell Papers, Hoover Institution.
13 Slim, *Defeat Into Victory*, 178–80.
14 Slim, *Defeat Into Victory*, 182–7; Hough, *Mountbatten*, 178–81. Emphasis in original.
15 Slim, *Defeat Into Victory*, 168; Hough, *Mountbatten*, 181. With over half a million men under command, Fourteenth Army was the largest single Allied field army in World War II.
16 Slim, *Defeat Into Victory*, 188–9; M. R. Roberts, *Golden Arrow: The Story of the 7th Indian Division* (East Sussex: Naval & Military Press 1951), 30–2. Roberts commanded 114th Brigade in the division.

17 Antony Brett-James, *Ball of Fire: The Fifth Indian Division In the Second World War* (Aldershot: Gale & Polden 1951), 249–53. Brett-James was a staff officer for Briggs. The entire chapter offers a view of Slim's reforms through the eyes of one division.

18 SP, 230–2. A list of Allied codenames for people is in the Stilwell Papers, Hoover institution.

19 SP, 232–3. Lieutenant General Brehon Somervell of the U.S. War Department was there on a fact-finding mission and helped broker the agreement. "This is the gosh darndest country I have ever had dealings with," he told Mountbatten that night.

20 Philip Ziegler, ed. *Personal Diary of Admiral The Lord Louis Mountbatten, 1943–46* (London: Collins 1988) 13–18. Hereafter cited as Mountbatten Diary.

21 Tuchman, *Stilwell*, 418–9; Romanus and Sunderland, *Stilwell's Command Problems*, 122–4, 142. A strength return for CAI, dated 15 October 1943, is in the Stilwell Papers at the Hoover Institution.

22 This is drawn from a paper titled *Ramgarh Training Center* by Col. John A. Andrews, dated December 20, 1943, in the Haydon Boatner Papers, Hoover Institution. British Enfield Rifles were cut down four inches and their sights modified to sit the shorter stature of the Chinese.

23 Ibid.

24 Ibid; see also Romanus and Sunderland, *Stilwell's Mission to China*, 214–20.

25 20th General Hospital Annual Reports for 1943 and 1944, I. S. Ravdin Papers, University of Pennsylvania Archives.

26 20th General Hospital Annual Report for 1943, I. S. Ravdin Papers, University of Pennsylvania Archives.

27 20th General Hospital Annual Report 1944, and Ravdin lecture dated November 15, 1945, I. S. Ravdin Papers, University of Pennsylvania Archives.

28 Tuchman, *Stilwell*, 416. For Ledo Road efforts, see Ulysses Lee, *The Employment of Negro Troops* (Washington DC: U.S. Army 1965), 609–18; and U.S. Army Engineer Office publication EP-870-1-42, titled *Builders and Fighters—U.S. Army Engineers in World War II*, 327–345. Except for the 92nd and 93rd Infantry Divisions, the Ledo Road project was the largest single deployment of African-American troops to a war zone in World War II.

29 The report, titled "Lessons from Experiences in the Akyab Area" and dated July 25, 1943, is in the MacArthur Memorial Archives, Record Group 3 (hereafter cited as MMA RG). It was captured in May 1944 in New Guinea and translated by the Southwest Pacific Area headquarters at the request of SEAC.

30 BOR, 38–49.

31 Raghavan, *India's War*, 276–95.

32 Ibid; see also Rudrangshu Mukherjee, *Nehru & Bose: Parallel Lives* (Haryana: Penguin India 2014), passim. For Bose's submarine trip, see Clay Blair, *Hitler's U-Boat War Volume II* (New York: Random House 1998), 231–2.

33 Raghavan, 276–95.

34 BOR, 39–49.

35 BOR, 76.

36 Tuchman, *Stilwell*, 416–19. Many Americans in CBI joked that the real meaning of the acronym *SEAC* was "Save England's Asiatic Colonies."

37 Slim, *Defeat Into Victory,* 205–7; McLynn, *Burma*, 242–4. See also Stilwell's diary for 18 November 1943, in which he sums up this discussion as "Long squabble over command. Finally told them, O.K. at Kamaing. Knocked down arguments of Giffard and Peirse."

38 Taylor, *The Generalissimo*, 245–252; see also Mountbatten Diary, 30–36; and SP, 242–50. John Paton Davies in September 1944 summed up the previous year by saying "Nowhere does

Clausewitz's dictum that war is only the continuation of politics by other means apply with more force than the Asiatic theater."

39 Ibid; Marshall is quoted in Matloff, *Strategic Planning for Coalition Warfare*, 350. Emphasis in the original.

40 Ibid. Stalin had refused to participate in a four-way meeting with Chiang because the Soviet Union was not at war with Japan. His participation also would have complicated relations with Mao.

41 Matloff, *Strategic Planning for Coalition Warfare*, 347–87.

42 John Paton Davies, *China Hand: An Autobiography* (Philadelphia: University of Pennsylvania Press 2012), 154.

43 Tuchman, *Stilwell*, 406; Taylor, *The Generalissimo*, 244.

44 Davies, *China Hand*, 152–4; SP, 251–4, contains a rough transcript by Stilwell (evidently reconstructed from memory) of the meeting. Additional notes are in SP, 255.

45 Davies, *China Hand*, 154; the quote is in the Stilwell Papers, Hoover Institution.

46 Romanus and Sunderland, *Stilwell's Command Problems*, 122–4. The *Washington Post* on November 21, 1943 wrote about Boatner that his "aggressiveness, informality, contempt for red tape, gags and command of invective have become legendary all over the theater."

47 Ibid.

48 Ibid.

49 Ibid.

50 Taylor, *The Generalissimo*, 261–4; Tuchman, *Stilwell*, 410–13; SP, 262–6.

51 SD, entry for 18 December 1943; emphasis in original. See also SP, 262–7. The previous foreigners to command a Chinese army in combat, American Frederick Townsend Ward and British Charles "Chinese" Gordon of the Ever Victorious Army in the 1860s, had considerable operational control of their troops but more limited administrative control. Stilwell's mandate for the X Force/CAI gave him full authority both operationally and administratively.

Chapter 3

1   Fred Eldridge, *Wrath in Burma* (New York: Doubleday 1946), 191–195. Eldridge was Stilwell's press officer throughout the latter's tenure as CBI commander, and wrote one of the best accounts from any American in CBI.

2   Slim, *Defeat Into Victory*, 217–18.

3   Romanus and Sunderland, *Stilwell's Command Problems*, 119–24; SD, entry for December 22, 1943.

4   BOR, 59–61. The chrysanthemum is an official symbol of the Japanese Emperor and his family. Chrysanthemum stamps appeared on all Japanese firearms and on dress uniforms.

5   This description is based on Stilwell's copy of a 1942 report titled *Hukawng Valley Route from China to India via Burma*, in the Stilwell Papers, Hoover Institution.

6   Romanus and Sunderland, *Stilwell's Command Problems*, 125–7.

7   Eldridge, *Wrath in Burma*, 192–3; Tuchman, *Stilwell*, 419–20.

8   SD, entry for December 26, 1943.

9   SD, entry for December 29, 1943; Romanus and Sunderland, *Stilwell's Command Problems*, 127–33.

10 The account of this meeting is based on SP, 275; and Mountbatten Diary, 53–4.

11 Prasad, *Reconquest of Burma*, 313–18.

12 This is drawn from a Summary of Operation of Special Force in the U.K. National Archives, 1–3. Hereafter cited as Special Force. The divisional artillery and reconnaissance troops were stripped

of their guns and vehicles and re-trained as infantry, retaining their former designations. See also Prasad, *Reconquest of Burma,* 313–18.

13 Michael Calvert, *Prisoners of Hope* (London: Leo Cooper 1971), 16–17; Thomas, *Back to Mandalay,* 155.

14 Wingate laid out the Stronghold concept in Special Force Commander's Training Note No. 8. It is quoted in full in Calvert, *Prisoners of Hope,* 282–8.

15 Tulloch, *Wingate,* 130–137–141.

16 Tulloch, *Wingate,* 160–1. See also SD, entry for January 3, 1944.

17 Ogburn, *The Marauders,* 61. These three designations will be used interchangeably. In 1944 the most common usage was 5307th or Galahad.

18 SP, 276; Romanus and Sunderland, *Stilwell's Command Problems,* 33–6; Ogburn, *The Marauders,* 64–5. The changed designation of the 5307th was to avoid the incongruity of a regiment, normally led by a colonel, being commanded by a general officer.

19 BOR, 76–8.

20 H. P. Willmott, *June 1944* (New York: Sterling 1984), 159–60; for a good overview of the Pacific War, see Ronald Spector, *Eagle Against The Sun* (New York: Vintage 1985), passim.

21 BOR, 77–8; Allen, *Burma,* 166.

22 Allen, *Burma,* 166.

23 BOR, 78. The order was Army Directive No. 1776.

24 Kirby, *War Against Japan,* 71–81. The 54th and 2nd Divisions were arriving in Burma in stages throughout the first months of 1944. There is evidence that some of the troops coming across the Burma–Siam Railway knew its nickname, Railway of Death, although many seemed to think it was a reference to the number of friendly troops killed by air raids, as opposed to its true meaning of mortality to thousands of Allied prisoners of war and Asian laborers.

25 BOR, 77–93.

26 BOR, 84–5.

27 Slim, *Defeat Into Victory,* 231–3, 289; see also *MAGIC and ULTRA in the China-Burma-India Theater,* a 1991 paper by Colonel Stephen K. Fitzgerald, in the collections of the U.S. Army War College, Carlisle, Pennsylvania, and Henry Probert, *Forgotten Air Force: The Royal Air Force in the War Against Japan, 1941–45* (Lincoln, NE: Potomac 1995), passim.

28 Slim, *Defeat Into Victory,* 231–3; a history of air supply is in the 20th General Hospital Collection, University of Pennsylvania. See also USAF Historical Studies No. 75, *Air Supply in the Burma Campaigns,* by Joe G. Taylor.

29 Romanus and Sunderland, Stilwell's Command Problems, 265–74; see also Steven Hantzis, *Rails of War: Supplying the Americans and Their Allies in China-Burma-India* (Lincoln, NE: Potomac 2017), passim.

30 Slim, *Defeat Into Victory,* 233.

31 Ibid, 291–3.

32 Romanus and Sunderland, *Stilwell's Command Problems,* 142.

33 CBI History, North Burma Campaign, Stilwell Papers, Hoover Institution. The information about Sun and Liao's language proficiency is from "Gillem's Loss," an undated manuscript (circa December 1945) by Stilwell for Marshall in preparation for the latter's mission to China, a copy of which is in the personal collection of John Easterbrook of Saratoga, CA.

34 Undated manuscript titled "BACK TO BURMA," Haydon Boatner Papers, Hoover Institution.

35 SD, entry for January 6, 1944; Romanus and Sunderland, *Stilwell's Command Problems,* 136–8.

36 Romanus and Sunderland, *Stilwell's Command Problems,* 127–38; SD, entry for January 17, 1944.

37 SD, entries for January 29 and 30, 1944.

38 SP, 277; Romanus and Sunderland, *Stilwell's Command Problems,* 133–4.

39 "Air Evacuation of Sick and Wounded" and "Some Experiences in Assam"; both in Ravdin papers, University of Pennsylvania.
40 Tuchman, *Stilwell*, 421; Rusk, *As I Saw It*, 106.
41 David W. Hogan, *U.S. Army Special Operations in World War II* (Washington DC: US Army 1992), 98–112. See also Richard Dunlop, *Behind Japanese Lines: With The OSS In Burma* (New York: Rand McNally 1979), passim. Carl Eifler's papers are in the Hoover Institution. Adolf Suehsdorf of Detachment 101 noted that "*Kachin* is a Burmese word meaning *Savage*. Kachins prefer their own term, *Jinghpaw* meaning mountain men."
42 Bernard Fergusson, *The Wild Green Earth* (London: Collins 1946), 22–3.
43 SD, entries for January 8, 20, and 30, 1944.

Chapter 4

1 SD, entry for January 8, 1944; Kirby, 67–70.
2 Pownall Diary, 138; SD, entry for January 31, 1944; Mountbatten Diary, 58–9.
3 SD, entry for January 31, 1944; Tuchman, *Stilwell*, 427–8. The first aid convoy via the Ledo Road entered China on January 28, 1945, 362 days after Wedemeyer made this prediction.
4 Matloff, *Strategic Planning for Coalition Warfare*, 435–6. Sultan recommended the sending of a delegation to Washington, and helped arrange its dispatch.
5 Davies, *China Hand*, 180–1; SD, entry for January 20 and 31, 1944; Matloff, *Strategic Planning for Coalition Warfare*, 435–7.
6 Mountbatten Diary, 59.
7 Ibid.
8 N. N. Madan, *The Arakan Operations, 1942–45* (New Delhi: Government of India 1954), 1–11, 98–109.
9 Slim, *Defeat Into Victory*, 165–6.
10 Kirby, *War Against Japan*, 133–6.
11 Brett-James, *Ball of Fire*, 162–3; Slim, *Defeat Into Victory*, 145; Geoffrey C. Evans, *The Desert and the Jungle* (London: Kimber 1959), 43. Both division commanders were born in the New World. Briggs was born in Minnesota to English parents, who returned to Britain when he was a boy and naturalized him a British citizen. Messervy was born in Trinidad to an English banker and his Trinidadian wife.
12 The best summary of the Japanese plan and order of battle is Madan, *Arakan*, 115–18; Sakurai is quoted in Roberts, *Golden Arrow*, 99.
13 7th Indian Division War Diary, entries for February 1–5, 1944. All War Diaries are hereafter cited as WD. See also Roberts, *Golden Arrow*, 55–69; Brett-James, *Ball of Fire*, 277; and Madan, *Arakan*, 120–4.
14 Madan, *Arakan*, 120–124; Allen, *Burma*, 174–5.
15 Madan, *Arakan*, 125–127; Allen, *Burma*, 175–7; see also 7th Indian Division WD, 6 February 1944.
16 Roberts, *Golden Arrow*, 74–75; Kirby, *War Against Japan*, 140.
17 Evans, *Desert and Jungle*, 127.
18 Ibid.
19 Ibid, 129.
20 Ibid, 129–31.
21 7th Indian Division WD, February 6, 1944; Evans, *Desert and Jungle*, 131; Roberts, *Golden Arrow*, 76–8.
22 Evans, *Desert and Jungle*, 132.

23 7th Indian Division WD, February 7, 1944; Evans, *Desert and Jungle*, 132–4.

24 Unless otherwise cited, this section comes from Roberts, *Golden Arrow*, 78–9 and 288–96; 7th Indian Division WD for February 7–9, 1944; and Kirby, *War Against Japan*, 142–3. The British referred to INA troops as JIFs (also rendered JIFFs), sort for "Japanese-inspired Fifth Column."

25 Evans, *Desert and Jungle*, 139–40.

26 Davies, *China Hand*, 181.

27 Tuchman, *Stilwell*, 430–1; Davies, *China Hand*, 182.

28 Tuchman, *Stilwell*, 430–1; Davies, *China Hand*, 181–3; Matloff, *Strategic Planning for Coalition Warfare*, 436–9.

29 Albert C. Wedemeyer, *Wedemeyer Reports!* (New York: Henry Holt 1958), 259–61.

30 Kirby, *War Against Japan*, 162–3.

31 Ibid, 162–4.

32 Kirby, *War Against Japan*, 161–7; Matloff, *Strategic Planning for Coalition Warfare*, 435–9.

33 Kirby, *War Against Japan*, 252; Wedemeyer, *Wedemeyer Reports*, 263–4.

34 Kirby, *War Against Japan*, 142–6; see also Roberts, *Golden Arrow*, and Brett-James, *Ball of Fire*.

35 Slim, *Defeat Into Victory*, 234–5.

36 Ibid, 236.

37 SD, entries for February 15 and 20, 1944; Romanus and Sunderland, *Stilwell's Command Problems*, 168; Kirby, *War Against Japan*, 145.

38 Scott Gilmore, *A Connecticut Yankee in the 8th Gurkha Rifles* (Washington, DC: Brasseys 1995), 139–41; see also 7th Indian Division WD. Gilmore had volunteered with the American Volunteer Service ambulance corps in North Africa. Gilmore and nine other Americans accepted commissions in the British Indian Army to help meet a shortage of officers, and swore "obedience but not allegiance" to King George VI. After the war, he was discharged and returned to the United States.

39 Evans, *Desert and Jungle*, 142–5.

40 Madan, *Arakan*, 118–19; see also Probert, *Forgotten Air Force*.

41 Roberts, *Golden Arrow*, 84; Evans, *Desert and Jungle*, 152–3. American light planes also flew out wounded from the 114th Brigade perimeter.

42 Roberts, *Golden Arrow*, 90–1; 7th Indian Division WD, February 1944. Emphasis in the original.

43 Roberts, *Golden Arrow*, 80–8.

44 Kirby, *War Against Japan*, 148–50; see also 7th Indian Division WD.

45 Kirby, *War Against Japan*, 149–50; Slim, *Defeat Into Victory*, 243; Roberts, *Golden Arrow*, 97.

46 Both are quoted in Roberts, *Golden Arrow*, 100–1. See also Evans, *Desert and Jungle*, 166–7.

47 7th Indian Division WD, February 24, 1944. Capitalization as in the original.

48 Barker, *March on Delhi*, 93.

49 BOR, 81–2.

50 Ibid.

51 Ibid; Barker, *March on Delhi*, 94.

52 Barker, *March on Delhi*, 93.

53 All quotes from Miyamoto come from an Order of the Day he issued on March 8, 1944 to his regiment. A copy was later captured, translated, and inserted into the IV Corps General Staff (GS) WD in May 1944 as Appendix A to that month. The 124th also fought in Borneo, the Southern Philippines, and Guadalcanal in 1942 as part of the Kawaguchi Detachment, before that force was expanded into the 31st Division and sent to Burma. It is not known how many Guadalcanal veterans were in the ranks in March 1944, although undoubtedly there were some.

54 NCAC's creation is outlined in General Orders No. 11, a copy of which is in the Stilwell Papers, Hoover Institution. The adjective *Combat* was added to the command's designation to limit

SEAC's control, as by agreement Mountbatten's headquarters directly controlled all supply and service commands within SEAC's boundaries.

55 SD, entries for February 2 and 21, 1944. Emphasis in original.

56 Robert M. Cannon remarks, Robert M. Cannon Papers, Hoover Institution.

57 Romanus and Sunderland, *Stilwell's Command Problems*, 139–42; I. R. Ravdin lecture, Ravdin Papers, University of Pennsylvania.

58 Ogburn, *The Marauders*, 79–81.

59 Romanus and Sunderland, *Stilwell's Command Problems*, 142–146; SD, entries for February 18 and 22, 1944.

60 SD, entry for February 9, 10, and 13, 1944; Robert M. Cannon remarks, Robert M. Cannon Papers, Hoover Institution; Eldridge, 205. A larger bodyguard of 10 men was first assigned, but after one day Stilwell dismissed most of them with the comment, "I was in a damn parade all day, so many men around me I couldn't see anything." Stilwell felt some concern about becoming a casualty; on February 9 he appended a note to his wife Win in his diary that read: "Just in case I get bumped off, let me tell how free in my mind I have been lately. I was wondering today why, and I believe it is because we have had everything worth while, including, for me, a full realization of your grand character. I wouldn't have fully realized it if it had not been for this war, which has made plain to me what a wonderful girl I married. Why you accepted a bum like me, I'll never understand, but I can sure pass on without regret."

61 Fergusson, *The Wild Green Earth*, 36–47. Half of Fergusson's brigade, the four rear columns, were made up of artillerymen and mounted reconnaissance men recently converted to infantry.

62 Ogburn, *The Marauders*, 71–88; SD, entry for February 21, 1944.

63 SD, entry for February 21, 1944.

Chapter 5

1 Romanus and Sunderland, *Stilwell's Command Problems*, 146–8.

2 Ogburn, *The Marauders*, 88–93.

3 SD, entry for February 21, 1944; Ogburn, *The Marauders*, 134; see also Hopkins, *Spearhead*, 85–91; Romanus and Sunderland, *Stilwell's Command Problems*, 149. Osborne was a veteran of Bataan who, as a captain, made an epic escape via sailboat to Australia in 1942 with Lieutenant Damon Gause. Roughly 300 men stayed behind to assist with supply operations and liaison duties.

4 Ogburn, *The Marauders*, 30, 65; see also Sam Wilson, "You Volunteered For This," in *World War II* August 2018, 20. Hereafter cited as Wilson Interview.

5 Hopkins, *Spearhead*, 154–7.

6 Hopkins, *Spearhead*, 163–5. Taken from an oral history.

7 Ogburn, *The Marauders*, 102–6; Dunlop, *Behind Japanese Lines*, 269–72; Hopkins, *Spearhead*, 166.

8 SD, entry for February 28, 1944; Eldridge, *Wrath In Burma*, 219. Eldridge mistakenly places the strafing on February 29.

9 Hopkins, *Spearhead*, 169–75.

10 Romanus and Sunderland, *Stilwell's Command Problems*, 148–55; Roy Matsumoto memoirs and questionnaire responses, MMA RG 15. Hereafter cited as Matsumoto Memoirs.

11 Hopkins, *Spearhead*, 178; BOR, 65–6.

12 Romanus and Sunderland, *Stilwell's Command Problems*, 148–55; Hopkins, 178–82, 188–90.

13 Ogburn, *The Marauders,* 116–18; Hopkins, *Spearhead,* 195–202. The 2nd Battalion drove a mule in front of it in case of booby-traps. It was a wise precaution, as the mule found one and was blown up.

14 Hopkins, *Spearhead,* 208–13.

15 Romanus and Sunderland, *Stilwell's Command Problems,* 148–55. See also SD, entries for March 2–8.

16 BOR, 66; Romanus and Sunderland, *Stilwell's Command Problems,* 152–3; SD, entry for March 6, 1944.

17 Romanus and Sunderland, *Stilwell's Command Problems,* 152–153; SD, entry for March 6, 1944; Hopkins, *Spearhead,* 216–18.

18 Romanus and Sunderland, *Stilwell's Command Problems,* 154; SD, entry for March 8, 1944.

19 Romanus and Sunderland, *Stilwell's Command Problems,* 158; Ogburn, *The Marauders,* 134.

20 BOR, 66; Hopkins, *Spearhead,* 218.

21 Special Force, 6.

22 Ibid; Tulloch, *Wingate,* 194–6. The landing zones were named for the major commercial streets in London (Piccadilly), New York (Broadway), and Calcutta (Chowringhee).

23 Special Force, 7–9.

24 Tulloch, *Wingate,* 197–8; Calvert, *Prisoners of Hope,* 23; Thomas, *Back to Mandalay,* 197.

25 Thomas, *Back to Mandalay,* 199–01.

26 Thomas, *Back to Mandalay,* 201–2, quotes verbatim Russhon's account of this process.

27 Slim, *Defeat Into Victory,* 260–1; Tulloch, *Wingate,* 198–201; Calvert, *Prisoners of Hope,* 21–4; Thomas, *Back to Mandalay,* 202–206; Special Force, 9.

28 Slim, *Defeat Into Victory,* 260–1; Tulloch, *Wingate,* 198–201; Calvert, *Prisoners of Hope,* 21–4; Thomas, *Back to Mandalay,* 202–6; Special Force, 9.

29 Slim, *Defeat Into Victory,* 260–1; Tulloch, *Wingate,* 198–201; Calvert, *Prisoners of Hope,* 21–24; Thomas, *Back to Mandalay,* 202–6; Special Force, 9.

30 Calvert, *Prisoners of Hope,* 24–8.

31 Calvert, *Prisoners of Hope,* 28–30; Tulloch, *Wingate,* 202–3. Pork sausage was a popular item in British rations, whereas the soya link version of the sausages was the most reviled.

32 Special Force, 9. Two gliders full of Gurkhas came down near Imphal and started a firefight with IV Corps under the mistaken impression they were in Burma.

33 Calvert, *Prisoners of Hope,* 27–33. Tulloch, *Wingate,* 207–8, has statistics on glider operations of the night 5–6 March.

34 Quoted in Tulloch, *Wingate,* 208. Emphasis in original.

35 Romanus and Sunderland, *Stilwell's Command Problems,* 169–70; SD, entry for March 6, 1944.

36 Mountbatten Diary, 77–8.

37 SD, entry for March 7, 1944; Mountbatten Diary, 78.

38 SD, entry for March 7, 1944; Mountbatten Diary, 79.

39 Mountbatten Diary, 79. Mountbatten was the only Allied Supreme Commander injured on duty and hospitalized for a significant time. Two others, Archibald Wavell in 1942 and Dwight D. Eisenhower in 1944, were injured in the back and leg respectively. Both were treated and released to duty.

40 Ibid; see also Scheie's notes and case file in the Harold G. Scheie Papers, University of Pennsylvania Archives.

41 Slim, *Defeat Into Victory,* 285–95; IV Corps GS WD, March 1–14, 1944. See also A. J. F. Doulton, *The Fighting Cock: Being The History of 23d Indian Division, 1942–1947* (Sussex: Naval & Military Press 2002), 75–82; and Kirby, *War Against Japan,* 187–193. Mountbatten was scheduled to attend this meeting, but his injury kept him in Ledo.

42 Personal visit, September 2018; see also Hemat Singh Katoch, *Imphal 1944: The Japanese Invasion of India* (Oxford: Osprey 2018), 24. Tulihal is today Imphal International Airport, while Palel is a base for the Indian Army's Assam Rifles. The other fields are in various states of overgrowth and disrepair.

43 Slim, *Defeat Into Victory*, 294–5; Barker, *March on Delhi*, 97.

44 BOR, 90–3.

45 17th Indian Division WD, March 8–14, 1944. M. A. Rahman, a Lieutenant in the Frontier Force Rifles stationed at Tiddim, noted that the Japanese had concealed themselves completely from Allied patrols. See M. Attiqur Rahman, *Back to the Pavilion* (Oxford: Oxford University Press 2005), 42–3.

46 BOR, 94–95; Calvert, *Prisoners of Hope*, 299.

47 17th Indian Division WD, March 8–14, 1944; Barker, *March on Delhi*, 97–8.

48 Unless otherwise noted, this section is based on Scheie's notes and case file on Admiral Mountbatten, plus remarks given by Mountbatten on April 21, 1964 when Scheie retired from the U.S. Army Reserve; both in the Harold G. Scheie Papers, University of Pennsylvania Archives.

49 Stilwell visited the hospital on March 12, and stopped by Mountbatten's ward among visits to the American and Chinese wounded. He noted in his diary that Mountbatten was "having a good time."

50 According to Scheie's notes, Mountbatten's regular vision tested at 20/15 in both eyes, and returned to normal on April 6, 1944. See also Mountbatten Diary, 80–1.

51 A land area approximately the size of Pennsylvania.

Chapter 6

1 Mountbatten Diary, 81; Slim, *Defeat Into Victory*, 304–6; Kirby, *War Against Japan*, 197–8.

2 Mountbatten Diary, 81; Slim, *Defeat Into Victory*, 304–6; Kirby, *War Against Japan*, 197–8.

3 Pownall Diary, 150–1; Kirby, *War Against Japan*, 198; Barker, *March on Delhi*, 120–5. The cargo capacity of 20 C-46s was equivalent to 30 C-47s.

4 BOR, 86–90; Record of Pack Bullock Tai, 15th Division, in IV Corps GS WD for May 1944.

5 Record of Pack Bullock Tai, 15th Division, in IV Corps GS WD for May 1944.

6 Kirby, *War Against Japan*, 201–3; Katoch, *Imphal*, 30–5.

7 Vicki Croke, *Elephant Company: The Inspiring Story of an Unlikely Hero and the Animals Who Helped Him Save Lives in World War II* (New York: Random House, 2014), 240–55.

8 Doulton, *Fighting Cock*, 83–94.

9 17th Indian Division WD, March 14–17, 1944 and Appendix B; Katoch, *Imphal*, 26.

10 17th Indian Division WD, March 14–17, 1944 and Appendix B; Katoch, *Imphal*, 26.

11 Doulton, *Fighting Cock*, 94–101.

12 17th Indian Division WD, March 17–24, 1944. The Japanese were seen joyriding in jeeps around the supply dump.

13 BOR, 101–2.

14 17th Indian Division WD, March 28–31, and April 1–4, 1944.

15 BOR, 103–4.

16 BOR, 104; Barker, *March on Delhi*, 131.

17 Doulton, *Fighting Cock*, 76; BOR, 88–90, 118. The 31st Division was based on the Kawaguchi Detachment as a cadre. The 124th Infantry had previously fought at Guadalcanal.

18 Kirby, *War Against Japan*, 236–8; Doulton, *Fighting Cock*, 102–123.

19 Brett-James, *Ball of Fire*, 299–301; statistics come from Appendix F of the IV Corps Quartermaster WD, March 1944. The numbers include 1550 men, 16 jeeps, and 11 motor-carriers flown in

via 113 sorties as advance units on March 14; the majority of the lift was March 20–26. Heavy transport and equipment was left behind, to come by road and rail later as best they could. The 5th Indian Division was relieved in the Arakan by 25th and 26th Indian Divisions.

20 Brett-James, *Ball of Fire*, 299–301. One pilot asked his passengers where they wanted to go; another asked for the name of the field they had just left. A third panicked when his load of mules started kicking, and shot them all.

21 Slim, *Defeat Into Victory*, 305.

22 Ibid.

23 Special Force, 9–10.

24 Ibid; see also Masters, *Road Past Mandalay*, 177–81.

25 Special Force, 9–10; Masters, *Road Past Mandalay*, 181–82.

26 Special Force, 9–10; Masters, *Road Past Mandalay*, 183–90.

27 Special Force, 10; Thomas, *Back to Mandalay*, 247–51. Cochran and Alison confronted Wingate about the Spitfires, which he had authorized to be based at Broadway. "I don't think the Japs would have seen anything to attack," observed Cochran, "if they hadn't spotted the six Spitfires flying in and out and sitting on the field during the day."

28 Tulloch, *Wingate*, 265.

29 Calvert, *Prisoners of Hope*, 47–51; Special Force, 9–10; Kirby, *War Against Japan*, 205–6.

30 Calvert, *Prisoners of Hope*, 51–3; Special Force, 9–10; Kirby, *War Against Japan*, 205–7. Cairns died of his wounds, and in 1949 received a posthumous Victoria Cross—the last one awarded for World War II.

31 Calvert, *Prisoners of Hope*, 54–9; Kirby, *War Against Japan*, 206; Special Force, 10–11.

32 Special Force, 10–11; Kirby, *War Against Japan*, 206; Calvert, *Prisoners of Hope*, 60–4. One of the Japanese prisoners was the battalion adjutant who begged to be shot.

33 Kirby, *War Against Japan*, 207–9; Fergusson, *The Wild Green Earth*, 72–99. Wingate's naming Aberdeen disappointed Fergusson, who had hoped to name the Stronghold himself.

34 Tulloch, *Wingate*, 222–6.

35 Romanus and Sunderland, *Stilwell's Command Problems*, 197; Calvert, *Prisoners of Hope*, 297–8; Tanaka interview typescript, in Robert M. Cannon Papers, Hoover Institution. Hereafter cited as Tanaka Interview. The regiments and strengths referenced were 55th (2,000) and 56th (2,500), 18th Field Artillery (1,000), and 18th Engineer (800). Regulation strengths in a division of this type for the infantry regiments were 5,685, the artillery regiments 2,380, and the engineers 1,010.

36 Calvert, *Prisoners of Hope*, 64–6.

37 Tulloch, *Wingate*, 227–41. Aboard were Wingate; Borrow; Hodges; 2nd Lieutenant Stephen A. Wanderer, USAAF; Tech Sergeants James W. Hickey and Frank Sadoski, USAAF; Staff Sergeant Vernon A. McIninch, USAAF; and British civilian war correspondents Stuart Emeny and Stanley Wills. The Americans were the plane's crew, while Wingate had allowed the two reporters to hitch a ride.

38 Ibid; Thomas, *Back to Mandalay*, 292–3; see also Philip Cochran's oral history in the files of the USAF's 1st Special Operations Wing, Hurlbut Field, Florida. Individual bodies were unidentifiable and unable to be separated in the crash and resulting fire. After the war, all nine were temporarily buried in a common grave in Imphal War Cemetery. Because the majority of those lost were American, the commingled remains were sent to Arlington National Cemetery in 1950 and buried in a common grave.

39 Masters, *Road Past Mandalay*, 204; Calvert, *Prisoners of Hope*, 94; Tulloch, *Wingate*, 227–41. That day Calvert had given Wingate the nomination packet for Lieutenant Cairns's Victoria Cross award, to recognize his actions at Pagoda Hill. Wingate had it with him on the flight, and it was lost in the wreckage. After the war, Calvert successfully re-started the award process.

40 Tulloch, *Wingate*, 265.
41 Tulloch, *Wingate*, 227–41; Masters, *Road Past Mandalay*, 203–6; Thomas, *Back to Mandalay*, 294. See also Special Force, 11–12.
42 BOR, 95–6.
43 BOR, 64–6; Romanus and Sunderland, *Stilwell's Command Problems*, 177–8. At that time, the end of U-Go was expected by early April.
44 Romanus and Sunderland, *Stilwell's Command Problems*, 175–6.
45 Romanus and Sunderland, *Stilwell's Command Problems*, 175–6; SD, entry for March 10–11, 1944. On 13 March Stilwell mused: "Begins to look like Shaduzup for the rainy season anchorage. We will make it strong, and go on as far as we can."
46 Romanus and Sunderland, *Stilwell's Command Problems*, 175–7. This omission is difficult to explain. Stilwell was not ignorant of those forces, as Detachment 101's commander Lieutenant Colonel William Peers was travelling with NCAC's headquarters. Stilwell also knew of their prowess fighting the Japanese; one day a Kachin Ranger emptied a satchel in Stilwell's desk, full of ears taken from Japanese he had killed. A horrified Stilwell ordered such practices to stop.
47 Ogburn, *The Marauders*, 141.
48 Ogburn, *The Marauders*, 136–42; Romanus and Sunderland, *Stilwell's Command Problems*, 176–7.
49 Hopkins, *Spearhead*, 279–94. The Marauders also secured a small supply of elephants which were used on the march. The elephant experience was unsuccessful, as elephants and mules proved to be afraid of each other and would immediately flee at the sight of the other.
50 SD, entries for 17–21 March 1944.
51 SD, entries for 13–17 March 1944; CBI History, North Burma Campaign, Stilwell Papers, Hoover Institution; Romanus and Sunderland, *Stilwell's Command Problems*, 185–8.
52 CBI History, North Burma Campaign, Stilwell Papers, Hoover Institution; Romanus and Sunderland, *Stilwell's Command Problems*, 185–8.
53 CBI History, North Burma Campaign, Stilwell Papers, Hoover Institution; Romanus and Sunderland, *Stilwell's Command Problems*, 185–8.
54 Hopkins, *Spearhead*, 294–6; Romanus and Sunderland, *Stilwell's Command Problems*, 178–81; Ogburn, *The Marauders*, 189–92.
55 Hopkins, *Spearhead*, 296–302; Romanus and Sunderland, *Stilwell's Command Problems*, 178–81.
56 Hopkins, *Spearhead*, 302–5, 311–12; Romanus and Sunderland, *Stilwell's Command Problems*, 178–81.
57 Romanus and Sunderland, *Stilwell's Command Problems*, 178–81; Tanaka Interview; BOR, 67.
58 Romanus and Sunderland, *Stilwell's Command Problems*, 178–81; Hopkins, 303–17.
59 Romanus and Sunderland, *Stilwell's Command Problems*, 178–81; Hopkins, 303–17.
60 Ogburn, 164188; Romanus and Sunderland, *Stilwell's Command Problems*, 184–5; Hopkins, *Spearhead*, 252–63.
61 Romanus and Sunderland, *Stilwell's Command Problems*, 184–5.
62 SD, entries for 26 March–8 April 1944.

Chapter 7

1 SD, entries for 28–30 March 1944; emphasis in original.
2 SD, entries for 27–31 March 1944; Romanus and Sunderland, *Stilwell's Command Problems*, 176–7, 297–314.
3 Hopkins, *Spearhead*, 295.
4 Ibid, 343, 349.
5 Ibid, 371, 376–7.

6   Ibid, 344–7. Some of the men were suffering from psychological issues ("battle fatigue") and received assignments to dig shelters and assist in the hospital. Of the seven such men assigned, five made a full recovery.

7   Ibid, 345–62.

8   Special Force, 12; Calvert, *Prisoners of Hope*, 79–83; Thomas, *Back to Mandalay*, 298–300; Prasad, *Reconquest of Burma,* 351–3.

9   Special Force, 12; Calvert, *Prisoners of Hope*, 79–83; Thomas, *Back to Mandalay*, 298–300; Prasad, *Reconquest of Burma,* 351–3. Some Japanese troops stabbed the fuselages of the light planes, thinking that would put them out of action.

10 Special Force, 12; Calvert, *Prisoners of Hope*, 79–83; Thomas, *Back to Mandalay*, 298–300; Prasad, *Reconquest of Burma,* 351–3.

11 Fergusson, *Wild Green Earth*, 96–102; BOR, 144–5; Prasad, *Reconquest of Burma*, 353–6. The defenders were the 24th IMB headquarters, 141st Battalion of 24th IMB, 3rd Battalion of the 114th Regiment (from 18th Division), 2nd Battalion of the 29th Regiment (2nd Division), and 2nd Battalion of the 51st Regiment (15th Division).

12 Fergusson, *Wild Green Earth*, 102–108; Tulloch, *Wingate*, 241; Masters, *Road Past Mandalay*, 201–3; Prasad, *Reconquest of Burma*, 353–6.

13 Special Force, 11–12; Fergusson, *Wild Green Earth*, 108–15; BOR, 144.

14 Special Force, 11–12; Fergusson, *Wild Green Earth*, 211–12. The Japanese refused to use the road for five weeks afterward.

15 Special Force, 11–12; Fergusson, *Wild Green Earth,* 115–20. Exact losses on either side are not recorded. The Leicesters' commander, Lt. Col. "Wilkie" Wilkinson, got the Distinguished Service Order for his leadership. He broke his arm during the battle, and was flown back to India to recover.

16 Special Force, 12; Calvert, *Prisoners of Hope,* 67–9. The Chindit order of battle for this attack is from Special Force. A slightly different force composition is given in Calvert. 50 Column came from the Lancashire Fusiliers, while 63 Column was from 3/6 Gurkhas.

17 Special Force, 12; Calvert, *Prisoners of Hope,* 67–9.

18 Calvert, *Prisoners of Hope,* 69. The Chindits also captured a lot of Japanese equipment, including swords. These were later distributed to Air Commandos as thanks for their services.

19 BOR, 112–14. Some British sources put the date of the road cut at March 29, which appears to be when the cut was discovered by some units.

20 A searing account of these battles is in C. E. Lucas-Phillips, *Springboard To Victory* (London: Heinemann 1966), 79–90).

21 Ibid.

22 Mountbatten Diary, 82; Slim, *Defeat Into Victory,* 271–3.

23 SD, entry for April 3, 1944; Slim, *Defeat Into Victory,* 271–3.

24 Kirby, *War Against Japan*, 247–8; SD, entry for April 3, 1944; Slim, *Defeat Into Victory,* 273.

25 Radio message from Stilwell to Marshall, April 4, 1944, in Stilwell Papers, Hoover Institution.

26 Rahman, Back to Pavilion, 44.

27 Personal visit, September 19–21, 2018; see also Prasad, 272–4. All Kohima sections are also based on Christopher L. Kolakowski, "'Is that the End or Do We Go On': The Battle of Kohima, 1944" in *Army History* 111 (Washington DC: US Army 2019). The hill known as Kuki Picquet had been an observation (known as picquet or picket) post since the 19th century, and retained its name and archaic spelling.

28 Ibid.

29 Lucas-Phillips, *Springboard to Victory*, 91–17; Slim, *Defeat Into Victory,* 311–13.

30 An excellent source on the Naga experience is Charles Chaise and Harry Fecitt, *The Road to Kohima: The Naga Experience in the 2d World War* (Norway: Barkweaver 2017), passim. The quote comes from page 83.

31 BOR, 119–23; Barker, *March on Delhi,* 247–8.

32 A detailed order of battle of the Kohima garrison is in Prasad, 416.

33 Prasad, Reconquest of Burma, 276.

34 Ibid, 277; Arthur Swinson, *The Battle of Kohima* (New York: Stein and Day 1966), 66–7.

35 Swinson, *Kohima,* 70–1. Harman is buried in the Kohima War Cemetery.

36 Kirby, *War Against Japan,* 301–2; Lucas-Phillips, *Springboard to Victory,* 160–5.

37 Kirby, *War Against Japan,* 305; see also Swinson, *Kohima,* 76–87.

38 Lucas-Phillips, *Springboard to Victory,* 119.

39 Brett-James, *Ball of Fire,* 325–6; Katoch, *Imphal,* 40–1.

40 Katoch, *Imphal,* 40–41; personal visit, September 16–20, 2018.

41 Unless otherwise cited, this section is based on BOR, 114–16; Brett-James, *Ball of Fire,* 324–33; Katoch, *Imphal,* 39–46; and Prasad, *Reconquest of Burma,* 244–5. One brigade of 17th Indian Division arrived at Sengmai on April 5, but was quickly withdrawn into corps reserve.

42 Hafiz is today buried in the Imphal Indian Army War Cemetery.

43 254th Tank Brigade War Diary, 12–13 Aril 1944 and Appendix XXIV. The tank unit's full designation at the time was 3rd Carabiniers (Prince of Wales's Dragoon Guards). The "3rd Dragoon Guards" is how they are referred in the brigade war diary, although some accounts of the battle refer to them as "3rd Carabiniers".

44 Today, the Dragoon Guards are part of the British Army's Royal Scots Dragoon Guards (Carabiniers and Greys), while the Dogra Regiment is part of the Indian Army. Each April 13, both units parade without officers to commemorate the Battle of Nungshigum.

45 Kirby, *War Against Japan,* 307–8; BOR, 115–16; See also a captured diary in IV Corps GS WD, May 1944, in which an unnamed Japanese NCO lamented on April 9/10 that he "cannot see how it can be done. At this rate the war will go on for ever. In the end the only results are loss of men by each side and there is no end to this bloody affair. Japan must win, but the enemy are fierce."

46 BOR, 116–18. See also the captured diary in IV Corps GS WD, May 1944, which notes that some men haven't slept in a week and were eating sporadically.

47 BOR, 108–11; Katoch, *Imphal,* 29; personal visit, September 18, 2018.

48 Mukherjee, *Parallel Lives,* 240; Raghavan, *India's War,* 424–5; personal visit, September 19, 2018.

49 BOR, p. 106; Katoch, *Imphal,* 32–4; Kirby, *War Against Japan,* 310; personal visit, September 17, 2018; 20th Indian Division WD. A report from the Devonshires noted that the first wave of attackers on April 16 wore British helmets and greatcoats.

50 Croke, *Elephant Company,* 256–80.

51 Kirby, *War Against Japan,* 320–5; IV Corps Q War Diary, April 1944.

52 Kirby, *War Against Japan,* 320–5; IV Corps Q War Diary, April 1944; Brett-James, 322.

53 This message is in IV Corps Q War Diary, April 1944. Loup reported to Fourteenth Army on April 11 and 18 that IV Corps was desperately short of paper and office supplies to conduct business.

54 Kirby, *War Against Japan,* 321–323; Prasad, *Reconquest of Burma,* 418–25.

55 BOR, 146–7.

56 Special Force, 13–15; BOR, 144–5.

57 Calvert, *Prisoners of Hope,* 112–13.

58 Calvert, *Prisoners of Hope,* 112–18; Special Force, 13–15. One of the Lancashire Fusiliers' mares foaled during a bombardment.

59 Calvert, *Prisoners of Hope*, 122–41; Special Force, 13–15; BOR, 144–5. Calvert's force included 77th Brigade HQ and 36, 63, 20, 50, 45, 54, 29 and 35 Columns, respectively representing 3/6 Gurkhas, 1st Lancashire Fusiliers, 45th Reconnaissance Regiment, and 7th Battalion Nigerian Regiment. Left in White City under Brigadier Gillmore was 3rd West African Brigade HQ with 38, 80, 12, 43, 17, and 71 Columns, respectively representing 1st South Staffordshire, 12th Battalion Nigerian Regiment, and 2nd Leicesters. The heavy weapons of the 3/6 Gurkhas and 1st Lancashire Fusiliers also stayed in the block.

60 Calvert, *Prisoners of Hope*, 119–20; Masters, *Road Past Mandalay*, 222–3. Masters visited White City a week after the battle and described how "Quicklime had been scattered everywhere and portable flamethrowers (Lifebuoys) used in an effort to dispose of the bodies, but the sickly sweet smell hung in the air, and stayed for hours afterward on my own sweaty shirt and trousers." He had stayed only a few hours before flying back to rejoin his brigade.

61 Robert F. Dorr, "The First Helicopter Rescue: Where the Special Operations Combat Rescue Mission Began," Defense Media Network, 15 January 2015.

62 Prasad, *Reconquest of Burma*, 359–70; Special Force, 15–17; Masters, *Road Past Mandalay*, 20921; Tulloch, *Wingate*, 246–7.

63 Prasad, *Reconquest of Burma*, 359–370; Special Force, 15–17; Masters, *Road Past Mandalay*, 209–21; Tulloch, *Wingate*, 246–7. The quote is from Special Force.

64 Hopkins, *Spearhead*, 359–448; see also a memo from Captain H. L. Greengus to Merrill dated May 17, 1944, and Note from 5307th Communications Officer, dated August 18, 1944, both in Stilwell Papers, Hoover Institution. The latter describes shelling of 2nd Battalion's radios.

65 Hopkins, *Spearhead*, 359–448; see also a memo from Captain H. L. Greengus to Merrill dated May 17, 1944, Stilwell Papers, Hoover Institution.

66 Hopkins, *Spearhead*, 359–448; Matsumoto Memoir; Romanus and Sunderland, *Stilwell's Command Problems*, 188–91. Several *Nisei* were from southern and western Japan, and understood the regional dialect and slang of the Kyushu-based 18th Division troops.

67 Hopkins, *Spearhead*, 359–448; Romanus and Sunderland, *Stilwell's Command Problems*, 188–191; Ogburn, *The Marauders*, 210–8.

68 Ogburn, *The Marauders*, 210–8.

69 Ibid; Tanaka Interview.

70 Ogburn, *The Marauders*, 210–8.

71 Ibid, 182–4; see also Kirby, *War Against Japan*, 301.

72 Swinson, *Kohima*, 81–4; see also Lucas-Phillips, *Springboard to Victory*, 185–95.

73 Ibid; see also Kirby, *War Against Japan*, 304–5.

74 Swinson, *Kohima*, 87–91.

75 Ibid.

76 Allen, *Burma*, 236–8.

77 This and preceding paragraphs are based on Lucas-Phillips, *Springboard to Victory*, 211–14. Colonel Richards related this exchange to Lucas-Phillips.

78 Unless otherwise cited, this section is based on Ziegler, *Mountbatten*, 278–280; and Mountbatten Diary, 96–102.

79 SP, 310–11.

80 Pownall Diary, 162–3.

81 BOR, 106, 117–18; 20th Indian Division WD, April 1944.

82 BOR, 110–11; Katoch, *Imphal*, 49–51. Point 5846 is so named because of its elevation in feet.

83 BOR, 110–11; Katoch, *Imphal*, 49–51; Denis E. Short, *To Burma: I Was Not To Reason Why* (unpublished memoir in author's collection), Chapter 9. The text has been lightly edited for clarity. Some men on both sides suffered altitude sickness as they ascended the heights in this sector.

84 BOR, 110–11, 123–5.
85 Kirby, *War Against Japan*, 322–3, 512–16; see also IV Corps Q War diary, April 1944.
86 Kirby, *War Against Japan*, 322–3, 512–16; see also IV Corps Q War diary, April 1944.
87 This report is in Prasad, *Reconquest of Burma*, 418–25. Emphasis is in the original.
88 Kirby, *War Against Japan*, 297–312; Swinson, *Kohima*, 95–6.
89 Ibid.
90 Quoted in Swinson, *Kohima*, 102–3.
91 BOR, 123–5. Some accounts say Mutaguchi's order arrived 17 April; this source says "about 19 April."
92 Prasad, *Reconquest of Burma*, 286–9.
93 BOR, 124–5; Swinson, *Kohima*, 111–14.
94 SD, entries for 9–17 April 1944; message from Stilwell to Marshall, 13 April 1944, in Stilwell Papers, Hoover Institution. Stilwell starts the message by saying "A lifesaver Galahad has been."
95 Romanus and Sunderland, *Stilwell's Command Problems*, 208–13.
96 SP, 289–90.

Chapter 8

1 Romanus and Sunderland, *Stilwell's Command Problems*, 316–27; see also the message draft and traffic in Stilwell Papers, Hoover Institution.
2 Special Force, 17–18; SD, entry for April 30, 1944.
3 Romanus and Sunderland, *Stilwell's Command Problems*, 200–2; SD, entries for April 13–May 6, 1944.
4 This message is in the Stilwell Papers, Hoover Institution. It was forwarded from Chungking and initialed by Stilwell upon reading.
5 SD, entry for April 17, 1944; Romanus and Sunderland, *Stilwell's Command Problems*, 223–5.
6 Hunter is quoted in a report in the Stilwell Papers, Hoover Institution; Ogburn, *The Marauders*, 218.
7 Ogburn, *The Marauders*, 218–21; Hopkins, *Spearhead*, 463–4.
8 SD, entries for April 10 and 20, 1944.
9 Romanus and Sunderland, *Stilwell's Command Problems*, 223; Hopkins, *Spearhead*, 512–13.
10 Wilson Interview; Romanus and Sunderland, *Stilwell's Command Problems*, 223–5; Ogburn, *The Marauders*, 227.
11 Ogburn, *The Marauders*, 229; Wilson Interview; Hopkins, *Spearhead*, 488–90. Stilwell had visited the men before their departure, and was disconcerted when a Kachin poured out a large quantity of Japanese ears to prove how many enemies he had killed. At the top of the pass, Wilson's men picked up Russian radio news, and a Russian-speaking soldier translated. At that moment, Wilson decided to study Russia after the war and learn "what gave these people the heart to hang on."
12 Romanus and Sunderland, *Stilwell's Command Problems*, 225–6. See also Hopkins, *Spearhead*, 495–506.
13 SD, entries for May 1 and 14, 1944; Hopkins, *Spearhead*, 516.
14 SD, entry for May 14, 1944.
15 Special Force, 18–20; Kirby, *War Against Japan*, 279–296, 401–408. Fergusson's men got out without loss, except for two aircraft that crashed, killing 7 mules and 12 men. The Special Force report notes that White City "had been held for 7 weeks, and … had reduced the steady flow of enemy supplies and reinforcements to their hard pressed troops in the north to a thin trickle." As for Broadway, "it was an ideal example of the late Major General Wingate's conception of the stronghold."

16 Unless otherwise cited, this account of Blackpool is based on Masters, *Road Past Mandalay*, 233–260; Special Force, 19–23; and BOR, 145–148.

17 Calvert, *Prisoners of Hope*, 159–62. Six Gurkhas from Calvert's 3 Column in the 1943 Chindit expedition managed to reach 77th Brigade's lines at this time. They had been captured by the Japanese and used as coolies before escaping.

18 BOR, 125; the 20th Indian Division and IV Corps Q WDs note the weather for the Imphal area.

19 BOR, 132–135; Doulton, *Fighting Cock*, 124–34; Kirby, *War Against Japan*, 334.

20 Kirby, *War Against Japan*, 334–5; 17th Indian Division WD, May 1944; Short, Chapter 10.

21 20th Indian Division WD, 2–3 May 1944; Allen, *Burma*, 226–227.

22 Katoch, *Imphal*, 58–9; 20th Indian Division WD, May 1944. The casualties quoted above are listed for "present ops" and include smaller actions along with the major fighting on the Shenam Saddle. Exact totals are: Japanese, 2,921 killed, 1,008 wounded, 24 captured; INA (JIF), 192 killed, 122 wounded, 133 captured; British, 470 killed, 1,880 wounded, 164 missing/captured.

23 Katoch, *Imphal*, 58–9; 20th Indian Division WD, May 1944.

24 Kirby, *War Against Japan*, 324–5; Barker, *March on Delhi*, 127–8.

25 Kirby, *War Against Japan*, 324–5; Barker, *March on Delhi*, 127–8. In the event, the 79 transports arrived back in the Mediterranean in July 1944, just in time to participate in the airborne part of the Southern France landing (Operation Dragoon) on August 15, 1944.

26 Swinson, *Kohima*, 106–7.

27 Swinson, *Kohima*, 108–25.

28 Swinson, *Kohima*, 114–31; see also Kirby, *War Against Japan*, 335–9; and Prasad, *Reconquest of Burma*, 288–91.

29 Prasad, *Reconquest of Burma*, 291–5; Kirby, *War Against Japan*, 335–9.

30 Roberts, *Golden Arrow*, 126.

31 Prasad, *Reconquest of Burma*, 291–5; Kirby, 335–9. Brigadier Goschen died in this action. He and Randle are both buried in the Kohima War Cemetery.

32 Chasie and Fecitt, *Road to Kohima*, 190–203. Among the British agents helping the Nagas was a woman, Ursula Graham Bower.

33 Roberts, *Golden Arrow*, 121–36.

34 BOR, 139.

35 Swinson, *Kohima*, 199.

36 Unless otherwise cited, this section is based on Romanus and Sunderland, *Stilwell's Command Problems*, 329–60.

37 These quotes are all taken from Dorn's notes and reports on Y Force, in the Frank Dorn Papers, Hoover Institution.

38 SD, entries for May 15–16, 1944; Romanus and Sunderland, *Stilwell's Command Problems*, 226; Ogburn, *The Marauders*, 242–245; Hopkins, *Spearhead*, 520–3.

39 Romanus and Sunderland, *Stilwell's Command Problems*, 226; Ogburn, *The Marauders*, 242–245; Hopkins, Spearhead, 520–3.

40 Hopkins, *Spearhead*, 525–8; Romanus and Sunderland, *Stilwell's Command Problems*, 226; see also the message form with time stamped 12:30 and MERCHANT OF VENICE written across it in the Stilwell Papers, Hoover Institution. A signal officer noted that messages between NCAC and Myitkyina were delayed 90 minutes or more because of atmospheric conditions; a six-hour delay was not unheard of.

41 SD, entry of May 17, 1944. Interestingly, two senior officers each flew over the field at midday and early afternoon, and reportedly saw nothing.

42 Larrabee, *Commander in Chief*, 567; Ziegler, *Mountbatten*, 274–5.

43 Hopkins, *Spearhead*, 529–49; SD, entries for May 18–19, 1944; Galahad draft history, Stilwell Papers, Hoover Institution.

44 Romanus and Sunderland, *Stilwell's Command Problems*, 230; Galahad draft history, Stilwell Papers, Hoover Institution.

45 Galahad draft history, Stilwell Papers, Hoover Institution.

46 Galahad draft history, Stilwell Papers, Hoover Institution; Tanaka Interview; BOR, 146.

47 Unless otherwise cited, this account of Blackpool is based on Masters, *Road Past Mandalay*, 233–260; Special Force, 19–23; and BOR, 145–8.

48 Lentaigne's new headquarters opened May 19. The date for this meeting is based on SD, entry for May 20, 1944. The order announcing Stilwell's assumption of control of Special Force as of 0900 May 17, 1944 is in Stilwell Papers, Hoover Institution.

49 SD, entry for May 25, 1944; Lentaigne's message is in Stilwell Papers, Hoover Institution.

50 Romanus and Sunderland, *Stilwell's Command Problems*, 211–16; Tanaka Interview.

51 Romanus and Sunderland, *Stilwell's Command Problems*, 211–16; Tanaka Interview. Like the 124th Regiment in Sato's 31st Division, the Japanese 2nd Division and its component units were veterans of the Battle of Guadalcanal.

52 Romanus and Sunderland, *Stilwell's Command Problems*, 229–34. See also Ogburn, *The Marauders*, 245–64, and Allen, *Burma*, 362–8. Louis Allen was an intelligence officer in SEAC and later historian of the campaign. He offered another theory as to why the 36th Division was held back: "After 'burning up' the Limeys, and with a dozen war correspondents describing to the world his great American triumph, it was unthinkable for Stilwell to call on the British to pick his chestnuts out of the fire."

53 Romanus and Sunderland, *Stilwell's Command Problems*, 229–34; Ogburn, *The Marauders*, 245–64. Of the original 2,997 men of the 5307th, only Colonel Hunter and Lieutenant Phil Weld were not evacuated due to sickness or wounds.

54 Tanaka Interview. See also Maruyama Fusayasu interrogation, in Robert M. Cannon Papers, Hoover Institution. Hereafter cited as Maruyama Interview.

55 IV Corps Q War Diary, May 1944. Stamina's transport planes were from the Royal Air Force and U.S. Army Air Force.

56 Probert, *Forgotten Air Force*, 190–3. Flight times from the Imphal Plain to the battlefront were so short that it was not unheard of for a fighter-bomber to take off on a mission, strike the target, and immediately return to base to reload and go back again.

57 IV Corps Q WD, May 1944; 254th Tank Brigade WD, June 1944; Rahman, *Back to the Pavilion*, 49; Doulton, *Fighting Cock*, 138–44.

58 BOR, 125–7; Katoch, *Imphal*, 53–4.

59 Kirby, *War Against Japan*, 351; 17th Indian Division WD, May 1944. The operations order for Cowan's attack is Appendix I.

60 BOR, 128–9.

61 Pownall Diary, 166–7; Sultan and Stilwell's messages are in Stilwell Papers, Hoover Institution.

62 Brett-James, *Ball of Fire*, 345; Bennett's reports from Imphal are in Stilwell Papers, Hoover Institution. They cover only the period May 19 to June 19, 1944. Hereafter cited as US LNO Reports. The quotation is from his May 21 report.

63 Personal visit, September 18, 2018.

64 Doulton, *Fighting Cock*, 150–1; Katoch, *Imphal*, 59–62; BOR, 108.

65 Doulton, *Fighting Cock*, 152–5; Katoch, *Imphal*, 59–62; BOR, 108.

66 Doulton, *Fighting Cock*, 152–5; Katoch, *Imphal*, 59–62; BOR, 108. As they advanced, Rajputs were seen throwing dead and wounded Japanese off Gibraltar's steep hillsides.

67 Unless otherwise cited, this section is based on BOR, 125–31; US LNO Reports, May 19–31, 1944; 17th Indian Division WD, May 1944. The tanks and trucks were supposed to be the first counterattack against the block, but the commanders misjudged its location and inadvertently drove into Cameron's perimeter unawares.
68 US LNO Reports, June 1 and 2, 1944.
69 Roberts, *Golden Arrow*, 128–34.
70 Ibid; see also Swinson, *Kohima*, 201–3. In some bunkers on GPT the Royal Norfolks found regimental cap badges of an early-war design; they had been taken from members of the regiment's 4th, 5th, and 6th Battalions who had surrendered at Singapore in 1942. The author had a relative in 6th Royal Norfolks who survived captivity.
71 Gilmore, *Connecticut Yankee in the 8th Gurkha Rifles*, 160; Swinson, *Kohima*, 203; Roberts, *Golden Arrow*, 133.
72 BOR, 139–42; Roberts, *Golden Arrow*, 121–36; Prasad, *Reconquest of Burma*, 294–300; 7th Indian Division WD.
73 Quoted in Swinson, *Kohima*, 230; see also BOR, 142–3.

Chapter 9

1 BOR, 131.
2 For Hump tonnage charts for 1944–1945, see Plating, *The Hump*, 239, 245.
3 This order has been reproduced in many places in slightly different forms. This one follows the version in Prasad, *Reconquest of Burma*, 426. Emphasis in the original. It has been lightly edited for clarity.
4 Allen, *Burma*, 260–4.
5 Allen, *Burma*, 264–5.
6 Allen, *Burma*, 264–6.
7 Ibid.
8 Prasad, *Reconquest of Burma*, 300–10; Roberts, *Golden Arrow*, 137–8.
9 Roberts, *Golden Arrow*, 137.
10 Ibid, 144, 146.
11 Allen, *Burma*, 289–93.
12 The best summary of this pursuit is Prasad, *Reconquest of Burma*, 305–10.
13 IV Corps Q WD, June 1944.
14 Doulton, *Fighting Cock*, 155–7.
15 Katoch, *Imphal*, 70–6; Allen, *Burma*, 276, 284; BOR, 131–2. Cowan's troops won four Victoria Crosses in these actions.
16 Brett-James, *Ball of Fire*, 345–53.
17 Prasad, *Reconquest of Burma*, 305–10.
18 Prasad, *Reconquest of Burma*, 305–10; Brett-James, *Ball of Fire*, 352–3.
19 Tanaka Interview; NCAC G-2 reports, in Stilwell Papers, Hoover Institution.
20 Romanus and Sunderland, *Stilwell's Command Problems*, 218.
21 Tanaka Interview; NCAC G-2 reports, in Stilwell Papers, Hoover Institution; Romanus and Sunderland, *Stilwell's Command Problems*, 218–20.
22 Calvert, *Prisoners of Hope*, 180–8.
23 Calvert had dropped the column designations and formed his units into regular battalions.
24 Calvert, *Prisoners of Hope*, 188–209; BOR, 147–9; Special Force, 23–4.
25 Calvert, *Prisoners of Hope*, 222.
26 Calvert, *Prisoners of Hope*, 222–45; Special Force, 2325.

27 Calvert, *Prisoners of Hope,* 245–6. Capitalization in the original.
28 Romanus and Sunderland, *Stilwell's Command Problems,* 238–48; see also Boatner's daily reports to Stilwell in Boatner Papers, Hoover Institution. In the collection there are also a few letters from Stilwell in reply, and letters to Colonel Cannon, the new NCAC Chief of Staff. Hereafter cited as Boatner Letters.
29 Boatner Letters, June 3 and 4, 1944. See also Special Force, 23–6.
30 Romanus and Sunderland, *Stilwell's Command Problems,* 238–48; see also Hopkins, *Spearhead,* 632–46.
31 Ibid; Gilbert Howland, conversation with the author, April 19, 2019. See also Ogburn, *The Marauders,* 266–7.
32 Romanus and Sunderland, *Stilwell's Command Problems,* 238–48; Ogburn, *The Marauders,* 265.
33 Romanus and Sunderland, *Stilwell's Command Problems,* 238–48; Ogburn, *The Marauders,* 266.
34 William Tunner, *Over The Hump* (Washington DC: Office of Air Force History 1964), 54.
35 Boatner Letters, June 12–15, 1944; SD, entry for June 4, 1944.
36 Maruyama Interview; Romanus and Sunderland, *Stilwell's Command Problems,* 238–48; see also "Psychological Warfare Operations in Myitkyina" in Suehsdorf Papers, Hoover Institution.
37 Boatner Letters, June 14–16, 1944; Romanus and Sunderland, *Stilwell's Command Problems,* 238–48.
38 Ibid.
39 SD, entry for 17–20 June 1944.
40 SD, entries for 23–6 June 1944. Capitalization in the original.
41 BOR, 154.
42 Mukherjee, *Parallel Lives,* 240. Various dates are given for this broadcast, but the most authoritative state July 6. The post-independence Indian constitution formally bestowed the title of "Father of the Nation" on Gandhi.
43 Slim, *Defeat Into Victory,* 347–52.
44 Swinson, *Kohima,* 244–53. Nicholson had previously commanded 21st Indian Division.
45 Swinson, *Kohima,* 244–53.
46 Brett-James, *Ball of Fire,* 357–8.
47 Slim, *Defeat Into Victory,* 347–52.
48 British losses come from Kirby, *War Against Japan,* 526–7; Japanese from BOR, 164. INA losses are difficult to tabulate, but are commonly estimated at one-third of the force. Prasad gives slightly different numbers, drawn from a report to SEAC at the end of the war. Regardless of the numbers used, Fifteenth Army was shattered.
49 Masters, *Road Past Mandalay,* 268; Special Force, 58; see also medical reports in the Stilwell Papers, Hoover Institution.
50 Special Force, 25–6; Masters, *Road Past Mandalay,* 268–81.
51 Slim, *Defeat Into Victory,* 279–80; SD, entries for June 30 and July 1, 1944. See also Stilwell's notes on meetings of June 30 and July 19, and related correspondence, in Stilwell Papers, Hoover Institution; and Romanus and Sunderland, *Stilwell's Command Problems,* 239–40.
52 Calvert, *Prisoners of Hope,* 248–9.
53 This section is based on Calvert, *Prisoners of Hope,* 252–4; SD, entry for July 11, 1944; and notes from the meeting dated July 11, 1944 in Stilwell Papers, Hoover Institution. Stilwell had a sore throat that day. Calvert got one of the five Silver Stars, the others going to the battalion commanders in 77th Brigade.
54 Masters, *Road Past Mandalay,* 279–82; Special Force, 26–7. See also the related paperwork and orders in Stilwell Papers, Hoover Institution. The fittest brigades, 3rd West African and 14th,

were the last two flown in, in late March and early April; 111th Brigade, by contrast, had landed between March 6 and March 10 at Chowringhee and Broadway.

55 Romanus and Sunderland, *Stilwell's Command Problems*, 360–400. See also Willmott, *June 1944*, 250–1.

56 The sketches are in Stilwell Papers, Hoover Institution.

57 Unless otherwise cited, this section is based on Romanus and Sunderland, *Stilwell's Command Problems*, 248–56. Some Chinese units had exacerbated the supply problems by indiscriminately firing off most of their ammunition during nighttime, something that continued during virtually the entirety of the siege. The Americans were annoyed, but so were several Chinese units. One Chinese regiment offered to fight the offenders to get them to stop.

58 Lentaigne's message is in Stilwell Papers, Hoover Institution; see also Special Force, 26.

59 "Psychological Warfare Operations in Myitkyina" in Suehsdorf Papers, Hoover Institution.

60 Maruyama Interview.

61 Hopkins, *Spearhead*, 679–87.

Epilogue

1 Of all the volume titles in the U.S. Army's official history of World War II, Stilwell's name is the only one of an individual that appears. He is in the title of two volumes—*Stilwell's Mission to China* and *Stilwell's Command Problems*.

Index